I0826191

CCAR Journal

The Reform Jewish Quarterly

Inspiration & Opportunity: The Arts and Jewish Life

Contents

At the Gates — בשערים

When I go to see certain works of art, the trip to the museum where they reside is a pilgrimage. I aim to look closely, delighting my eyes and expanding my world, but I also aim to pay homage—to touch base with something sacred, for my own sake and also, somehow, as an act of witnessing. This is the way I felt when approaching Michelangelo's *David* the first time, and on subsequent visits. It's how I felt lining up at the Uffizi to see Botticelli's *Birth of Venus* and taking the tube to the Tate to see William Blake's drawings. And it's always how I feel when setting out to view the work of my favorite artist, Johannes Vermeer.

My favorite Vermeer used to be *Girl with a Pearl Earring*. Then I came to love *The Little Street*, after a smart docent explained the way in which every Vermeer contains at least one secret. But now my favorite is *De Keukenmeid*, variously translated as *The Milkmaid* and *The Kitchen Maid*. An inadequate but still wonderful lucite version hangs next to my washbowl. Not infrequently, I pause to study and restudy the way in which the milkmaid looks down with deference and concentration at the earthenware pot where milk is accumulating, the posture of her body while pouring, and the ethereal yet earthy stream of milk that connects pitcher to pot.

How can it matter the way in which a servant girl pours milk? Of course, it's also the vibrant blue and yellow of the woman's dress, as well as the milky white of her cap and the translucence of the window across from her, that matter. From the colors and forms of this picture, as of art in general, our sense of sight is reanimated and our appreciation for this gorgeous world is heightened. Still, with a representational painting like this, what is shown also conveys ideas and feelings, possible teachings and ideals. From this Vermeer painting I learn the beauty and value of focused concentration upon the ordinary acts of daily life, and also the generous plenitude that suffuses the universe if only we have the proper receptacle in which to gather it.

Shortly after having, as it were, fallen in love with *De Keukenmeid*, I came upon the following statement by the poet W. S. Merwin in a publication brochure that included his new collection, *The Shadow of Sirius*: "When you listen to Mozart or when you listen to Shakespeare, you don't know what part of yourself is responding to it, and you don't know what part of them it's coming from. Somewhere in between is this poetry. It's that girl pouring milk from the pitcher." After gasping in recognition, I read and reread the enigmatic statement, and then thankfully cut it out and pasted it to the back of my bathroom version.

"Somewhere in between is this poetry. It's that girl pouring milk from the pitcher." Notice the way in which the poet reaches across the centuries and miles, blurring the distinction between one art medium and another as he strives to capture in words the magical, mysterious, liminal space where artist meets audience.

Merwin's meditation on how art affects us, with its invocation of Vermeer's painting, came into my mind early in the process of planning this symposium issue of the *CCAR Journal.* It seems to me that the "somewhere in between" where viewer meets painting and where listener hears Mozart or Shakespeare is also the space where Jew encounters Torah and God. For different people and at different times, the stream of milk will be represented by a different passage, prayer, or *nigun*; or by one among the various names by which we call God, one aspect of the heightened reality we seek in God.

So much of our lives focuses on what Wordsworth calls "getting and spending" and Freud groups within "love and work" (*leiben und arbeiten*). The two great vehicles that carry us beyond these vital but limiting dimensions, beyond ourselves, are religion and art. Surely then the truth of art and that of religion must intersect. Surely then the world of Jewish practice and living needs to open itself up to the world of artistic fashioning.

The *Journal*'s editorial board, Director of the CCAR Press Hara Person, and I are most grateful to Eve Ben-Ora and Vicki Reikes Fox for having taken on themselves the major responsibility of guest editing (curating) this issue. Their ability to conceptualize and organize the issue will be apparent as soon as you turn to the Contents. You'll notice their ability to attract and bring out the best in a wide range of authors as you progress through the articles. Congratulations to everyone associated with this issue, including its readers.

Susan Laemmle, Editor

Introduction to This Issue from the Guest Editors

Eve Ben-Ora and Vicki Reikes Fox

Imagination is more important than knowledge.

—Albert Einstein

Introduction

A rabbi and an artist walk into a bar . . . . The punch line is the story of how it came to be that we're working together on this symposium issue of the *CCAR Journal: The Reform Jewish Quarterly*. What brought us into that bar in New York? Vicki inhabited the arts world comfortably. Being a working artist and a Jewish museum professional, she was attending the Council of American Jewish Museums Conference in the winter of 2010. Eve had been working in the Jewish communal world serving congregations and JCCs for many years. What brought us together was a creative force known as Carole Zawatsky, who was then serving at the JCC of San Francisco as associate director of Arts, Ideas, and Jewish Life with Eve and has been a museum colleague and friend of Vicki for many years. Through this relationship, Eve and Vicki began working on various projects. Then an opportunity was presented to use our respective interests and talents to collaborate on a symposium issue of the *Journal;* this project would never have happened without our New York bar meeting.

The importance of collaboration has been fundamental to conceptualizing this issue of the *Journal* and bringing it to fruition. The

---

EVE BEN-ORA (MAJCS 1981, C86) is the director of Education at Congregation Beth Torah in Fremont, California. After serving sixteen years in JCCs in Houston and San Francisco, she has returned to her roots as a synagogue educator.

VICKI REIKES FOX (MAJE LA78) is a museum professional, artist, and educator who specializes in art as it relates to the Jewish experience. Fox was the founding project director of the Museum of the Southern Jewish Experience and author of *Shalom Y'all, Images of Jewish Life in the American South.*

process of working with another person so closely had not been a core part of Eve's experience in her rabbinic training. The need to have independent ideas played a much bigger role in her development as a rabbi. But the art world flourishes when nourished by collaboration. The exchange of ideas that sometimes contradict and other times reinforce one another results in a more thoughtful and thought-provoking piece of work, no matter what the medium. Hara Person, director of the CCAR Press, had the initial idea to focus an issue of the *Journal* on the topic of the arts. Her willingness to let us take it in new and unexpected directions brings us to this point. The power of two—with the support of an organized, insightful, and supportive editor, Susan Laemmle, and the fine attention to detail by a patient and all-seeing copy editor, Mike Isralewitz—allowed us to do even more than we could have alone. Putting two creative minds together with different skills and backgrounds, and the backing of the CCAR, allowed us to soar.

We approach this *Journal* issue as curators approach an exhibit. We have brought together writers and developed the framework and content through which their opinions would be viewed. We sought to collect a wide array of written pieces that would shed light on new ways of looking at the merging of the visual world and the text-based world of Jewish scholarship. We hope that our curatorial vision will encourage new ideas to flow.

At the beginning of our working on this issue we sought to have the most well-rounded representation of the world of Jewish art today. Our Call for Papers elicited responses from working artists, rabbis, educators, and scholars—so many people thinking about the issues of the place of the arts in Jewish life. We were committed to including a broad array of voices in order to bring attention to the creativity happening in the Jewish world today. Proposals for articles included the visual arts, movement, music, theater, puppetry, and more. But after we reviewed them, we decided that our strengths best supported a focus on the visual arts.

The visual arts are easily incorporated into synagogue life through study both formal and informal; through life's special moments and trying times. There is great untapped potential through the use of visual media to welcome both the trained and the uninitiated into Jewish life. What would it look like if someone's first experience with collage, photo transfer, or calligraphy became the vehicle to transmit Jewish family stories or the retelling of the

Passover story? The arts can be a significant entry point for people to find a way into Jewish life who may not have previously seen themselves as having such a place. Consider that words alone are an inadequate language for religious expression.

Structure of This Symposium Issue

The core of the Jewish people from the beginning until today is Torah. The Five Books of Moses represent the foundation of Jewish belief and practice. The divisions of the Torah will serve as our organizing principle, both as a reminder that we always keep Torah as a central object and that the messages contained in the Torah are beyond the textual. According to Ori Soltes, the main question is: "How [can] the People of the Book . . . also be a People of the Image?"

Our primary purpose is to explore the results of what happens when an artist looks at Torah. What a nonartist might typically skip over in a classic text, an artist will see with all the depth and possibility, nuanced or overt. When an artist sees Torah the view takes on many more dimensions: They see meaning in the letters, their shapes, in the words, and even the spaces. A *soferet* is not only copying a Torah scroll—she is actively passing on the tradition and teaching God's word. This method of seeing the world is what we want to highlight.

We also want to give credence and legitimacy to the notion of using a visual element in the process of doing traditional text study. The tradition has been to give serious attention to scholars who focus on the words and the words that are built upon the words. We want to bring attention and focus to the space between the words and how those spaces can be filled and reshaped to bring even deeper meaning.

And yet we strive to ground this issue of the *Journal* in the texts of our tradition. After all, what has been the foundation of Judaism? To that end, the Five Books of the Torah provide titles for the sections of this issue. We use an artistic lens to view Jewish tradition as we work our way through the articles that were so graciously submitted to us.

By using the structure and thematic ideas of the Five Books of Moses as the organizing principle, we invite the rabbinic mind into our conversation about using the visual as a means to inspire Jewish creativity. Please understand that the order of the articles does not reflect a hierarchy of importance. Similar to how the Rabbinic mind in classical text does not concern itself with sequence, in this issue there is no before or after. Also there is no definite conclusion to the process. Rather it is an ongoing evolution.

Genesis/*B'reishit*: A New View

Pioneers take a calculated risk when they enter new and uncharted territory. The artists, curators, and rabbis in this section are the pioneers because they were the ones who took the first steps into new arenas. Their goal was to provide meaningful identity development and build toward a solid future for Judaism and the Jewish people.

Marcia Josephy and Meira Josephy describe the process of developing a model for a Jewish artisans festival at a time when nothing like this had been done before. This creation of a celebration of Jewish artisans was designed to give Jewish artists a broader audience and make Judaica available to that audience. This was during a time when people were interested in reclaiming their Judaism and searching for the means to do so. The festival produced results beyond all expectations.

Gary Rosenthal tells the story of how he became a Judaica artist. With the inspiration of Bezalel he found a way to incorporate his artistic talents with his Jewish upbringing. He had the personal mission of filling a gap in the world of contemporary Judaica, seeking to make it possible for everyone to fulfill the commandment of *hidur mitzvah* and to proudly assert their Jewish identity by beautifying their homes with contemporary objects celebrating Jewish life.

Tal Gozani brings a broadening worldview of the role of Jews in the artistic realm in France. Her essay documents Jewish participation in all the major artistic trends of the day and provides context for understanding the role of art in modern Jewish life. The involvement of Jews and especially women in the major art salons during the second half of the nineteenth century gives a remarkable insight into the ability of Jews to be full participants in French culture.

Miriam Terlinchamp brings her passion for the arts and for Judaism to light because she believes strongly that "The problem is not how to bring art into the synagogue walls but how to make congregants active participants in Jewish art." A self-described "rabbi-artist," her commitment to using art as a central aspect of her rabbinate articulates the revolutionary idea that practical rabbinics must also include an artist's palette.

Exodus/*Sh'mot*: Art as a Guide to Where We Are Going

The Book of Exodus is the prime example of taking a journey into the unknown. Human beings rebel against change, even if it is good for them! The Israelites leaving slavery in Egypt felt challenged and yet they forged ahead anyway. Someone must be willing to be the first to go boldly into unchartered territory in spite of the challenges to be faced. The following authors have either observed or been the instigators of change:

Anne Hromadka asks the important question of how Gen X, Y, and Echoes can be connected to the organized Jewish community. They are much less likely to automatically join a synagogue in the same way as previous generations. They need to feel that community speaks to their understanding of a world that has been deeply influenced by popular culture. The arts are an ideal way to allow them a seat at the table.

Yael Rooks-Rapport investigates the definitions of post-ethnicity in light of contemporary identity politics and the landscape of a specifically post-Jewish identity. These insights arise as a result of a deep exploration of the exhibit *The New Authentics: Artists of a Post-Jewish Generation* at the Spertus Museum. She discusses the new paradigms of creating identity and the challenges and opportunities presented by each.

Richard Siegel talks about the significance of the cultural elements in Jewish identity that have the potential to have a powerful impact on what being Jewish means today in America. In order to address the ever-changing paradigm of identity, he stresses the importance of nurturing, employing, and supporting the cultural innovators so that they can create.

Joel Schwartzman's experience as a chaplain in the Air Force provides us with a firsthand account of what is required in a world that is built around order and discipline when it needs to change paradigms. Using finesse and charisma, Schwartzman's narrative about choosing art for the Air Force Academy Chapel depicts one such journey.

Leviticus/*Vayikra*: Artists' Voices

The Book of Leviticus focuses a great deal on describing physical elements. Priestly vestments, ornaments for the Tabernacle, the structure of the dwelling place of God—indeed this is the most visually oriented section of the Torah. This is also where we find the clearest articulation of holiness. Holiness results from actions that reflect our divine spark. Just as the center of the Torah includes the Holiness Code, so too have we placed in the center of this *Journal* issue a group of artists who are engaged in the process of interpreting holiness through the works of their hands.

Art Historian and Artist Richard McBee makes a distinction between Jewish art and craft. Crafts have the function of concretely facilitating our service to God, which is not insignificant. Art encourages us to think differently. Each serves an important function and both are necessary in order to create an authentic relationship to the Divine.

These select voices share some insights into the diverse worlds of camp, synagogue, commissioned art work, collecting, and documenting. They provide some examples of what can occur when we are open and receptive to the role of the arts in Jewish life:

Flora Rosefsky
Isaac Brynjegard-Bialik
Mark Hurwitz
Peretz Wolf-Prusan
Lisa Sloane
Yehudis Barmatz-Harris
Josh Plaut

Leon Morris creates a model for visual artists that exemplifies their responsibility to serve as commentators on traditional Jewish text using their unique skills to keep classic text alive and vibrant. Through integrating the text study process with the creative process, a group of Jewish artists found their voice as they engaged with text on a regular basis. His essay includes the voices of four artists—**Barbara Freedman, Susan Kaplow, Larry Frankel,** and **Rachel Kanter**—as he reflects on this concept via the Artists' *Beit Midrash* that he founded at the Skirball Center for Adult Jewish Learning at Temple Emanu-El in Manhattan. This model could easily find its way into other communities.

Numbers/*B'midbar*: Challenge and Perspective

The desert experience created a time and place for the Israelites to make the transition from being slaves to becoming a nation. This section provides the opportunity to consider who has been left out of Jewish life and what we miss when we ignore artistic expression. When we add the depth and meaning of the visual, we will be able to create a community that embraces the richness of all modalities of expression, holiness, and spirituality.

Historian Ori Soltes lays out the fundamental questions that Jewish art raises in trying to incorporate the inherent issues of portraying visual images. What artists produce invites the ongoing commentary that has engaged us for centuries. There are no easy ways to define the question of what is Jewish art and what makes a Jewish artist.

Curator Michal Friedlander writes about the place of Jews in the cultural world in Germany today. Jewish popular culture takes on a unique role in Germany that is not the same as Jewish communities around the world. Jewish kitsch, not typically considered part of high culture, should not be ignored. Upon close analysis of this genre we gain insights into the impact of German life on the Jewish psyche.

Adina Allen and Pat Allen's collaborative effort seeks to present an integration of text study and art therapy into a new model for creatively understanding the Divine. The ancient and modern combine to give new voice to an eternal desire.

Jean Abarbanel and Anne Hromadka collaborate on an essay that tells the story of how the Skirball Museum was preparing to move from the HUC-LA campus when they realized that the role of the arts in a seminary education would be missing. How would they be able to preserve the impact of the loss of a world-class collection of Judaica on campus?

Jean Bloch Rosensaft and Laura Kruger reflect on how the noted collections in the HUC-JIR Museum in New York have historically and currently provided opportunities for students to elevate their knowledge and integrate their experiences with the visual arts.

Curator and Art Historian Daniel Belasco writes about how Jewish ceremonial art becomes a means for a younger generation to apply their worldview. Pushing the boundaries of the assumptions of what a ritual object should look like reveals the reality that the eternal messages of the traditions can hold up under critical questioning and radical experimentation.

Deuteronomy/*D'varim*: Moving Forward Creatively

In this section, *D'varim* brings us back to the importance of words; at the same time it does not diminish the exploration of the visual world. In order to be able to communicate the visual, especially in a journal such as this, the written word must still be skillfully employed. The very last word of the Torah is "Israel," and that topic also needs to be included albeit from a unique perspective.

HUC–JIR Professor Bill Cutter shows us how the words of modern Israeli poetry incorporate the visual imagery that we can often relate to but can easily look beyond without gaining a heightened awareness of the value of the visual and the power it contains. Both the process of creating poetry and the objects the poets describe result in a modern visual midrash that potentially has the same enduring quality as the classic midrashic texts that have defined Judaism for centuries.

Artist and Architect Amy Reichert raises important questions about aspects of *hidur mitzvah* that have implications for the way that sacred space is conceived. Her interweaving of the inspirations from Torah text with her knowledge of design and architecture challenges our preconceived notions of what can happen in a synagogue.

Roy Walter and Garey Marks think about the need to consider synagogue architecture and art. What does it look like to incorporate into a place of worship a visual sensibility that goes beyond just putting pretty things up on the wall or finding a place for well-meaning donations? This article provides a model for how to thoughtfully engage in this process.

Jewish Educator Cheri Ellowitz provides a detailed description of how one congregation went through an intense process that began with rethinking the way that their educational program could be transformed. Through a thoughtful planning-and-implementation process, teachers, children, and adults discovered the arts as a means of expression as well as a way to build community.

Historian and Rabbi Lance Sussman urges us to enter the twenty-first century by incorporating visual culture into synagogue life. The assumption that this is a new phenomenon is a misunderstanding and to ignore this is at our peril.

Conclusion

Jewish art is commentary that contains deep and important ideas; it is a creative response to traditional sources. The goal is to use art as an expansion, extension, and elucidation of Jewish text sources through the use of one or more of the five senses. Even if we are not personally involved in using the tools to create, our senses are responding. As we look around the Jewish world today we see the opportunity for Jewish institutions to be open to creative possibilities and become places of creativity in conjunction with deep learning and meaningful prayer. In this period of new possibilities it could be argued that we are seeing a level of creativity that would indicate we are indeed in another Golden Age.

And finally, we want to express our thanks to our wonderfully supportive families, especially to Avi and Steve, for putting up with our phone calls and many hours engaged in this process.

A Gift to the Community: The Los Angeles Temple Isaiah's Festival of Jewish Artisans

The Dream and Reality of Twenty-Five Years of the Nurturing of Jewish Arts and Artists

Marcia Reines Josephy and Meira Josephy

Dedicated in memory of Karl Josephy and Rose Ann Chasman

> Artists in their work sell soul, work, dreams, and inspiration and at the Isaiah Festival many people understood this.
>
> Sari Srulovitch, silversmith, interview, Jerusalem, Israel, April 2, 2012

So how did this phenomenon all begin? In the fall of 1981 Temple Isaiah, a midsized Reform Temple on the west side of Los Angeles, created a Jewish Arts Lecture Series. Until that point, the synagogue had been known for its social action activities rather than any involvement in Jewish art. This was new, uncharted

---

MARCIA REINES JOSEPHY has an MA in Anthropology and worked in Jewish and Holocaust museums in the United States, curated and curates exhibitions, and is available to consult with Jewish artists and collectors throughout the world.

MEIRA JOSEPHY has an MA in the History of Art focusing on Contemporary Judaica, grew up and participated in the Festival, and consults and creates artists websites from her Jerusalem base. Writings about Judaica and Jewish crafts can be found at her blog: http://birkatchaverim.com/wordpress.

Information for this paper was derived from the archives of Jean Abarbanel, Marcia Josephy, Shelia Gan, and Susan Needleman and discussions with organizers and artists. Since all of the informants referred to the Festival of Jewish Artisans as "the Festival," this article also uses this term. In addition, some interviews and survey results used were derived from work by Meira Josephy from the MA course "Sacred and Secular" as well as a paper for Jonathan Sarna's American Jewish History course given at Hebrew University.

territory for them and the community. An organizing committee was formed with, what in retrospect, may have seemed like lofty goals, difficult to achieve.[1] The committee members recognized the search for Jewish identity by many Jews in the general population and in particular, within the Jewish artist population.[2] They felt that a Jewish Artisan's Festival could become an educational format that would address both the needs of the artists to show and sell their work and the needs of the general Jewish population[3] to learn about the history of Jewish art and view and purchase Judaica. Through many discussions and meetings with a lot of laughter and camaraderie, the committee fine-tuned and worked towards meeting their goals. Their original intent was to focus on California artists.[4] Rules were developed but there was always flexibility.

The series opened on October 12 and included a lecture series and events focusing on art, music, and drama.[5] Lectures included two talks on Jewish art,[6] a lecture by photographer Bill Aron, and a lecture on Art and Artists in Israel.[7] There was also a guided tour of Jewish art and artists in Los Angeles.[8] The series culminated with a Festival of Jewish Artisans on Sunday December 13, 1981,[9] when the committee realized that while they had successfully introduced the concept of contemporary Judaica, in fact no venue existed for the community to view and purchase objects and meet Jewish artists.

The Festival did not begin in a total vacuum. When it began, there was already a strong interest in Judaica, attested to by the proliferation of Jewish Publication Society books on Jewish art subjects beginning in 1971.[10] Remember, this was the beginning of the 1980s, and Jews had been influenced by ethnic pride movements and the search for their own identities, particularly for their Jewish identities. Many Jews became more interested in Jewish history and Jewish culture but did not want to access it in a formal, traditional manner. Part of that quest led many Jews to Judaica in general and contemporary Judaica in particular. Although Jewish art books dealt mainly with the history of Jewish art, *The Jewish Catalog* (1973) was one example of Jewish counterculture,[11] one way for Jews to take control of their Judaism. *The Jewish Catalog* and *The Second Jewish Catalog* (1976) included do-it-yourself articles on Hebrew calligraphy and Jewish folk art. They also included examples of contemporary Jewish ritual art. Not everyone in the broader community knew about these resources, and educating and informing the community became part of the greater goal of the Festival.

Many fine art and craft artists saw that through creating works with a Jewish aspect or use, they found an impetus for returning to the Jewish community.[12] This occurred in varying degrees not only through their art but also through study of traditional Jewish sources as a source for iconography and purpose, something many had never thought they would do or ever need to do. Others felt encouraged to create Judaica because they did not see any Jewish ritual objects that reflected their own identity.[13] Books began to appear encouraging Jews towards "creative participation in a Jewish-American Folk Art movement."14 Many discovered that they had become Judaica artists almost by default. In some cases, through making a ritual object for themselves, a family member, or friend they suddenly found that other community members were demanding their work.[15] The interest by a broader group of artists and artisans as well as the sudden rise in interest by community members made a craft show like Temple Isaiah's Festival of Jewish Artisans timely and, it turned out, necessary. Its format became a guideline for shows that were to follow both at Isaiah and other venues.

During the planning phase in October of that year, the Festival committee searched out and sent letters to Jewish artists and artists who created Jewish art. In the letter, Jay Abarbanel, the chairperson, was explicit in expressing the hope that the Festival would eventually become an annual event. He shared that a primary goal of the Festival was "to educate the public to the rich variety and endless possibilities of Jewish art."[16] The organizers hoped to bring recognition, artistic and financial, to artists who were donating their time, their souls, their inspiration, their dreams[17] towards producing Jewish art. At the same time, the Festival hoped to reach out and attract Jews affiliated with a wide variety of Jewish communities.[18] Towards that end, Isaiah's show was not sponsored by the Sisterhood or Men's Club, but was a distinct arts committee. Two members of the committee were not only not Isaiah members, but were in fact from the Orthodox community, as were many of those providing home hospitality to the artists. The Festival's purpose was not to create an insular synagogue community but rather to appeal to the broader community, and its committee and publicity reflected that.

The Festival's title—The Festival of Jewish Artisans—was carefully crafted and expresses the ties the show had to folk tradition. The term "artisans" suggests that the organizers saw a closer connection to a folk artisan tradition rather than an academy art tradition. Much of the exhibited works were to be ritual art, very rarely were paintings included. Since ritual, craft, and folk art works are usually viewed as beautiful but primarily utilitarian in nature, Festival organizers saw a strong connection between the Festival and both the American craft and folk art movements and the Jewish folk art movement,[19] with a heavier focus on actual ritual objects.

The first year the show maintained the California emphasis and included only artists from California. The organizers set a $15 registration fee[20] and expected artists to cover transportation expenses. They did not believe artists outside of California would want to participate due to cost. Twenty-six artists were in the Festival the first year.[21] Given the spatial constraints of the exhibition area, no more than twenty-nine artisans participated in any given year. Over the years there was an effort by well-meaning people to suggest moving to a larger venue to enable participation by more artists. But because this had become a truly special Isaiah event, and its gift to the community, there was no desire to change. Remaining a small community of artists and organizers had the benefit of allowing the nurturing and support of artists to continue and even expand.

The response to the show was overwhelming. The first Festival was visited by about six hundred people,[22] representing the spectrum of the Jewish community. This pleased the organizers, who had taken many steps toward its goal of educating the public regarding contemporary Jewish art. In addition to displaying the works of the artists, the Festival also featured demonstrations by some of the artists to reveal the techniques they employ in their creative process.[23] This gave the visitors a unique opportunity to ask the artists questions about their work or their process. As a result, the visitors were learning about their Jewish heritage and creating their Jewish present.

In 1983 the Festival added educational programs to include hands-on workshops[24] such as papercutting and calligraphy. These workshops added a dimension to the artwork by emphasizing that old and new techniques have a place in contemporary Judaica. Programs were additionally expanded to include lectures such as "The Challenge of the Visual Arts in Judaism" by Dr. Stephen S. Kayser, *a"h*, Professor Emeritus in the department of Art History at UCLA and a director of the Jewish Museum, New York. Starting in 1987 other Jewish arts such as dance and music were added as evening programs.[25] Innagural performances included those by Yale Strom and the Zmiros Klezmer Band. The original single day was expanded at the artists request[26] to include Saturday night as well as the original Sunday program. However, the committee emphasized the educational importance of the overall show by creating an evening program that always had to have an educational component, including *Havdalah*. It was never purely entertainment. The Saturday night program had a higher entrance fee and included refreshments. This proved to be one of the most difficult aspects of the committee's work, being creative for Saturday night.[27] In addition, there were children's art workshops and programming so that families could come together and each enjoy the Festival at their own level. The children's workshops were devised to keep the children occupied so their parents could focus on purchasing their own Judaic heirlooms for the future. Many of the visitors purchased Judaica at the Festival. It is important to note that at this time the Festival of Jewish Artisans was one of the few places where people could go to buy contemporary Judaica in Los Angeles.[28] During this period, due to an economic downturn, there was a number of closings among galleries where Jewish artists with Jewish content were able to sell their work. Some artists turned to folk art festivals and craft shows as a medium for selling their works.[29] In truth, there were also Chanukah boutiques, but these were really smaller shows intended solely to fund-raise for the organizing synagogue. There really wasn't a place that focused on educating about and promoting the sales of Judaic art.

The Isaiah show was one of the few places aimed at educating the Jewish community about contemporary Jewish art, one of the few places where Judaica helped define contemporary Jewish identities in the Los Angeles region. The Festival opened the way for local Los Angeles Jewish patronage of contemporary Jewish artists. This rise in demand by the Los Angeles Jewish community meant that the artists needed to raise their production.[30] The artists began to view the Festival as an important segment of their annual income.

It should be noted that in the beginning, there was a tension between existing Judaica galleries in the Los Angeles area and the

Festival. Some galleries felt that a festival of this type would take away business and make the business climate more difficult for galleries focused on Judaica. Over time, most of the galleries came to see the Festival as an asset, both as a place to find new artists and a way to gain new customers. After all, the Festival was only once a year and people's desire for contemporary Judaica grew all year long.

The demand for the contemporary Judaica found at the Festival suggests that members of the Los Angeles Jewish community saw these works as enhancements to their Jewish identities, as contemporary pieces reflecting contemporary Jewry.

A major part of the Festival was the magic that happened when bringing Judaica artisans together. Artists could network about the business of being artists, talk about iconography and symbolism, and cross-pollinate ideas. Creating[31] and nurturing a community of Judaica artisans were important goals.

To encourage artist growth, Festival organizers created Sunday morning events specifically for the artists. These breakfast discussions served a cohesive and educational purpose. There were presentations and discussions related to how artists chose symbols, how to market oneself as an artist, portfolio management, and copyright laws. These events as well as the overall culture of the Festival did seem to have an impact. Some participants have commented on the fact that they felt a part of the Isaiah Festival artist community and have collaborated, swapped pieces, and made good friends from their experience at the Festival. Many continue to interact to this day.

Organizers also saw that works by some of the participating artists might not sell during the show due to their prices. For instance, artists with works above a certain price point (highly intricate textiles, silver candelabras, or personalized ketubbot) may not immediately sell those works. Organizers did not, however, want the artists to leave without making any sales. This was particularly true later on, when artists were coming from greater distances. Attempts were made to arrange meetings outside of the Festival between these artists and potentially interested community members. Thus, although these artists did not necessarily get outstanding sales at the Festival, they might leave Los Angeles with a sale, contact, or commission to make their travels worthwhile. And in truth, many on the committee felt compelled to see that each artist had some sales.

Earning a profit was never a high priority in planning which artists and programming to include.[32] While it was necessary to cover costs,[33] the organizers never saw the Festival as a temple fundraiser. Festival income was used to promote the Festival (advertisements, brochures, and the like) and create community workshops and lectures. This is not to say there was never any profit from the Festival. Temple Isaiah always received the entrance fee from the Festival, the proceeds of which were often used, along with other donations, to purchase Judaica for Temple Isaiah.[34]

In 1981 the idea of having an annual Festival was only a dream.[35] The fact that it became an annual event was a result of a number of important factors.

The process of choosing the artists involved a committee.[36] Not every artist was chosen. The members of the committee needed to establish and understand the criteria for selecting the artists; thus the jurying process also became an educational process for committee members.

This selective process also benefited the artists. Participation in juried shows was a significant enhancement to an artist's resume. The fact that the Artisan's Festival is a juried show helped it and the artists to rise in prominence. Though many artists were invited, including participants from previous years, no artist was guaranteed spots for the following year.

As the reputation of the Festival grew each year, the committee felt it was important to reach out to new artists. At the same time, new artists sought out the opportunity to show at the Isaiah Artisan's Festival. The original focus on Californian artists in 1981[37] evolved in subsequent years so that eventually the Festival had participants and applications from throughout the United States[38] and as far away as Israel,[39] Brazil,[40] and Italy.[41] This occurred despite the costs incurred due to travel. Artists from far away might combine participation in the Artisan's Festival with "selling trips" throughout the United States. In addition, other Jewish artisans festivals were planned so that artists could include trips to these shows as well. Today international artists travel to the Judaica shows in White Plains, New York, and Skokie, Illinois, as well as the URJ Biennial. (Though the Biennial is seen as more of a trade show, important for contacts and future sales, whereas artists felt that the Isaiah Festival was "promoting art for art's sake"[42] and never compromised on those standards.)

No two juries use the same criterion in their methods of choosing participating artists. The Artisan's Festival organizers felt that it was important not only to support former participants but to open the doors to new artists. Rules were developed to encourage the educational goals. Organizers felt that participating in a festival encouraged artists' growth through the exchange of ideas between fellow artists.[43] Newer artists could learn from more established artists and all could learn from one another.

The committee made an attempt from the beginning to try to diversify types of artists by price, method, and materials used. In this way visitors would be exposed to a diversity of works in a variety of media. This also meant that a greater potential for sales could occur since even if there were overlapping in object types there would still be variety within a medium. This allowed visitors to compare works and purchase within their price ranges.

The variety of media also resulted in the diversity of the ritual objects included. Metalsmiths do not make challah covers and textile artists do not make candlesticks. The display provides a wider variety of opportunities for educating the viewing community. New objects were created and introduced.

Media represented over the course of the Festival have included ceramics, silver, paper (papercut/calligraphy and printmaking), wood, glass, textiles, stone, photography, jewelry, and mixed media.

The backgrounds of the artists varied as well. Artists ranged from those who were semiliterate Jewishly to those who had a good Jewish education. From the self taught to those who hold Fine Art degrees. Some artists were graduates of Bezalel, the Tobe Pascher workshop,[44] or other fine arts programs. This range is common in all contemporary Judaica.

Besides choosing artists who fall within a variety of media, the Festival attracted artists representing a range in prices. The Festival attracts a broad spectrum of the Jewish community from collectors able to afford larger purchases to young couples with young families and modest budgets. Organizers wanted any visitor to be able to come away with a beautiful item of Judaica. Thus, it was necessary to maintain a varied price scale. Visitors could buy holiday cards or a silver Chanukah lamp.

A significant rule, strictly enforced, was that organizers expected the artists to be present to exhibit, sell their own work, and meet the community. Representatives were not allowed. This is again related to the educational aspect of the Festival. For it was important for artists to meet and speak both with other artists and the community. But there were rare occasions when this rule was waived.

The ultimate decision of who to include was a committee decision based on slide (and later digital images) review and discussion. Everyone's vote was equal. Over the years committee members changed, but the rules for deciding remained essentially consistent. Committee members each received a list of potential participants. Images from each potential participant were presented and the committee discussed each artist as an individual and in relation to the mandate of the Festival.[45]

Outgrowth of the Isaiah Festival

The Artisan's Festival was created simultaneously with the desire of Jewish artists to explore their identity and create ritual works that they and others could relate to. Throughout the years of the Artisan's Festival many new objects, techniques, materials, and forms were introduced that spoke to the various visitors. Among the mezuzot, *Kiddush* cups, tallitot, and *ketubot*, Miriam's cups, amulets for learning or to prevent earthquakes, blessing bowls, lace fringed *kippot*, and sculptures and cups made out of shards of the glass broken at a Jewish wedding have been displayed, bought, and sold. Some artists, particularly those with expensive pieces, wanted their work to be viewed and displayed as "art" when not in ritual use.

Isaiah's show was successful in creating a community of Jewish artists based on participation in this show.[46] Since its creation, communities of artists appeared[47] such as JACOB,[48] SPIRAL,[49] and the East Coast Jewish Artists Association, among many others.[50]

After its inception, other festivals of Jewish artisans began throughout the United States and throughout the world.[51] A number of their organizers visited the Isaiah show for inspiration and many implemented the artists breakfast as well as other features. In a recent conversation with founding White Plains Judaica Craft Show organizers, a show that continues to this day, they expressed their thanks for the inspiration and lessons learned from the Festival.[52] Today there are many more locations for Jewish artisans to display and sell their work. Galleries, including artist-owned galleries, museum shops, and even synagogue shops offer selling opportunities today.

Following the creation of the Isaiah show came the creation of large-scale Judaica competitions such as the Jesselson Prize, Jerusalem; Spertus Competition, Chicago; and the Adi prize, Jerusalem. Like the Artisan's Festival these competitions encouraged artists to explore their Jewish identity and create contemporary Jewish ritual articles and art. In addition, there are many more exhibition venues for contemporary Judaica than there were in the early 1980s.

After more than twenty-five years, the Artisan's Festival finally wound down.The founders, their relatives, and member have been asked, "Why did the Festival stop?" "Aren't you considering starting the Festival again?" Given the many opportunities that grew over time for artists both from an educational and business perspective (as well as the extensive amount of work necessary to create the Festival) after a more than a twenty-five-year run, it was decided to end the Festival of Jewish Artisans. Informally, many of the organizers continue to support artists with advice, connections, and sometimes purchases, but the Festival itself is now over.[53]

Historian of Jewish art Moshe Davidowitz, himself the son of a major collector, pointed out the special role that Jewish ritual objects play in Judaism. He said that "when one uses the objects, is aware of their meaning, participates with *kavanah,* focuses on the mitzvah, and enhances it with beauty, then one transforms a ceremony into a sacred event."[54] At the Isaiah Festival artists and visitors often learned together the meaning of the objects and developed their own private understanding of these objects, their own *kavanah*. They explored new ways of enhancing traditional objects with beauty as well as new ways to enhance their Jewish identities through the introduction of new or traditional ritual items. The development of the Temple Isaiah model, the influence it had, the lessons learned, and the ripple effect it produced in support for Judaica artists throughout the world, had an impact beyond the wildest dreams of its founders.

Notes

1. The founding committee included Jean and Jay Abarbanel and Fred and Nancy Golub, who were members of Temple Isaiah and Karl and Marcia Josephy, members of Orthodox synagogues.
2. Jean Abarbanel, "Temple Isaiah's Festival of Jewish Artisans: A Jewish Community Art Outreach Program" (grant application submitted to the Jewish Community Foundation, 1984), 1. The

grant requested funds to build appropriate display boards for the artists' work. This grant was received.

3. Ibid., 1.
4. Ibid., 2.
5. "For the Fall, 1981 Temple Isaiah Presents: A Celebration of Jewish Arts" (advertising flyer).
6. Ibid. Lectures presented by Marcia Reines Josephy.
7. Lecture by Linda Steinberg.
8. Series advertisement mailer, 1981. The studios visited were those of photographer Bill Aron, printmaker Marion Baker, and ceramicist Verna Kaufman.
9. Ibid., side 2.
10. Jonathan D. Sarna, *JPS: The Americanization of Jewish Culture, 1888–1988* (New York: JPS, 1989), 280–81.
11. Ibid., 282–83.
12. Jean Abarbanel and Marcia Reines Josephy, "Renaissance of the Jewish Craft Movement" (paper presented at Art Culture Future American Craft '86 National Conference, Oakland, CA, June 6, 1986).
13. In a survey of over fifty artists by Meira Josephy between November 2001 and October 2002 quite a number indicated that they began creating Judaica because they saw a lack of Judaica they could relate to or felt was aesthetically pleasing. To view that paper or artist responses please contact the author at mjosephy@alum.barnard.edu. See also Mae Shafter Rockland, *The Work of Our Hands: Jewish Needlecraft for Today* (New York: Schocken Books, 1972), viii: "What is currently available in crafts for Jewish-Americans, either to buy or to make, is paltry indeed."
14. Rockland, *The Work of Our Hands,* viii. See also Ita Aber, *The Art of Judaic Needlework: Traditional and Contemporary Designs* (New York: Charles Scribner's Sons, 1979); Jay Greenspan and David Moss's articles on scribal arts in *The Jewish Catalog: A Do-It-Yourself Kit*, ed. Richard Siegel, Michael Strassfeld, and Sharon Strassfeld (Philadelphia: JPS, 1973); and Rockland's article on Jewish folk art in *The Second Jewish Catalog,* among others.
15. This information was also relayed by a large number of survey respondents to the question "what encouraged you to begin work in ritual art?"
16. Jay Abarbanel, artist invitation letter, October 12, 1981.
17. Sari Srulovitch, silversmith, interview, Jerusalem, Israel, April 2, 2012.
18. Jean Abarbanel, "Temple Isaiah's Festival," 2.
19. Neither folk art nor craft are easily defined and have often been used interchangeably. The *American Folklore Encyclopedia* defines

folk art as "objects of aesthetic expression usually appreciated for their traditional aspects." See Kristin G. Congdon, "Art, Folk," *American Folklore: An Encyclopedia,* ed. Jan Harold Brunvand (New York and London: Garland Publishing, Inc., 1996), 46., There has been debate as to whether folk artists must only be self or traditionally taught or whether formal instruction will not impede on a work's folk aspect. See Gary Schwindler, *Interface: Outsiders and Insiders* (Athens, OH: Ohio University, 1986), 4, in Roger Cardinal, "Toward an Outsider Aesthetic," *The Artist Outsider: Creativity and the Boundaries of Culture*, ed. Michael D. Hall and Eugene W. Metcalf, Jr. (Washington, DC, and London: Smithsonian Institution Press, 1994), 31. Craft is usually defined as objects handmade by craft workers utilizing local materials and local techniques. The workers are taught through demonstration. See Jean Haskell Speer, "Craft," *American Folklore: An Encyclopedia* ,173. For a new analysis of the meaning and relevance of craft, see M. Anna Fariello, "Making and Naming: The Lexicon of Studio Craft," *Extra/Ordinary Craft and Contemporary Art*, ed. Maria Elena Buszek (Durham and London: Duke University Press, 2011).

20. Jay Abarbanel, artist invitation letter, 1981.
21. Series advertisement mailer, 1981, side 1.
22. Jean Abarbanel, "Temple Isaiah's Festival." Isaiah wanted to enable families with children and single parent families to equally participate in the event. Therefore, they provided children's programming. Over the years thousands of people attended.
23. Advertisement for the 1982 Isaiah show explains that there will be "Exhibit, demonstrations, and sale of works by well-known Jewish artisans, including calligraphers, weavers, embroiderers, illuminators, ketubah makers, sculptors, print makers, photographers, paper-cutters, ceramicists, metal workers."
24. Jean Abarbanel, "Temple Isaiah's Festival." A grant was requested to support workshops, which would be a new feature of the Festival programming, and lectures on Jewish art.
25. An almost complete list of lectures and workshops can be found at http://birkatchaverim.com/isaiahfestival.
26. The initial request came from Claire Sherman, a ceramicist from Northern California.
27. Programs included: "Reflections on Contemporary Jewish Art: The Artist's Perspective" (Bill Aron, photographer; Rose Ann Chasman, paper-cutter and calligrapher; Laurie Gross, weaver; Peachy Levy, textile artist; Peretz Wolf-Prusan, printmaker; moderator: Linda Steinberg, Director of Marjorie and Herman Platt Gallery, University of Judaism), "Drawing from Judaica: A Slide Presentation" (Mark Podwal, illustrator and author of *A Book of*

Hebrew Letters and A Jewish Bestiary), "Collecting Judaica:The Passion and the Quest; Views of the Vendor, Artist, and Collector of Jewish Art and Artifacts: A Panel Discussion" (Nancy Berman, then Director of HUC Skirball Museum; Herb Bernhard, collector; Laurie Gross, artist; Alex Lauterbach, collector; Joy Schonberg, Judaica International, formerly with Christie's Judaica department), Margalit Oved in "Travel with Me My Dove and Listen to Me, based on a poem by Shalom Shabazzi" (dance performance combining traditional with contemporary), Klezmania! Golden State Klezmer Band and the Buddy Collette Trio, The Sounds of Jerusalem (featuring Bruce Burger of RebbeSoul and Evan Kent, cantor at Temple Isaiah), The Ellis Island Klezmer Band, and Mariachi Mundiale de Mexico.

28. Ellen Friedberg, "Annual Festival of Jewish Artisans Kicks-off 14th Year" *California Jewish Press*, November 4, 5, and 6, 1994.
29. Lila Wahrhaftig, printmaker; interview, Berkley, California, June 13. 2002.
30. The following year organizers approached artists earlier to give them time to produce enough work for the following year's show.
31. Jay Abarbanel, artist invitation letter, 1.
32. Linda Estrin, "The Chai Year of the Festival of Jewish Artisans," *The Isaiah* (November 1998): 2.
33. In 1982 in addition to the $15 registration fee, Temple Isaiah requested a 10 percent commission "to cover our costs, which we discovered are considerable." Jay Abarbanel, artist invitation letter, 2.
34. Estrin, "The Chai Year," 2.
35. Jay Abarbanel, 1981.
36. The committee expanded and over time also came to include Susan Needleman, a former president of Temple Isaiah, and Sheila Gan (who both came to chair the committee), Susan Bartholomew, Barry and Helene Korn, Pamela Deitch, Vicki Reikes Fox, Joan Hess, Even Kent, Charlene Kodimer, Dawn Revel, Joan Sales, Jackie Trauberman, and June Wynbrandt.
37. Jay Abarbanel, 1981.
38. For instance, Robert Lipnik, ceramicist from Davenport, Iowa; Roseann Chasman, *z"l*, Chicago, IL., papercut; and Arel Mishory, found metal from Denver, Colorado.
39. For instance, Dan Givon, Avi Biran, Eitan Amiel, Emil Shenfeld, and Sari Srulovitch, metalworkers; Sara Einstein, *z"l*, jewelry; Corrine and Robert Kleinman, and Adina Gatt, textile; Catriel, woodwork; and Yehudit Shadur, *z"l*, papercut.
40. Norma Grinberg, ceramics.
41. Luigi Del Monte, silver.

42. Robert Kleinman, Shizrei Kodesh, interview, Jerusalem, Israel, April 2, 2012. A similar sentiment about the importance of the artist at the Isaiah show was expressed by Sari Srulovitch.
43. This phenomenon did occur from year to year at the Artisan's Festival. Marcia Reines Josephy has relayed an incident wherein Roseann Chasman, a papercut artist had been using a catalog on Jewish amulets and superstitions in her amuletic work. This book was from an exhibition on amulets at the Spertus organized by Marcia Reines Josephy. The concepts of amulets and the catalog made their way to a ceramic artist, Claire Sherman, who began to create amulets such as the amulet against earthquakes. Other artists also began designing amulets as well.
44. In 1956 the Jewish Museum in New York opened the Tobe Pascher workshop and brought Ludwig Wolpert from Israel to serve as the master craftsman. See Grace Cohen Grossman, *Smithsonian Studies in History and Technology, no. 52: Judaica at the Smithsonian:Cultural Politics as Cultural Model* (Washington, DC: Smithsonian Institution Press, 1997), 204. Abram Kanof was a main force behind the creation of the Tobe Pascher workshop and in bringing Wolpert to the United States.
45. Temple Isaiah Festival of Jewish Artisans Outline, 1995.
46. David and Michelle Plachte-Zuieback, survey response, August 14, 2001.
47. Jean Abarbanel and Marcia Reines Josephy, "Renaissance of the Jewish Craft Movement."
48. Jewish Arts Community of the Bay.
49. Midwest Jewish artist group.
50. Many of these groups are currently defunct or officially inactive. However, informally participants still create a community of artists. The Pomegranate Guild of Judaic Needlework and Pomegranate Guild of Judaic Textiles, Toronto, also began at around the same time as the Festival and provide support to artists in an amateur to professional environment. The American Guild of Judaic Art provided and provides professional support to artists.
51. Many of these shows' organizers contacted the Isaiah show founders for help in setting up their shows. Calls were received not only from all over the United States but also from other countries.
52. Betsy and Don Landis, founders of the White Plains Judaica Art Show, Jerusalem, Israel, March 28, 2012.
53. It was gratifying, I must admit, that when I visited the Biennial, former Festival participants told each other I was there and many came to find me to say hello and thank you. (M.R.J.)
54. Moshe Davidowitz *"See and Sanctify": Exploring Jewish Symbols* (New York: Yeshiva University Museum, 1979), 9.

Becoming a Modern Judaica Artist: A Stranger in a Strange Land No More

Gary Rosenthal

The Bible provides a description of the ultimate Judaica artist when it describes the role and responsibilities of Bezalel when he is tasked with the creation of the Tabernacle. But when I dropped out of Cornell in 1972 to become a sculptor, I was not inspired to follow in Bezalel's footsteps to create beautiful Judaica. The shoes were too big to fill and I perceived them as being way out of date and covered with the dust of the ages. I was focused on creating art and the issue of my Jewish identity played no part in this endeavor.

During my year off from college, I taught myself how to weld and shape metal. Success came easily and my art very quickly became popular because it looked good over sofas and my table-top items made great gifts. Before I knew it, the Dance Masters of America asked me to create a bronze trophy for their Miss Dance America contest. At the same time, I had received a letter from President Carter letting me know that my work had been accepted into the White House Library Collection. I was doing well, traveling the artist circuit, when my life was changed one day, in 1978, at the Baltimore JCC Art Show.

"Do You Think You Could Make a Menorah?"

What an amazing question to be asked in that setting, a room filled with Jews who had all come there to buy art. There was not a piece

GARY ROSENTHAL has been sculpting in welded metals for almost forty years using copper, brass, and steel with brilliant fused glass. His work has been presented to presidents from Jimmy Carter to Barack Obama, and to celebrities as varied as Bette Midler, John Travolta, and Tony Randall. The Collection can be found throughout the world in many fine galleries, private collections, and museum shops.

of Judaica to be found. In fact, at that time, Judaica was not found in any gifts shops or fine craft galleries across the country. In 1978, to get a menorah, you either inherited something from the old country—that looked like it was made in 1785—or you brought something back from Israel or bought it in a Sisterhood gift shop. In either case, it was sure to have a blue-green patina and broke shortly after it was used for the first time. In all likelihood, the reason you bought it in the first place was because you were supporting Israel.

The fact that I was in a room filled with Jewish artists and Jewish buyers, with no Judaica to be found, today seems impossible. *Hidur mitzvah* (the mitzvah of beautifying Jewish ritual) is one of the 613 mitzvot that we are commanded to perform. Furthermore, since the destruction of the Second Temple and the ending of the priesthood, observation of Judaism became personalized and centered in the home rather than the synagogue. As a result, every observant Jewish family has a pair of Shabbat candlesticks and every doorway a mezuzah. If this was indeed the case, why weren't twentieth-century American Jewish artists making Judaica?

A History of Exclusion

The answer most likely lies in the diaspora history of Jews in Europe, starting with the Middle Ages and continuing to as recently as twenty years ago. During the Middle Ages, European Jews were not allowed to join craft guilds. A Jew could not serve as an apprentice or become a master silversmith or other tradesman. If he was caught working as a craftsman, the penalty could be death. As a result, while there were many finely wrought Christian artifacts, Judaica items were simple and fairly limited. In addition, throughout history, up to the years following the Holocaust, most Jews, like my parents, first-generation Americans, were unwilling to celebrate their Judaism in public view. As a result of these two factors throughout much of our history, Jews creating identifiable Jewish ritual objects remained a rarity. I believe there was an interruption in our creative history from the time of Bezalel in the Torah until perhaps the mid-twentieth century when Ludwig Wolpert opened his studio in New York City and began creating the most beautiful silver Judaica that had been produced in many centuries.

By 1985 American Jews found themselves in an ever-changing environment. I benefited from this transition when I embraced the question posed to me at the Baltimore JCC and produced several menorot to bring to the next show. They turned out to be so popular that I immediately put all of my energy into creating a whole line of new, modern Judaica—everything from mezuzot to *Havdalah* sets. Everything I made sold as soon as it was made. I was in the right place at the right time!

A New Way of Being in the World

When I was growing up, my family had a single menorah, one set of brass candlesticks for Shabbat, and a *Kiddush* cup. These pieces were consigned to a drawer or cabinet in the dining room until Friday night. By Sunday, they were back in their hideaway until they were called into service the following Shabbat or holy day. I knew other families who may have had a *Havdalah* set, and maybe a second set of silver candlesticks, for when company came for Shabbat dinner, but no one thought of these items as art, or worthy of permanent display.

All of this began to change after the Six-Day War and into the early 1970s as American Jews began to feel comfortable and even proud of their religion. Many baby boomers were growing up without a full set of Judaica in their homes. Many of their congregations were encouraging the visible celebration of holidays that, heretofore, had only been recognized in religious schools or when the Orthodox kids stayed out of secular school in the middle of the week. As their incomes and education levels rose substantially higher than those of their parents and they began to have their own children, these newly established and visible Jews wanted to have both art and Jewish ritual items to display in their much larger homes.

As for me, I was just ahead of the curve where baby boomer Jews would become Judaica collectors and a menorah would become the ultimate wedding present. As a result, my success at art shows was extraordinary. As the only artist selling Judaica at many of these shows, even those sponsored by Jewish Community Centers, my work would sell out at every show. I was soon exceeding the capacity of my garage, where I had my studio, and I hired my first employee to help keep up with the demand. I'll never forget the day I showed my dad a table full of mezuzah cases and he said, "Who is going to buy all those mezuzahs?" No one in his generation, including my eighteen aunts and uncles, thought I could earn a living making Judaica. Even as the menorot were flying off the table, customers at shopping mall art shows and outdoor festivals where I would show my work would quickly put their new purchases in their bag and say, "Aren't you afraid of showing Judaica in public?" The fear of being recognized as a Jew in America was still strong in the 1980s into the 1990s. It was not until later in the 1990s that this changed and Jews finally found a new way of being in the world, comfortable in their own skins.

A Jewish Johnny Appleseed

By the late 1980s I had a wife and a son and was tired of spending my life on the road. I decided to build my business by selling my work wholesale to galleries and gift shops, instead of directly to retail customers. As it turns out, most of the galleries and fine gift shops were owned by Jewish retailers; but, contrary to expectations, we had the hardest time convincing them to buy the work. They didn't want the store to seem "too Jewish." Once again, the fear of being visible as a Jew was evident, and I truly believe that many of these merchants thought that if they had a menorah in their store window, a brick was soon to follow.

Despite this resistance, I loved creating Judaica and it became a mission for me to popularize modern and contemporary Judaica. I began advertising in Jewish media from *Reform Judaism Magazine* to *Outlook* to *Hadassah* to secular American craft magazines like *Niche* and *American Crafts*. We always placed full-page ads with the most prominent placement we could afford. My favorite ad ever was a two-page spread in *Reform Judaism* that featured a selection of two dozen of my latest mezuzot, with a caption that read, "thank G-d you need more than one mezuzah." In those years, I frequently felt as if I were the Jewish Johnny Appleseed, out to popularize fine American Craft Judaica.

Even with all the advertising and clear success at art shows, the Jewish gallery owners still would not purchase our Judaica. I really believe that their fear of reprisal and desire to be invisible as a Jew prevented them from making a good economic decision. Finally, several of the best-known American crafts galleries in the country, owned by non-Jews, agreed to take my work. I'll never forget when Arthur Grohe, owner of Grohe Galleries of Boston, among the first to sell my work, said to me, "Gary, I always knew that most of my best clients were Jewish, but who would have ever thought that they would want to buy Judaica!" This "revelation" drove my business for the next twenty years. I eventually had fifty employees creating nothing but Judaica.

One day a writer for Associated Press paid a visit to my studio for an article about Chanukah, where he saw a clothesline with one hundred menorot hanging up for the varnish to dry. In his article, he described my studio as "Santa's workshop for Jewish people."

Over the years, the many artists and craftspeople who have worked for the Gary Rosenthal Collection helped to create and then rode the wave of contemporary Judaica so that, by 1994, the cover of *Niche,* the wholesale craft industry's feature magazine, was a picture of a menorah, with a headline that read, "Judaica, the hottest trend in American crafts!" By that time, collectors of mezuzot and menorot had emerged across the country; and Judaica was purchased not only for function, but also for display as a home decorator item. It felt as if I were back to the days of making sculptures that looked good over sofas, as now clients were sending me color swatches to match for their newest menorah. It was clear that the growth of the Judaica "industry" in America correlated with the rise of popular Judaism in late twentieth-century America. As the second millenium C.E. drew to a close, it was finally okay to own a menorah, and it was okay for the world to know that you were Jewish.

The Best of Times

I didn't have a role model for creating contemporary Judaica; but I did feel as if I had an instruction manual in the Bible and in the thousands of years of history, which, believe it or not, I learned in Hebrew school. It practically came in the form of a blank check to be creative. I knew that families everywhere light and bless the candles on Shabbat, that the mezuzah scrolls hang on the doorway, and that the story of our escape from Egypt needs to be told in foods held on a plate. But somehow, I also realized that what holds the candles, contains the scrolls, or displays the foods is up to the artist's imagination! Without a role model I started creating very contemporary Judaica. I took on, as a mission, the job of making Judaica popular. My goal was always to create each work of Judaica that was both functional and, at the same time, beautiful enough to leave out year-round and that families could be proud to own and share with everyone. As artists, we try to put our *ruach* (spirit) into every piece of Judaica that we create. I feel blessed to have helped so many families beautify their ritual through my art and lucky to be a Jewish artist. I like to think that if Bezalel were still around, he might approve of the state of Judaica today. With so many Jewish artists around the world creating beautiful Judaica, I believe that this just may be the best time in the history of the Jewish people to be looking for a new menorah. Thank you for the inspiration, Bezalel!

Painting by Numbers: Reporting on the Emergence of Modern Jewish Art

Tal Gozani

Nearly four hundred Jewish painters, sculptors, engravers, enamellists, and architects, including more than one hundred Jewish women, exhibited at the official annual art exhibitions of the *Académie des Beaux-Arts* in Paris, commonly known as the Salon, in the half-century preceding World War I.[1] Jewish artists, deeply ensconced in the French art world, won prestigious public art commissions and juried awards, including the Salon's highly coveted *Prix de Rome.*They were selected for France's highest civilian tribute, the Legion of Honor, and chosen to represent France at that extravagant new venue of national pride, the World's Fairs. Jewish artists also increasingly exhibited at such alternative art venues as the revolutionary Impressionist salons.

The Jewish press, which as recently as 1851 lamented the failure of French Jews to make *any* kind of mark in the visual arts, proudly reported on these achievements and were responsible for introducing Jewish audiences to the growing number of Jewish artists and their work. Journals such as *L'Univers Israélite* and *Archives Israélite* set aside special columns describing official Salon entries by French Jewish artists. These columns focused on the major accomplishments of Jewish artists and their remarkable integration into the mainstream French art scene. They also speculated about the significance of these accomplishments for modern French Jewry. In the process, the journals legitimated this field of endeavor among

TAL GOZANI is Vice President of Young Adult Programs at the Jewish Federation of Los Angeles. Previously, she was a curator at the Skirball Cultural Center and Museum for over a decade. She has curated dozens of exhibitions and published articles on the intersection of modern Jewish art and Jewish history and is currently completing her doctoral dissertation on the emergence of modern Jewish art in nineteenth-century France.

Jews and helped dispel the ever-persistent prejudice that Jews were innately incapable of producing genuine art.

This article's historical survey of the dramatic explosion of Jewish interest and participation in the arts relies heavily on reports contained in the contemporary Jewish press. These reports—skewed towards artists who exhibited at the official Paris Salon and World's Fairs—offer intriguing glimpses at the careers of leading Jewish artists across a broad range of art styles. In annual reviews, the press described with formulaic consistency each Jewish artist's training, the masters with whom they studied, and any honors they received. The Jewish press seemed more interested in recording lofty artistic pedigrees than independently evaluating the artistic merits of specific work. In many ways, it was these official markers of success, and not necessarily the artistic brilliance of any individual artist, that rendered these artists the idealized embodiment of French Jewish integration.

The Jewish press also reported with pride on Jewish participation at the extravagant *Expositions Universelle* (World's Fairs), which were designed to showcase national industrial and artistic accomplishments.[2] Jewish reporters rejoiced that Jewish artists were among celebrated artists chosen to represent France at these prominent affairs. This inclusion of Jewish artists, both French and foreign, was taken by the Jewish press as authentication of the success of Jewish integration and the deep-felt patriotism of Jewish artists.

The Jewish press reviewed all the World's Fairs held in France, but discussions of the 1878 Exposition were particularly enthusiastic. For one thing, the 1878 World's Fair came to symbolize France's successful national "rebirth" as a socially, culturally, and politically progressive Third Republic after a series of humiliating military defeats. *Archives* art critic David Schornstein, for instance, took note of the Exposition's symbolic importance for the fledgling young Republic and a Jewry closely intertwined with its fate. In his view, active Jewish participation in the Exposition not only affirmed the ideals of French Jewish integration but also proved that Jews embraced their patriotic duty to help the young Republic succeed.[3]

Jewish enthusiasm for the 1878 Fair also reflected the Exposition's inclusion of an unprecedented pavilion dedicated to an exclusively Jewish exhibition.[4] This *Musée Hebraique* was groundbreaking. Previously, some Jewish observers had sighed about the absence of serious discussions concerning Judaism at the World's Fairs (and in the arts more generally), expressing hope that "one day there will be a Universal Exposition just for us."[5] Now, with this prominent display of Jewish ritual objects, these observers got their wish.

The secularized presentation of Jewish ceremonial objects to a broad Jewish and non-Jewish audience was something new and radical.[6] Jewish observers felt a keen pride that Jewish ritual objects, converted into *objects d'art,* were worthy of inclusion in an exhibition of national, and even international, importance.[7] Moreover, the prominent inclusion of the *Musée Hebraique* in the grand Exposition of 1878 helped legitimize among both Jews and non-Jews the notion of a Jewish national affinity for art. One critic, who in his writings on the art of ethnic nationalities in Russia had frequently championed the idea that art could (and should) promote strong national identities, saw in the exhibited Judaica collection a powerful expression of a distinct Jewish national identity independent of French Jews' sociopolitical situation as citizens of the French state. He vigorously encouraged Jewish artists to further articulate and cultivate this Jewish national sensibility.[8]

For the Jewish press, the inclusion of the *Musée Hebraique* in the World's Fair of 1878 signified an important moment in the building of a modern French Jewish culture. The landmark exhibition offered concrete proof that Jewish creativity was valued as part of the new French national entity and that Jewish particularity could fruitfully coexist with French patriotism. Moreover, going forward, the successful development of an appropriate Jewish aesthetic sensibility depended not only on a critical mass of competent Jewish artists, which by now had begun to emerge, but also on such artists' active engagement with the types of religious and historical subject matters and materials embodied by the exhibited Judaica collection.

Jewish Women in the Arts

Overall, between 1846 and the outbreak of World War I in 1914, the Jewish journals reported on 384 French Jewish artists who participated in the official and most respected art Salon.[9] While some of these artists exhibited only once or twice, others were frequent contributors, including some who exhibited at the Salon for decades.

Initially, the journals listed all Jewish artists exhibiting in the Salons alphabetically. However, as these lists became ever longer and unwieldy, the journals started, around 1877, to subdivide the listings by art categories, such as painting, engraving, sculpture, watercolor and drawing, etc.

Women were not separately listed, but as early as 1847, the Jewish press reported on a female Jewish artist.[10] Beginning in the 1870s, and especially after the emergence of the French women artists' union in 1881, female Jewish participation in the Salon escalated dramatically.[11] To be sure, female artists tended to restrict themselves to media deemed appropriate for women, such as watercolor, pastel, and ceramics, and largely confined their art to such domestic themes as still lifes and portraits.[12] Nevertheless, by the turn of the twentieth century, Jewish female artists constituted, both in numbers and skill, an important segment of the vibrant Jewish art scene in France.

The Jewish press valued the contribution of these women to the overall goal of increased Jewish participation in the arts and treated female Jewish artists to the same praise and criticism as their male counterparts. Jewish art critics did not shy away from praising the artistic quality and potential of female artists, encouraging them to venture beyond so-called feminine subject matter.[13] At the same time, the Jewish press felt free to criticize female artists whose choice of subject matter or artistic execution failed to meet their expectations.

The two most recognizable female Jewish personalities in the French art world during this period were the Baroness Charlotte de Rothschild and Sarah Bernhardt. Taking after her parents, bank magnate James Mayer and Betty de Rothschild, Charlotte de Rothschild was easily the most recognizable French Jewish art patron and collector of the last third of the nineteenth century.[14] She socialized with such creative luminaries as Gioachino Rossini, Frédéric Chopin, Honoré de Balzac, and Eugène Delacroix and was a talented watercolorist in her own right, regularly exhibiting at the Salon and the newly formed *Société des Aquarellistes Français*. The Jewish journals proudly reported on this French Jewish celebrity's participation at France's most famous art events.[15]

Sarah Bernhardt, "the Divine Sarah," gained fame as Europe and America's premier tragedienne over the course of a sixty-year acting career and established herself as a very productive sculptor and painter as well. Noted Russian art critic Wladimir Stassoff proclaimed Bernhardt a "wildly talented woman," singling out her bronze sculpture of a prominent French scholar and politician as one of the "magnificent" artistic achievements on display at the 1878 World's Fair in Paris.[16] Her sculptures earned an honorable mention at the 1876 Salon.

Academic Art

In the 1850s, Jewish involvement in the arts was primarily confined to the medium of painting.[17] By the 1870s, Jewish artists were well-represented not only in painting but also in sculpture, drawing and engraving, and the decorative arts. In 1872, for instance, *Archives* featured master engraver Gustave Lévy, the accomplished sculptor Anthony-Samuel Adam-Salomon, watercolorists Jeanne Samson and the Baroness Charlotte de Rothschild, as well as several enamellists.

Many Jewish artists initially established their reputations in the neoclassical style, which sought to revive the ideals of ancient Greece and Rome—its art, culture, history, and landscape—through emphasis on formal composition and monumentality of subject matter. These artists created a broad range of historical and genre paintings, including many with Christian or classical mythological themes.

History

For much of the nineteenth century, history painting remained the dominant form of academic art and hence the most conspicuous at the official Salon.[18] History paintings depicting historical events from ancient Greece and Rome, Christian and medieval scenes, and important recent events were customarily large and frequently commissioned by the state. Artists exhibiting historical topics at the government-sponsored official Salon were more likely to receive awards and additional commissions. Despite the field's waning popularity in the latter decades of the nineteenth century, history painting retained its dignity as "the most elevated category of art" as long as it retained its academic art status.

Several Jewish artists gained prominence as history painters, including Benjamin Eugène Fichel and Benjamin Ulmann. Trained and influenced by renowned neoclassicist painters and teachers, such as Michel Martin Drölling, François-Édouard Picot, and Alexandre Abel de Pujol, Fichel produced grand commemorative tableaus of France's great leaders and military achievements, including Napoleon's victorious Italian campaign, as well as compositions relating to the infamous St. Bartholomew's Day massacre.

Benjamin Ulmann embraced the narrative approach to history painting made famous by the great neoclassicist painter Jean Auguste Dominique Ingres. The Jewish press, recognizing Ulmann's reputation as a history painter in the Salon, proudly introduced him in their annual Salon reviews as the Jewish artist most "faithful to historical subjects."[19] Inspired by his master's treatment of the same subject, Ulmann produced a sympathetic portrait of the future king of France welcomed back to Paris after the suppression of the peasant insurrection of 1358.[20] Another painting addressed the more recent political crisis of 1877 and captured the dramatic moment credited with saving the Republic. Ulmann also produced several prized portraits of significant literary and historical personalities and icons.[21] Ulmann received numerous medals for works he exhibited at the Salon, including the *Prix de Rome*, as well as the Legion of Honor.

Religion and Mythology

Religious painting resurfaced as an important artistic trend during the 1850s and 1860s. Following the divisive 1848 Revolution, artists and government officials loyal to the Second Empire (1852–1870) worked together to prevent future uprisings by imbuing art with moral values that portrayed a unity between church and state.[22] Many neoclassical artists looked to Christian iconography and Greek mythology to find religious or legendary personalities and biblical or allegorical stories as models for demonstrating the power of religious healing. Ironically, while stories from the Hebrew Bible were a popular theme for several non-Jewish artists who were inspired by its characters and stories, most Jewish artists who took an interest in religion or the Bible were specifically interested in the New Testament. Several of these, including Émile Lévy, Alexandre Laemlein, and Henri-Léopold Lévy, achieved prominence as painters of sacred history and mythology.

Émile Lévy rather surprisingly began his career painting Jewish themes, including a noteworthy treatment of Noah cursing his son, Canaan, exhibited at the 1855 World's Fair.[23] However, after winning the prestigious *Prix de Rome* and studying classical art in Rome with his colleagues Edgar Degas and Gustave Moreau, Lévy largely abandoned Jewish subject matter.[24] Profoundly influenced by his teachers—the great neoclassical artists Picot and Pujol—Lévy dedicated the remainder of his long and productive career as an artist to painting Christian and Greek mythological scenes, including monumental historical works of the death of Orpheus and the mythological tale of Cupid and Psyche.

Lévy's mastery of neoclassicism earned him a reputation as a first-rate academic painter and made him a favorite of academically inclined Salon jury members. As a result, he regularly gained government commissions to enhance the gravitas and beauty of important public structures. Among his most significant commissions were a series of Catholic tableaus for the newly reconstructed *Hôtel de Ville* in Paris and neoclassical genre paintings for the town hall of Paris's sixteenth district.

Lévy's prolific, gifted, and highly decorated career epitomized the hopes and disappointments of the Jewish press. The press celebrated Lévy's artistic accomplishments and his induction into the French Legion of Honor as a credit to all French Jews.[25] And yet, the fact that Lévy's work became synonymous with Christian and mythological scenes (and, presumably, his marriage to a non-Jewish woman) caused consternation among certain Jewish journalists who chastised Lévy and other Jewish artists for ignoring their own Jewish heritage.[26]

The Jewish press similarly invested great hope in Alexandre Laemlein, the first identifiably French Jewish artist to exhibit in the Salon. The Bavarian-born Laemlein exhibited in the Salon for decades beginning in 1836, winning medals for several of his works. The Jewish press was impressed by the artist's unique upbringing in Germany and France and emphasized Laemlein's reputation as a distinguished student of the great painter Picot.

Laemlein interspersed biblical art scenes throughout a long career best remembered for a single, socially progressive tableau touting the equality of the human races in 1846. Laemlein's mythological composition, *La Charité*, engendered one of the first sustained discussions about art in the Jewish press.[27] Jewish art critics, who enjoyed Laemlein's interpretations of the biblical Jacob, Job, and Adam, held out great hope that Laemlein would regularly treat Jewish topics in his art and pleaded for encores.

Interestingly, Laemlein later joined the chorus of media critics, himself becoming a lecturer and frequent contributor to the Jewish press, and pleading for the emergence of inspired, and inspiring, Jewish artists who could help cultivate a greater appreciation for the arts among Jews.[28] Ultimately, despite his occasional artistic forays into the world of the Bible and his belated literary efforts to inspire a more profound connection between Jews and the arts, Laemlein was primarily remembered for being a great talent of the French school of academic art and not for his Jewish contributions.[29]

Like Émile Lévy, Hénri-Léopold Lévy devoted his artistic career to Christian subject matter. Trained by Picot as well as the neoclassicist Alexandre Cabanel, and the landscapist and Orientalist Eugène Fromentin, Hénri-Léopold Lévy produced numerous scenic, allegorical tableaus based on ancient Greek and Christian myths as well as contemporary landscapes depicting customs of the Orient. Like Émile Lévy, Henri-Léopold Lévy was awarded several important public commissions, including ceiling decorations for the town hall of the seventh district in Paris.

Genre

History painting remained the most academically valued style of art throughout the nineteenth century even as genre painting—that is, depictions of subjects and scenes from everyday life, ordinary folk and common activities—gained ascendancy in the Salon. Out of the juxtaposition of these two distinct artistic styles emerged an amalgamation of the two, historical genre painting, which sought to democratize the grandeur of the classical past by depicting heroes at non-heroic moments or grandly treating commoners engaged in the quotidian activities of daily life.

In the field of genre painting, Jewish artists were influenced by such notable teachers and painters as Eugène Delacroix, Paul Delaroche, Jean-Louis Ernest Meissonier, and Jean-Léon Gérôme, who each offered innovative approaches to classical themes.[30]

Benjamin Eugène Fichel was a disciple of Delaroche but more commonly described in the Jewish press as the leading disciple of his other main mentor, Meissonier.[31] Meissonier's quaint scenes of musicians or men playing chess had a lasting impact in the Salon and on several Jewish artists, including Fichel, who thoroughly grasped Meissonier's genius in carefully crafting scenes of everyday life. Like Meissonier and Delaroche, Fichel enjoyed success as a historical painter before becoming renowned for his genre scenes. Fichel was famous for the great technical execution of his compositions and his meticulous depiction of historically accurate costumes. Fichel's small genre paintings of card or chess games, of musicians, and café scenes were executed with "rigid exactness, reproduc[ing] the morals of eras past...style[d] in modern compositions."[32] The art world rewarded Fichel during his nearly five decades of participation in the Salon with a Gold Medal at the 1857 Salon and later with the French Legion of Honor.

The celebrated Émile Lévy, who like Fichel excelled in several different artistic fields, also gained a fine reputation for his genre scenes of modern life. His genre scenes, including a controversial depiction of a prostitute in the grand style reserved for Greek heroes, were said to "masterfully capture the infinite diversity of contemporary man" in a neoclassical style and setting.[33] Other Jewish artists in this field included Auguste Hadamard who aggrandized trivial moments of modern daily life into classically styled scenes.

Orientalism

Several of the great genre painters, including Delacroix, Gérôme, and Delaroche's Swiss disciple, Charles Gleyre, spent time in the Orient observing and painting the religious customs and scenes of everyday life of various Jewish and Berber communities. Exemplifying the ever-growing European fascination with the Middle East and North Africa, these artists visually introduced European art audiences to the significant religious features of daily life in North Africa, Egypt, Palestine, and Arabia. In the process, they established genre painting as a leading vehicle of nineteenth-century Orientalism in France.

Alexandre-Auguste Hirsch was the Jewish artist with the most sustained commitment to depicting the Orient. He was primarily a disciple of Gleyre, whose profound fascination with the Orient was shaped by his travels to the Middle East.[34] However, Hirsch's folkloristic scenes of Jewish life in North Africa and his interest in

Moroccan Jewish customs also closely resembled those of Delacroix, who—like an anthropologist—had scrupulously documented the Moroccan Jewish community for six months in 1832.[35]

Starting with an 1857 drawing of a biblical Moses fleeing for his life, and continuing for more than five decades, Hirsch exhibited in the official Salons of Paris and Lyon. He first introduced his favored topic, the Jews of Morocco, at the 1870 Paris Salon. That year, the *Archives* singled out Hirsch's portrait of a Jewish girl as an impressive "report of a wealth of charming inspirations from Morocco" and noted with some sadness that Hirsch was the only Jewish painter to treat Jewish subjects at the Salon.[36]

Hirsch continued to delight the Jewish press with his sincerity in capturing the North African atmosphere, earning praise from an *Univers* critic for his felicitous choice of subject matter and the brilliant colors evoking the Levant sky.[37] Hirsch continued to depict all aspects of daily life of North African and Middle Eastern Jews until 1909. His numerous genre paintings include folkloric depictions of street scenes, landscapes, studies of religious rituals and rabbis, as well as portraits of singers and dancers.

Reviews in the Jewish press consistently commended Hirsch for his tender and evocative renditions of Moroccan Jewish customs.[38] However, Jewish critics never fully embraced Hirsch as a paradigmatic "Jewish artist." It is not altogether clear why the Jewish press, which at other times seemed so desperate to identify Jewish champions in the arts, did not adopt Hirsch as one of its primary heroes. Perhaps the Jewish press overlooked Hirsch's efforts because the quality of his artwork failed to impress Salon juries. Or perhaps his romanticized depictions of Moroccan Jewry, far removed from the complex realities of contemporary French Jewish concerns, failed to excite Jewish art critics hoping for art that could inspire its viewers or could profitably be used to oppose malicious Jewish stereotypes.

The Jewish press's subdued reception of Hirsch contrasts sharply with its enthusiastic embrace of the caricaturist Alphonse Lévy, whose depictions of Algerian and Alsatian Jews were regularly included in avant-garde French journals and Jewish illustrated novels as well as at the official Salon. The press warmly welcomed Lévy's quaint, compassionate illustrations of "his Jews" because they not only allowed Parisian Jews to reminisce nostalgically about a more innocent moment in recent Jewish history, but also helped defuse the impact of increasingly virulent anti-Semitic imagery.[39]

Lévy's ethnographic interest in Near Eastern physiognomy—adopted from his mentor Gérôme's pioneering ethnographic representations of the physiognomies, typography, and architecture of the Near East—resulted in a graphic approach to the traditional communities of Alsace and Algeria.[40] Lévy intended his presentation of the seemingly exotic, curious behaviors of traditional Alsatian and Algerian Jews to attest to the purity of traditional Jewish life, which was being lost to the newly urbanized Jews of Paris.

Lévy's countless illustrations established him as the principal contemporary documentarian of Jewish peasant life. They also earned him the honorific appellation, *"le Millet des Juifs,"* in reference to the great French painter of rural life, Jean-François Millet.[41] *Archives* critic Bezalel dubbed Lévy the "designer emeritus of Jewish scenes."[42]

Jewish Topics

The impressive efflorescence of Jewish artists on the French art scene in the second half of the nineteenth century was a source of great pride for Jewish observers. The scope and quality of active Jewish participation in the arts was deemed worthy of frequent discussion, and indeed regular columns, in the Jewish journals. The journals relished the fact that Jewish artists followed the same career path as their successful non-Jewish peers, which was taken to validate and embody the desired Jewish integration into the world of French high culture, an area previously outside the sphere of Jewish interest and accomplishment.

However, just below the surface of this obvious Jewish pride festered a nagging sense of anxiety and discontent. It rankled Jewish art critics that while the number of Jewish artists grew every year, the number of Jewish artists treating specifically Jewish subject matter did not.[43] For decades, the Jewish press harped on this unfortunate juxtaposition. An *Archives* critic bemoaned the fact that "Jewish history is still ignored by Jewish artists, in love with everything except Judaism."[44] And *Univers*'s chief editor and former chief rabbi of Paris, Lazare Eliezer Wogue, similarly complained: "This year [1881], more than ever, our artists shone in both number and in terms of the value and merit of their productions. However, more than ever, we must also say that their sense of Judaism was lacking. This painful observation, which we make every year, becomes harsher and more justified each time."[45]

Some Jewish artists did occasionally produce work dealing with Jewish or biblical themes but by and large Jewish artists preferred treating pagan and Christian mythologies to engaging their own Jewish heritage or history.[46] The critics could not understand why Jewish artists loyal to a classical approach in art did not, for instance, harvest material from the Hebrew Bible. Classically trained Christian artists, they pointed out, frequently did just that.[47] The Jewish artists' lack of active engagement with Jewish concerns tempered the excitement of Jewish journalists reporting on the remarkable successes of Jewish artists in the Salon world.

Jewish critics, perhaps unfairly, expected Jewish artists to serve not only as paradigms of Jewish integration but also as proactive campaigners for a regenerated Jewish image and as front-line soldiers in the fight against escalating anti-Semitism. But for the first generation of academically trained Jewish artists, success was defined not so much by satisfying the expectations of the Jewish community as by mastering the artistic parameters of Salon culture.

Most Jewish artists—like their non-Jewish contemporaries—entered the Salon world with classical training and pursued history and genre painting in the neoclassical style. They were more likely to mimic the artistic path of their (non-Jewish) mentors than to artistically engage Jewish topics.[48] Moreover, Salon juries traditionally did not reward artists who used their canvases to delve into subjects that strayed too far from the neoclassical repertoire. It cannot be too surprising, therefore, that most Jewish artists, having internalized these expectations through years of training, focused their paint brushes squarely on classical and Christian mythology without seriously considering subject matter that might be deemed specifically Jewish.

French Jewish artists who did dedicate their careers to Jewish topics were rare.[49] As mentioned above, the caricaturist Alphonse Lévy was known as *"le Millet des Juifs"* for his loving portrayals of rural Jews. Another was Édouard Moyse, who was crowned *"le peintre du rabbin"* for his many dignified portraits of rabbinic figures. Moyse, who remarkably exhibited at the Salon for fifty consecutive years, expressed a powerful vision of French Jewish integration based on the compatibility of French and Jewish commitments to the religious and civic virtues of truth and justice by visually recasting rabbis as monk- or judge-like figures. The values and agenda of Moyse's oeuvre resonated with the Jewish press, which embraced him for remaining faithful to the Jewish element in his art.[50]

Another Jewish artist consistently recognized by the press for his positive representation of Jewish subject matter was the Bordeaux-born Édouard Brandon. Brandon, who began his career as an award-winning painter of Christian iconography, became his era's preeminent painter of synagogues.[51] Harnessing the same powerful sense of simplicity, piety, and emotional intensity he earlier applied to church interiors, Brandon created atmospheric synagogue scenes that were innovative in both content and style. Jewish art critics were impressed with Brandon's modern depictions of Jewish religious life and discussed his paintings with great interest.[52]

Conclusion

The dramatic explosion of Jewish participation in the arts in France was a source of great pride for the Jewish community. It also ignited considerable discussion about the importance of art in the completion of the long project of French Jewish integration. By documenting Jewish participation in the major artistic trends of the era and the interest of the Jewish press in these developments, this article provides important historical context for understanding the emergence of art as an integral element of the discourse about modern Jewish life.

Notes

1. From 1725 to 1890, the annual Salon was arguably the greatest art event in Europe, if not the world. See Nigel Blake and Francis Frascina, "Modern Practices of Art and Modernity" in *Modernity and Modernism: French Painting in the Nineteenth Century* (New Haven: Yale University Press, 1993); see also Albert Boime, *The Academy and French Painting* (London: Phaidon, 1971).
2. Paris hosted the *Exposition Universelle des produits de l'Agriculture, de l'Industrie et des Beaux-Arts de Paris* in 1855, 1867, 1878, 1889, and 1900.
3. David Schornstein, "Chronique Israélite de la Quinzaine," *Archives Israélites de France* (1878): 291. On the Jewish embrace of the Third Republic, see Paula Hyman, *The Jews of Modern France* (Berkeley: University of California Press, 1998), 94–95; Pierre Birnbaum,

Jewish Destinies: Citizenship, State, and Community in Modern France, 1st ed. (New York: Hill and Wang, 2000); and Philip G. Nord, *The Republican Moment : Struggles for Democracy in Nineteenth-Century France* (Cambridge, MA: Harvard University Press, 1995), ch. 4.

4. The *Musée Hebraique* featured an impressive collection of Jewish ceremonial objects and manuscripts, some dating as far back as the twelfth century, assembled by Joseph Isaac Strauss, an Alsatian Jew who had served as Napoléon III's music director. The collection was later purchased by the Baroness Charlotte de Rothschild on behalf of the French chief rabbi and French Jewish Consistory, and then gifted to the French government. On the history and significance of the Strauss Collection, see Grace Cohen Grossman, "Jewish Museums of the World: Observations on the Cultural Politics of Interpreting the Jewish Heritage," *The Chronicle* 66 (2005): 22–25; Ezra Mendelsohn and Richard I. Cohen, *Art and Its Uses: The Visual Image and Modern Jewish Society*, Studies in Contemporary Jewry (New York: Institute by Oxford University Press, 1990); Richard I. Cohen, *Jewish Icons: Art and Society in Modern Europe* (Berkeley: University of California Press, 1998); and Joseph Gutmann, "On Medieval Hanukkah Lamps," *Artibus et Historiae* 20, no. 40 (1999): 187–90.
5. See Simon Bloch, *Univers 11* (1867): 505.
6. One noted art critic called the Strauss collection "one of the most distinctive achievements of our century [and] one of the most significant expressions of intellectual thought of our era." Wladimir Stassoff, "L'art Israélite à L'éxposition Universelle," *Archives* 40 (1879): 409.
7. "Now, for the first time, Jewish ritual objects were presented as historical and aesthetic phenomena, beyond their own framework of religion and religious practice." Cohen, *Jewish Icons*, 155.
8. Stassoff, "L'art Israélite à L'éxposition Universelle,"*Archives* 41 (1880): 410. In his ruminations about the existence of a Jewish national aesthetic sensibility, Stassoff referred to the tendentious Christian archaeologist and numismatist, Louis-Félicien Caignart de Saulcy, who for decades waged a single-minded battle to prove—against the conventional wisdom of most contemporary scholars—that the ancient Israelite nation, like other ancient civilizations, had its own distinct artistic style.The scholarly community largely rejected de Saulcy's specific assertions about the ancient Israelites' penchant for the arts but de Saulcy's singular obsession with ancient Jewish art was instrumental in galvanizing academic interest in Jewish antiquity. On Saulcy, see Hélène Nicolet, *Louis-Félicien-Joseph Caignart de Saulcy, 1807–1880* (Paris: Bibliothèque Nationale, 1981). A large collection of archaeological fragments relating to the ancient Israelites eventually found their way into a specifically designated "*Salle judäique*" at the national Musée du Louvre.

9. The first mention in the Jewish journals of Jewish participation in the Paris Salon occurred in 1846. In historical fact, we know that Alexandre Laemlein exhibited at the Salon as early as 1836, earning official honors for work he exhibited there in both 1841 and 1843.
10. The *Archives* praised the "talent of [this] young, distinguished artist [Delphine Bernard]" and noted her "graceful" pastel portraits. R, "Salon de 1847," *Archives5* (1847): 275.
11. Female artists started to exhibit their work at the official Salon during this period but continued to be excluded from official art institutions, including the *École des Beaux-Arts,* until 1897. Without the official imprimatur of the *École,* it was difficult—although not impossible—to gain entry into the halls of the Salon. It is no coincidence that the number of female Jewish artists grew dramatically as French women waged a successful battle to establish a presence for female artists in the French art world. The first time Jewish women made a truly enduring and noticeable impression as a group was at the Salon of 1876. That year, an unprecedented six Jewish women, out of a grand total of thirty Jewish artists, exhibited in the Salon. J. Schule, "Salon Israélite de 1876, " *Archives* 37 (1876): 376–77. Tamar Garb, "Gender and Representation," in *Modernity and Modernism: French Painting in the Nineteenth Century,* 219–89. See Tamar Garb, *Sisters of the Brush : Women's Artistic Culture in Late Nineteenth-Century Paris* (New Haven: Yale University Press, 1994).
12. For a discussion of "appropriate" arenas for women in the arts, see Garb, *Sisters of the Brush,* 154.
13. "We recommend, especially to girls who do not wish to limit their subjects to flowers and fans, to choose Ms. Formstecher as a teacher." J. Schule, "Salon Israélite de 1876," *Archives* 37 (1876): 345.
14. Charlotte de Rothschild gifted the Strauss Judaica collection to France's national Cluny museum. See Moise Schwab, "La Collection Strauss au Musée de Cluny," *Gazette des Beaux Arts* 5, no. 3 (1891): 245; G. David de Champclos, "Le Musée Strauss," *Univers* 46 (1891): 683. For a study of the Rothschild women's involvement with the arts, see Laura S. Schor, *Women, Religion, and Philanthropy in Nineteenth-Century France : The Case of the Baroness Betty de Rothschild* (New York: Hunter College of the City University of New York, 2006).
15. In the 1875 issue of *Univers,* the art reviewer proudly introduced Charlotte's Salon entry by acknowledging the artist's continued faithfulness to the arts. Isidore Loeb, "Le Salon," *Univers* 30 (1875): 595. See also David Champclos, "Le Musée Strauss," *Univers* 46 (1891): 683.
16. Wladimir Stassoff, "L'art Israelite à L'éxposition Universelle," *Archives* 41 (1880): 38. For more on Bernhardt, see Carol Ockman et al.,

Sarah Bernhardt : The Art of High Drama (New York/New York and New Haven: Jewish Museum/Yale University Press, 2005). Rothschild and Bernhardt were not only well-known among their peers as artists but also as subjects. Jean-Louis Gérôme's 1866 portrait of Charlotte de Rothschild—which pays homage to Ingres's 1848 portrait of the model's mother, the Baroness Betty de Rothschild—was one of the few female portraits the celebrated painter ever made. See Laura S. Strumingher, *The Life and Legacy of Baroness Betty de Rothschild* (New York: P. Lang, 2006). Sarah Bernhardt sat for the most fashionable artists of her time, including the pioneering photographer Félix Nadar. She was arguably the most photographed woman in the world during her day and captured in such famous theater roles as Hamlet, Camille, Cleopatra, and Joan of Arc.

17. See Isidore Cahen, "Les Israélites à l'Éxposition Universelle de 1855," *Archives* (1855): 445 ("Speaking of fine arts, painting is in first place, there is very little etching and even less sculpture. Architecture is not represented at all."). See also Cahen, "Les Israélites au Salon de 1861," *Archives* (1861): 337–38 ("One sees that, in painting, both French Jews and those from abroad comprise our contingent. However, there is much less to say about sculpture . . . This same lack, even more palpable, manifested itself in architecture and we are sorry for this.").
18. On the development of nineteenth century artistic styles, see Albert Boime, *Art in an Age of Counterrevolution, 1815–1848* (Chicago: University of Chicago Press, 2004); Patricia Mainardi, *The End of the Salon : Art and the State in the Early Third Republic* (Cambridge: Cambridge University Press, 1993); and Paul Duro, "Giving Up on History? Challenges to the Hierarchy of the Genres in Early Nineteenth-Century France," *Art History* 28 (2005): 687–711.
19. See David Schornstein, "Salon Israélite de 1877," *Archives* 38 (1877): 340, and "Salon Israélite de 1879," *Archives* 40 (1879): 191.
20. Ingres used the image of Charles V's return to Paris as a transparent celebration of the restoration of order and stability in the guise of monarchy embodied by the return of Louis XVIII after his short exile during Napoleon's brief return and as he awaited the outcome of the Battle of Waterloo. On Ingres's work, see Boime, *Art in an Age of Counterrevolution*, 86–89.
21. Ulmann's portraits reveal the influence of another of his mentors, Picot. Picot, who was famous for his grandiose historical portraits and Versailles commissions, influenced an entire generation of history and portrait artists including William-Adolphe Bouguereau, Alexandre Cabanel, and Gustave Moreau. See Boime, *Art in an Age of Counterrevolution*, 294–95.
22. Ibid., 458–63; Gabriel Weisberg, *The Popularization of Images: Visual Culture under the July Monarchy* (Princeton: Princeton University Press, 1994), 79–82.

23. Isidore Cahen, "Mouvement des Arts chez les Israélites et sur des Sujets Juifs," *Archives* 13 (1852): 322. See Cahen, "Les Israélites à l'Éxposition Universelle de 1855," 446. Émile Lévy, *Noé, ayant appris comment l'avait traité son second fils, dit: Que Chanaan soit maudit!* (Noah, having learned of how he was treated by his second son said: A curse upon Canaan!, 1855).
24. On Lévy and Degas's friendship, see Linda Nochlin, *The Politics of Vision: Essays on 19th Century Art and Society* (New York: Harper & Row, 1989), 149.
25. Jewish journalists proudly proclaimed that "Everyone knows the talent of the distinguished and talented master [Lévy]" and lauded his "incontestable superiority as an artist." Schule, "Salon Israélite de 1876," 346. Interestingly, Lévy's obituary in *Archives*, written by French-Cuban poet José María de Heredia, silently passed over Lévy's early interest in Jewish themes, focusing instead on Lévy's "fierce Greek mythological paintings" and his "idyllic historical and Christian compositions." In fact, Heredia's tribute largely ignores Lévy's Jewish background altogether, except for a brief physiognomic description of Lévy's "oriental" facial features, which apparently had the noble, priestly traits of a Jewish warrior. See José María de Heredia, "Le Peintre Émile Lévy," *Archives* 51 (1890): 414.
26. *Archive* chief editor, Isidore Cahen, alludes to Lévy's marriage to a non-Jewish woman in an article discussing the most prominent Parisian Jewish artists. Isidore Cahen, "Art et Judaisme," *Archives* 50 (1889): 202.
27. See "Salon de 1849," *Archives* (1849): 239–40. See also Nochlin, *The Politics of Vision*, 7.
28. The Jewish press often discusses Laemlein as an artist-philosopher. In the annual Salon review of 1857, critic Isidore Cahen explains that the public and critics have difficulty in appreciating Laemlein as "not only a painter, but a thinker." Isidore Cahen, "Le Salon de 1857," *Archives* (1857): 510.
29. For a remembrance of Laemlein's career, see "Les Artistes Israélites au Salon de 1872,"*Archives* 33 (1872): 374.
30. On the distinct approaches of these artists, see Boime, *Art in an Age of Counterrevolution*, 380–88.
31. David Schornstein, "Les Artiste Israélites au Salon de 1866," *Archives* 27 (1866): 528.
32. At times, Fichel was roundly criticized for imitating his mentor to such an extent that he didn't produce anything of his own and for being repetitive. See Maurice Dreyfous, "Salon de 1870," *Univers* 25 (1870): 664, and *Univers* 28 (1873): 624–25. A critic in *Archives* similarly rebuked Fichel for "spend[ing] so much time working on each individual aspect [of the painting], that one forgets the

ensemble of the piece as a whole." Schule, "Salon Israélite de 1876,"*Archives* 37 (1876): 345.

33. Heredia, "Le Peintre Émile Lévy,"414.
34. On Gleyre, see Boime, *Art in an Age of Counterrevolution*, 372–74.
35. On Delacroix's depictions of the North African Jewish community, see Cissy Grossman, "The Real Meaning of Eugène Delacroix's *Noce Juive au Maroc*," *Jewish Art* 14 (1988): 64-73; and Boime, *Art in an Age of Counterrevolution*, 82–85, 362.
36. Maurice Dreyfous, "Salon Israélites de 1874," *Archives* (1874): 343.
37. Edouard André, "Salons de 1897," *Univers* (1897): 278. Hirsch's Moroccan suite in the late 1890s was described as "full of grace and poetry." Isidore Loeb, "Le Salon," *Univers* (1898): 593–94.
38. Dreyfous, "Salon de 1870,"*Archives* (1870): 666, and "Salon Israélites de 1874,"*Archives* (1874): 343.
39. Lévy referred to Jews from his native Alsace as "my Jews," in Alphonse Lévy, letter to the editor, *La Plume*, (1895): 334–35. Lévy's deftly subverted anti-Semitic caricatures helped popularize a new Jewish literary form, the genre of "ghetto novels."
40. Gérôme sought to modernize neoclassical genre scenes by capturing contemporary, everyday moments in such far-off places as Turkey and Egypt. He was convinced that these contemporary Near Eastern societies shared important cultural similarities with the civilizations of ancient Greece and Rome. Boime, *Art in an Age of Counterrevolution*, 380–81.
41. Jean-François Millet was best known for his extensive, if ambivalent, treatment of peasant life. Millet's work was deemed revolutionary for its realistic, and sometimes critical, portrayal of the hardships and rigors of the working class characterized by the peasantry. See Christopher Parsons and Neil McWilliam, "'Le Paysan de Paris': Alfred Sensier and the Myth of Rural France," *Oxford Art Journal* 6 (1983): 41.
42. Bezalel, "Les Salons Israélites de 1897," *Archives58* (1897): 180.
43. See Prague, "Le Salon Israélite de 1884," *Archives* 45 (1884): 192, and "Art et Judaisme," *Archives* 55 (1894): 169. In 1873 and 1880, respectively, *Univers* and *Archives* began dedicating a discreet section of their art columns to specific works dealing with Jewish themes by both Jewish and non-Jewish artists. However, mentions were made sporadically and informally before these dates, including in *Archives* in 1867. See Schornstein, "Les Peintres Israélites au Salon de 1867," *Archives* (1867): 514.
44. Hippolyte Prague, "Le Salon Israélite de 1883," *Archives* 44 (1883): 191.
45. Lazare Eliezer Wogue, "Le Salon de 1881," *Univers* 36 (1881): 651.

46. For instance, Levy Coblentz and Benzion-Gerson Cahensky occasionally submitted biblical compositions to the Salon. See Prague, "Le Salon Israélite de 1884," *Archives* 45 (1884): 192, and "Art et Judaisme," *Archives* 55 (1894): 169.
47. As early as 1846, an article in the *Archives* lamented that of the many biblical subjects presented in that year's Salon—including depictions of the biblical Rebekah, Daniel, Moses, as well as Jephthah's daughter—none were depicted by Jews. R, "Salon de 1846," *Archives* (1846): 240.The press complained that "rare Jewish subjects were most often painted by Christian artists" and even hyperbolically expressed the fear that "Christians [would] exhaust Jewish subject matter themselves." See Prague, "Le Salon Israélite de 1881," *Archives* 42 (1881): 213, and "Le Salon Israélite de 1883," *Archives* (1883): 191. See also Bezalel, "Les Salons Israélites de 1897," *Archives* 58 (1897): 140.
48. Jewish artists trained at the *École des Beaux Arts* were heavily influenced in their choice of subject matter by the official Academic styles promoted in the Salon, the artistic predilections of their mentors, and the latest vogues of the art market.
49. See Tal Gozani, "Images and Jewish Identity: Three Jewish Artists in Nineteenth-Century France," *Judaism* 50 (Summer 2001): 307-318.
50. See Prague, "Le Salon Israélite de 1882," *Archives* 43 (1882): 185; Bezalel, "Les Salons Israélites de 1895," *Archives* 56 (1895): 173–74, "Le Salon Israélite de 1900," *Archives* 61 (1900): 124, and "Les Salons Israélites de 1901," *Archives* 62 (1901): 158.
51. See Gozani, "Images and Jewish Identity," 310–12.
52. See, for example, David Schornstein, "Les Artistes Israélites au Salon de 1866," *Archives* 27 (1866): 528, and "Les Peintres Israélites au Salon de 1867," *Archives* 28 (1867): 511–12; Bezalel, "Le Salon Israélite de 1889," *Archives* 50 (1889): 173.

Visual Art as a Spiritual Practice

Miriam Terlinchamp

> Such a command as that of the Decalogue would have been impossible to a nation possessed of such artistic gifts as the Greeks, and was carried to its ultimate consequences . . . only because the people lacked artistic inclination, with its creative power and formative imagination.
>
> "Art Among the Ancient Hebrews," in the *Jewish Encyclopedia*

There is no way around it. Jews are a people of the book. We label ourselves as a people who laud text above all else. It is a concept ingrained in our liturgy. We pray *Eilu D'varim* every morning for the ability to do important acts with the culminating phrase being, "Studying Torah is above them all because it leads to them all." It is an identity that was shaped by the concept of ongoing revelation. Rabbis of the third century studied text in order to elaborate on the words of our religion through Mishnah, Gemara, and Talmud. Even history had a hand in enforcing the text-oriented nature of the Jewish people. Through burning synagogues and destroyed villages, the only thing that could be carried with the Jews was the word of their tradition on their hearts. Through the wilderness of Egypt and on into the wilderness of Ellis Island, text was portable. Jews are the people of the book for both interior and exterior reasons. However, it is not conclusive whether or not being text-centric is the exclusive core of Jewish identity.

Surely we know that text is not the only thing that defines the Jewish people. Jews are known for their contributions of music, poetry, storytelling, social action, political involvement, garment making, and visual art to the greater world. However, it is not as evident if these other Jewish passions are as vital or meaningful to the Jewish story as text. The various gifts in our history in the arts compete with text when it comes to validating different avenues

---

RABBI MIRIAM TERLINCHAMP (LA10) serves Temple Sholom in Cincinnati, Ohio. She graduated from Scripps college with degrees in Religion and Studio Art.

of accessing tradition and personal truth. When the yeshivot were destroyed and whole Jewish communities ruined, one might have thought that another medium other than text might rise from the ashes. With our Sages gone and the great Rabbis surrendered to the camps, the Jews remained people of the book. I wonder then, not if text continued being a central value, but rather, if being the "people of the book" changed its meaning.

If we deconstructed the term "people of the book" to something more fluid like, "people of Torah," there might be more range in how Jews conceptualize their identity. Torah does not only mean text. Torah is revelation, tradition, ritual, history, the story and plight of both community and the individual. Torah is what we received at Sinai, what was written down by Sages through the generations, what was and is the experience of God in the human life span. With this definition, Torah is certainly not just text. Text is not the only thing that is portable and can survive persecution. Torah is the lifeblood of a people.

In everything in life, not just this subject matter, it can be easy to look at life issues as dualities. They are black or white, right or wrong, and either/or. Is it possible, in light of seeing Torah as a multifaceted entity, to see the complexity of our identity as multi-valued rather than dichotomous? Contradictions only occur when we present them as oppositional. We set ourselves a trap when we phrase our identity as either/or, better/worse, Jewish/not Jewish. We force ourselves to defend a nonexistent duality like being people of the book, as if it precludes us from being anything else as well. I am no historian or theologian or great master of text, but I am a Jew. I believe that there must be an encircling truth that can hold both visual art and text in a manner that is not contradictory. If we are people of Torah, then we are a people not of text and either/or's, but rather, a people that acknowledge the many layers of partnership between humans and the Divine.

Judaism, in the most classical sense, imagines itself to be transmitted from Sinai by two distinct methods: written media and memory.[1] The written revelation of Judaism is Scripture, while the more nebulous, and ongoing, revelation is oral. Both text and verbal narrative are considered Torah. The Jews are people of Torah, and therefore shaped by multiple sources of authentic revelation.

The oral Torah is referred to as midrash. Midrash can be difficult to define as it is an interpretative tool that utilizes parable and allegory to fill in information in biblical text. This does not mean that Rabbis "made up" the answers to questions left in scripture. Rather, midrash complements written Torah. It serves as an ongoing source that "uncovers" possible halachachic mandates and aggadic parables that were not mentioned when the written Torah was originally revealed. Midrash is a process of unveiling meaning and reimagining relevance of an ancient text for each generation.

Midrash in academic circles is always considered a body of literature. However, its imprecise existence as a process rather than a distinct body of work allows room for doubt that midrash should be defined as solely a body of literature. Midrash interacts with the Bible in very specific ways and times.

> Primarily we can see the central issue behind the emergence of Midrash as the need to deal with the presence of cultural or religious tension and discontinuity. Where there are questions that demand answers, and where there are new cultural and intellectual pressures that must be addressed, Midrash comes into play as a way of resolving crisis and reaffirming continuity with the traditions of the past.[2]

Midrash offers what is missing from the written text. It offers the chance to see something new in Scripture or to practice Judaism in ways that have new meaning for the community.

Midrash as a tool of interpretation can be a useful lens when trying to understand a specific text or habit of the Jewish community. The relationship between Jewish identity and visual art is one such situation. The second commandment tells us:

> You shall have no other Gods beside Me. You shall not make for yourselves a sculptured image, or any likeness of what is in the Heavens above, or on the earth below, or in the waters under the earth. You shall not bow down to them or serve them. For I the Lord your God am an impassioned God, visiting the guilt of the fathers upon the children, upon the third and upon the fourth generations of those who reject Me, but showing kindness to the thousandth generation of those who love Me and keep My commandments.[3]

When reciting the Ten Commandments, Exodus 20:3, regarding other gods, is always paired with Exodus 20:4, regarding images.

The Hebrew word for image used in Exodus 20:4, *t'munah*, is seen four other times in the entire biblical canon. Twice, it is connected with the word *pesel* (sculpture), as in the Ten Commandments. Two other times it is connected with the words *lo reitem* (you shall not see them), which are also references to idolatry. When searching for the English word "image,"[4] it occurs forty-nine times in the entire canon. In every case, image is connected with words such as molten, sculpture, carved, engraved, cut down, idols, altars, and broken. The words of sun gods, Asherim, Baalim, and names of foreign priests and gods surround the word for image. Clearly, the Bible sees images as directly correlated with idolatry, which is considered the gravest offense.

Rabbinic commentaries in the Talmud, with midrash woven throughout, have plenty to say about the role of imagery and idolatry. Rambam claimed that the second commandment was so extensive, that it not only precluded individuals from creating images but also forbade idolatrous thoughts.[5] He believed this, and other Rabbinic commentators agreed, that other gods could only exist in one's mind.[6] *M'chilta* claims that the prohibition is about holding idols made by others in one's possession and not forging any new ones. Some Rabbinic sources spend time differentiating the levels of punishment one might incur by physical acts of idolatry. For instance, possession of an idol is a sin but carving an idol is a sin that merits the death penalty. The largest problem for the Rabbis seems to be a fear of accepting the idols and gods in one's possession as one's God.

Somehow, with all this commentary regarding idolatry and fear of taking on new gods, the Jewish people eschewed common forms of visual art. Or at least that is the story most of us learned for many years! Jews do not believe in making images of heaven, earth, and water because it is akin to idolatry, so we do not do it. However, as more art history has revealed itself, this has been more myth than truth. We have long known of illustrated *haggadot*, *ketubot*, and scriptures as well as ritual ornaments, mosaics, and Torah mantles. In 1932 in Syria at the Dura Europos Synagogue a wall was uncovered with Jewish depictions of God's hands and human faces dating to the year 244. Proving that Jews may not have been as reticent to depict the heavens and earth as we imagined. Regardless, art and Judaism have long been entrenched in a complicated relationship, but it has never been absolutist.

The rich relationship of illustrated Haggadot, sacred manuscripts, and mosaics are part of classic Jewish visual history. Complexity arises when scholars attempt to define or discuss "Jewish art" rather than illustrated art.

> The term "Jewish art" remains something of an oxymoron. Jews may have made images, but that does not make the images, themselves, Jewish for every onlooker, for the images may not reflect the Jewish experience and might better be described as American, for example, or Socialist. Almost by definition, or rather by commandment, Jewish art does not exist.[7]

The second commandment prohibits any rendering of a likeness in the Heavens or on earth. Scholars continue to argue over what that actually means for artists. However, what makes something Jewish that a Jew creates is a more contemporary discussion regarding Jewish art. Regardless of whether one is allowed to represent images on earth or not, Jews have done so for centuries.

The inartistic Jew is a stereotype that many argue is anti-Semitic, reinforcing the idea that Jews are uncultured rather than struggling with definitions of tradition. Art has been used as a marker for racist distinction for centuries, reaching its height in the nineteenth century, where the exotic "Oriental" and "Jew" were peoples thought of interchangeably.[8] Nationalism and art-historian scholarship were deeply intertwined, art of the East "could neither reach a high degree of development nor any positive progress."[9] Biblical manuscripts and ancient art were appreciated for their historical value and relationship to sacred text. However, the nations who had created these works were also artificially limited to these works, ever reduced to labor without artistic sensitivity, never to progress.

Jewish artists have reacted to the notion of emerging from a people of primitive artistic competence by valuing their own contributions in a multitude of ways. "Critics debate whether Jewish American art need only be art made by a Jewish American, independent of content, or if both the artist and the artwork's identity must be Jewish."[10] This debate is ongoing, though in order to acknowledge some of the greatest and most popular artists in history as Jewish artists, one must relinquish the requirement for Jewish subject matter. American artists in this category would be: Elizabeth de Kooning, Roy Lichtenstein, Mark Rothko, and Judy Chicago. Some scholars claimed that though the artworks were not outwardly religious, they could be seen as Jewish when discerned through a Jewish lens. When reviewing art with the artist's biography, cultural history, and religious affiliation in mind, the art might feel Jewish even if the subject matter does not seem outwardly Jewish.

With American Jewish artists leading the world in abstract expressionism during the late 1940s and well into the 1960s, what it meant to create something as a Jew had to be thought of differently. With a war raging in Europe that was killing Jews who did and did not identify themselves outwardly as such, in America the artistic world reacted. Stateside the Jewish artist could be free to rail against the popular expressionist art form of the time. Nazi propaganda had usurped socialist avant-garde as their own art form, and so a new art form was born. Abstract expressionism was a new language to discuss the atrocities abroad for which there were no words. It was also an artistic modality that allowed the Jewish artist to reimagine what it meant to be a Jew and an American.

> [The Jew] did not want his Jewish heritage to be his mark of self-definition. Instead, he wanted to develop a Jewish consciousness that encouraged self-realization and that liberated him from outworn parameters of belief and behavior. He said that he wanted to feel free to be whatever he needed to be as a Jew or even as an American.[11]

Abstract expressionism was the Jewish American answer to anti-Semitism and to the nation who was said to be without art.

At the time, abstract expressionism was not widely accepted as a Jewish art form. Only with a half-century of hindsight, are we able to look back and see abstract expressionism as a form of Jewish responsa to war-torn Europe. In 1965 the Jewish Museum in New York showcased an exhibit of abstract expressionism. By then abstract expressionism was part of American cultural mainstream. Jackson Pollock brought the new wave of art through a featured article in *Life* magazine in 1949. In the 1960s and early 1970s pop art was already catching on, and a new wave of art was on the frontier. However, despite abstract expressionism's popularity, with its bright colors and lack of symbols, many Jews did not believe that the Jewish Museum should host the exhibit, as the work was not "Jewish enough."

I imagine that some of the rebuke over insufficient Jewish content in Jewish art is what makes something or someone authentically Jewish. The fear is that once we agree that art without images or distinctive Jewish characteristics is Jewish, how can we ever recognize Jewish art when we see it? Deciphering what makes an artwork or an artist Jewish, and for that matter, what makes a Jew a Jew, changes depending on who you ask. Nevertheless, there is common ground where everyone may come together to appreciate the artistic contributions of Jews regardless of content.

Currently, there are two distinct centers on the East Coast and West Coast of North America, which testify that Jewish art is alive and well. The Jewish Museum, in New York, was originally founded in 1904. It was reconstructed in 1989 and expanded to include gallery space in 1993.[12] On the West Coast, the Contemporary Jewish Museum, in San Francisco, which was originally founded in 1990, completed its construction of Daniel Libeskind's design of a full gallery in 1998.[13] Each focuses on very different aspects and definitions of Jewish identity and art.

To commemorate the new gallery in 1993, the Jewish Museum of New York opened with an exhibition titled "Too Jewish?"[14] The show included humorous depictions of bar mitzvah parties in eighties regalia and a large collection of prosthetic noses. Ruth Weisberg, dean of the USC Roski School of Fine Arts comments,

> Varying degrees of irony and humor were the permissible modes, but not affirmation and celebration. Perhaps the fear remains that if Jews engage [in] sentiment we will become sentimental, but every direction has its dangers. Tapping deep feelings does not automatically condemn one to nostalgia.[15]

In many instances Jewish artists have become apologists when they want to reference their Jewish identity. They often poke fun at themselves, using imagery from our history and culture as kitsch, rather than a source of expression.

Unfortunately, many Jewish artists who orient their subject matter around their identity can become categorized by other Jews as "too Jewish." There have been times in our history where acculturation has benefitted the Jewish people, times where whole art forms became possible in our struggle to hide and untangle our Jewish identity from our national identity. Yet, is it still that time? Have we reached a point where Jewish artists no longer need to dwell in the arena of craft and ritual items? Now is the time once more to expand back out into the greater art world without irony, with proudly identifiable Jewish subject matter. Clearly, America is ready, selling out the Jewish Museum in New York's show on Man Ray (born Emmanuel Radnitzky, 1934) and the new popular exhibit of Kehinde Wiley, *The World Stage: Israel*.

Perhaps there is hope on the West Coast too with The Contemporary Jewish Museum's current exhibition, *California Dreaming: Jewish Life in the Bay Area from the Gold Rush to the Present*. The show is an ongoing series of photographs, video, and interactive maps of what Jewish looks like in Northern California. Playful possibilities are evident in the show, as are celebration, affirmation, and continuity. The show challenges exhibitions of the past decade across the country to rethink what it means to discuss Jewish identity openly and unapologetically. Acknowledging who we are as a people maintains our connection to being a people of Torah.

In 1992 Jo Milgrom published *Handmade Midrash*, revolutionizing the way art and Jewish biblical exegesis interacted. By weaving together Jungian theory, art therapy technique, and biblical text, Milgrom created a new way for Jews to imagine midrash.

> "Handmade midrash" is a visual theology. It is an approach to biblical narrative that draws on the traditional study of Bible, midrash (rabbinic commentaries), the cognate disciplines of literature, history, archeology and linguistics. However, it moves beyond these to form a new synthesis with comparative symbolism, art history, and psychology—to create a new discipline. This study was provoked by the limitations of academic study of Scripture in addressing present day spiritual needs.[16]

Milgrom imagines midrash to be something beyond narrative. Midrash for Milgrom is an art form not to be left to a singular medium.

Her work is workshop based. She challenges her students to "play" rather than to "create art for art's sake."[17] She emphasizes sensuality in all her exercises.[18] She asks her students to rend cloth, tear paper, and search for expressions on the page that cannot be expressed in recognizable shape or symbol. I think the Rabbis of the Mishnah played in their narrative too. Not in the way a child plays, but as the adage goes, "Turn it and turn it again, for everything is contained therein."[19] Milgrom is not looking for fine art. Milgrom is looking for soul art.[20] By staying close to the biblical text, the projects have the feel of midrash in that the artists create the missing narrative in scripture.

Visual art, if permitted, may be the one element that can bridge the multilayered worlds of the people of Torah. Art as a valid form of midrash might be the transcending channel from our dualistic text-oriented tendencies. Art frees us from being people of the book and helps us become people of Torah, allowing truth to come from a variety of sources rather than from text alone. Midrash situates a given story in a specific time and place and allows for readers to bring in their own situation and experience.[21] Midrash is something that reverberates for people beyond their immediate condition, connecting the past with the present and vice versa. What better medium for transcending space and time than art? When we look into midrash as a tool for accessing knowledge, the same strengths as visual art seem to appear: connecting people to tradition, accessing wisdom in different ways, exploring identity, and enacting *hidur mitzvah* in a text format (beautifying the gaps that traditional texts may not encompass). Midrash is no second-rate Torah. It is not a novelty nor is it any less substantial than halachah. Midrash is a meaning maker in the places where no meaning can be found. Art, in its best moments, is a midrashic tool, in that it brings forth meaning.

Art, like prayer, should be the soul's food. Art as a decorative/illustrative force is part of the Jewish tradition. The commandment of *hidur mitzvah* is the act of beautifying another commandment. We tend to extend the definition of *hidur mitzvah* to mean making anything more beautiful (which, for example, is how modern Jews justify ear piercing). However it has to do more with "doubling" a mitzvah, if such a concept were possible. Doubling rather than intensifying a commandment, because *hidur* cannot be separated from the mitzvah it is serving. Yet, it serves its own specific purpose outside of the mitzvah in practice. When you take extra time to beautify a commandment that you are already in the act of doing, like making Shabbat or visiting the sick or studying Torah, by making an amazing Shabbat meal or bringing flowers to the sick or creating a decorative Torah ark, one heightens the mitzvah at hand. *Hidur mitzvah* does not stand on its own. The beautification piece, the art, is not its own mitzvah unless it is partnered with the mitzvah of glorifying God. Generally speaking, all mitzvot are supposed to be equal in the eyes of God. The concept that one can raise a given mitzvah beyond its scope is an exception rather than a rule. There are only two places where we see this notion of expanding a commandment: *hidur mitzvah* and making love to your partner on Shabbat. This latter act is seen as a way of communing with the Divine on a holy day, thereby aligning divine time and space with a divine act. I would also argue that it could fall under the scope of *hidur mitzvah* since it may be seen as a way of making the Shabbat more beautiful.

Hidur mitzvah as a codependent commandment makes the argument for art as a necessity a bit more complicated. Traditionally Jews have seen art as something that must partner with something else in order to have meaning; it cannot stand on its own. Art must serve a function beyond just existing.

Many artists have very definite opinions on this as well. Some believe that art exists for art's sake, and nothing more should be read into it. Others believe that all art is experience, and no art can be seen separate from the identity and experience of the artist. John Dewey, in his work, "Art as experience," formulated an artistic philosophy that shapes my personal foundations of the purpose of art.

> The significance of purpose as a controlling factor in both production and appreciation is often missed because purpose is identified with pious wish and what is sometimes called a motive . . . It is in the purposes he entertains and acts upon that an individual most completely exhibits and realizes his intimate selfhood. Control of a material by a "self" is control more than just "mind" . . . the object finally created is the purpose both as a conscious objective and as an accomplished actuality.[22]

Dewey explains that both the process and the result are the purpose of art making. The self is an active participant in the creation and in the result. Dewey writes that subject matter comes from the mind rather than outside of one's self. Therefore, the subject and the object are both the artist and the artist's creation. For Jews this can feel esoteric in that creating art may not on the surface seem to fulfill a functional capacity. However, there is place for meaningful art in Jewish life that exists for the sole reason that it is created by a Jew for a "Jewish reason," which would be through *hidur mitzvah*. *Hidur mitzvah* elevates human acts and creation, human offerings, to divine standards.

Art as a mitzvah can be a rarity. However, if given the chance, *hidur mitzvah* may partner with other mitzvot in a multitude of ways. If one looks carefully there is a place for prayerful art in the lives and spaces of our community. *Hidur mitzvah* in its simplest sense can be decorative and functional. It is the art on synagogue walls, the architecture of its sanctuaries, and the creation of ritual objects. In this capacity, art may push the functional limits by serving as a tool for education and the creation of community. If the whole community is involved in the creation or commissioning of art for their environment and collective use, then art is the agent that brings them together. It is a way of nurturing new relationships and bringing together people who might not naturally gravitate towards one another. It is very rare in weekly communal synagogue activities (like religious school, Torah study, parent education, worship services, etc.) to have a physical reminder of that community presence. The power of the physical result cannot to be denied.

Art in the synagogue can look like an illustration of a story, a Torah ark, architecture, a communal art show, a religious school bulletin board, sanctuary lighting, photos from a trip to Israel, paintings of the old country, modern tapestries, mosaic tiling, or a meditative art service. Art might be part of prayer or a place where prayer happens. In the congregational world art is everywhere, if you are willing to look for it. The problem is not how to bring art into the synagogue walls but how to make congregants active participants in Jewish art.

Funding and involvement in musical art projects have a longstanding history in the synagogue world. Music is not seen as a luxury. Music is the gateway for the Jewish community to access worship. Choirs, specialty classes, and unique musical services abound, because music is the chosen artistic craft of the Chosen People. Is it possible to elevate visual art as a midrashic tool and format for prayer the way music has been lauded?

Executive Director Ken Schlegel, of Temple De Hirsch Sinai in Seattle, Washington, claims that in the same way music has been changed, art is all about marketing.[23] When he was first applying for grants for his synagogue's Raq Shabbat programs no one wanted to support a Shabbat rock and roll band. The reason was not because of traditional understandings about how a synagogue service should sound, but because no one believed it would be successful. Six years later, twice a month, Raq Shabbat has the largest attendance in town. It costs the synagogue approximately $2,500 a service but, as Schlegel laughingly says, "For standing room only, what price wouldn't you pay?" Schlegel knew Raq Shabbat would be successful, but it would take work to get it to where it is now. People fund and attend successful programs but one has to find a way to brand them as such so that they may become successful. He claims that visual art will have no harder a time being worked into a synagogue community culture than Raq Shabbat; what it will take is some creative market branding. "You start with the rabbi," claims Schlegel.

Branding oneself a musical rabbi seems pretty obvious. You pick up a guitar or sing something in a creative way and people will see the rabbi as musical pretty quickly. Seeing one's rabbi as an artist, is a little less clear cut. The issue within the synagogue context is more about the rabbinate than about the art world. However, without delving too much into the subject, it is important to note the struggle in branding a rabbi as a rabbi-artist.

Having a rabbi who is an artist (rather than a rabbi who is simply artistic) shapes her rabbinate. Everything becomes filtered through an additional lens with which most congregants are not used to grappling: personal history, collective history, community, text, tradition, and art. Art for a rabbi-artist is a channel to the Divine as unique and meaningful as ritual and prayer. What is unique for the rabbi-artist is that art does not take the place of traditional worship nor does it serve an accessory role; rather, art occupies a place of equal footing in the rabbinic tool kit.

The congregational sphere is accustomed to a stagnant understanding of visual art in the synagogue world. The rabbi-artist turns that supposition on its head. Art becomes active. When one begins a new physical workout cycle, our muscles need time to awaken to the new movements; so too when we bring new lenses into a worship community. They have to exercise and stretch their praying muscles in order to incorporate a new understanding of the role art may play in the synagogue framework.

All that being said, once a rabbi-artist, always a rabbi-artist. Once there is a call to art in the community and outreach has begun, the whole community becomes encouraged to participate and pay attention to their visual environment. Art will be on people's minds, and hopefully, it will never stop. Therefore much care and forethought must be given to how the rabbi-artist wants to brand herself and her programs. When we talk about art, do we really mean that we want everyone to participate? Do we truly believe that everyone is an artist at heart? I do not ask these questions cynically, but with great awareness. As soon as you open up to a community, one must surrender to whatever outcome may arise. Therefore thinking about what communal involvement actually entails is an important first step.

The power of community involvement is immeasurable, though not all forms of visual art can be accessible to every individual. It is important to have places where we mean it when we say, "everyone is an artist" and allow for the whole community to participate, regardless of ability, if they so choose. Just as important is our need to have places where professionalism and artistic talent are valued. There must be a balance between experiential art and art appreciation. By creating a place for both professional art and community art we create more access points for congregants to engage in visual art. This way people may connect with the experiential elements of art as prayer, the communal aspects of creating together, and the joy in appreciating a piece of art that is separate from yourself.

In the best of worlds, visual art in the synagogue would incorporate a place for visual art as prayer, a space for a Jewish art collective to be formed, and a safe place for studio work and text study to go hand in hand. There would be a place for professional art shows, commissioned pieces that change the shape of the synagogue walls, congregants who would be partners in the creation of sacred space, and experiential art services in addition to musical and traditional services. People would take to heart the Jewish notion that we are cocreators with God. They would mimic our idea that God creates everyday and use this concept to fuel their passion for art.

Of course this is not yet the best of all worlds. In the most realistic of worlds, the synagogue might try for a few elements of visual art. The synagogue would open itself up to a communal art space or collective as well as commission a work of art or have an occasional experiential service. Art in the synagogue for many Jews may remain stagnant. They may forever hold pictures of orthodox rabbis praying at the western wall as their concept of what "real" Jewish art looks like. However, it is my deep hope that slowly this may change. "Artwork can be a way of exploring Jewish identity and a way of expressing Jewishness in concrete terms."[24] Perhaps Jewish art in the synagogue could become more multifaceted and widen congregants' scope of what it means to be creators of a Jewish worship space.

In both the most ideal and the most realistic of senses, the goal of introducing visual art to the congregational world is to embody the sense of being a people of Torah and not just people of the book. Art should not replace text and text should not have a hierarchical position above art. Nor should art be text's lesser, illustrative, and decorative cousin. We do this by building art into the psyche of a community where art does not have to exist as an "alternative" or "special event" but simply function as part of the picture of what it means to be people of Torah. Art needs to be one of the ways to enter the synagogue, prayer, and personal Jewish identity.

Notes

1. Jacob Neusner, *What Is Midrash*? (Philadelphia: Fortress Press, 1987), 3.
2. Barry Holtz, *Back to the Sources: Reading the Classic Jewish Texts* (New York: Summit Books, 2006), 179.
3. Exodus 20:3–6 (translation: Jewish Publication Society of America, *The TaNaKh*: *Student Edition*, 2000).
4. JPS student edition translation.
5. *Hilchot Yesodei HaTorah*, ch 1.
6. Yehuda Nachshoni, *Studies in the Weekly Parashah: The Classical Interpretations of Major Topics and Themes in the Torah* (Jerusalem: Mesorah Publications, 1988), 477.
7. Margaret Olin, *The Nation without Art: Examining Modern Discourses on Jewish Art* (Lincoln: University of Nebraska Press, 2001), 5.
8. Ibid., 7.
9. Ibid., 12.
10. Samantha Baskind, *Encyclopedia of Jewish American Artists* (Cleveland: Greenwood Press, 2006), xviii.
11. Matthew Baigell, *Jewish Art in America: An Introduction* (Lanham, MA: Rowman and Littlefield, 2006), 99.
12. www.thejewishmuseum.org.
13. www.thecjm.org.

14. Norman Kleeblatt, ed., *Too Jewish? Challenging Traditional Identities* (New York: Jewish Museum, 1996).
15. Ruth Weisberg, "Between Exile and Irony," in *You Should See Yourself: Jewish Identity in Postmodern American Culture*, ed. Vincent Brook (New Brunswick, NJ: Rutgers University Press, 2006), 170.
16. Jo Milgrom, *Handmade Midrash* (Philadelphia: Jewish Publication Society, 1992), ix.
17. Ibid., 7.
18. Ibid, 80.
19. *Pirkei Avot* 5:26.
20. This is my own term and analysis of what I believe Milgrom is searching for in her students' work.
21. Rabbi Rachel Adler on Fackenheim's use of midrash as a tool for explaining the Holocaust.
22. John Dewey, *Art as Experience* (New York: Penguin, 1934), 288–89.
23. Interview, November 15, 2008.
24. Anita Diamant, *Living a Jewish Life: Jewish Traditions, Customs, and Values for Today's Families* (New York: HarperCollins, 1991), 19.

Exodus/Sh'mot: *Art as a Guide to Where We Are Going*

A Nu Way Forward: Reaching Jewish Young Adults in Creative Ways

Anne Hromadka

> Over and over again for 350 years one finds that Jews in America rose to meet the challenges both internal and external that threaten Jewish continuity— sometimes, paradoxically, by promoting radical discontinuity. Casting aside old paradigms, they transformed their faith, reinventing American Judaism in an attempt to make it more appealing, more meaningful, more sensitive to the concerns of the day.
>
> Historian Dr. Jonathan D. Sarna

Anyone who is part of the secular or Jewish nonprofit sector is aware of the vast research regarding Generation Y (Millennials), Echo Boomers, and Xers. Most of this research points to current young adults (in their twenties and thirties) needing individualized approaches to encourage community involvement, fund-raising, and affiliation with religious organizations. The perception is that young adults want everything personalized, stylized, and packaged to conveniently fit their on-the-go lifestyles as evidenced by the fact that they are often called the MTV Generation or Generation Me.

How Do We Engage Jewish Young Adults?

As a young professional committed to the organized Jewish community, I have found answers to this question debated at

ANNE HROMADKA is the founder and director of NuART Projects [Insert Jewish Culture Here], independent curator, art consultant, and educator. In addition, she manages the Hebrew Union College Jack H. Skirball Los Angeles campus art collection and exhibition program.

every conference, via online media, in professional gatherings, and through scholarly journals. Typically, answers range from using flashy social media, planning big parties, organizing singles events, and offering freebies and/or discounts. The number-one mistake repeated at these gatherings and in much of the literature on this topic is not asking young adults to be part of the conversation about how to approach their cohorts. Often this conversation is led by seasoned professionals, historians, and researchers. It almost never includes professionals in their twenties, thirties, and forties. Often young professionals are being talked *at* rather than *to*.

When confronted with this debate, it reminds me of the improvisational game "Yes and." An example of this would be asking the following question: Is using social media, creating fun parties, and giving discounts the way to reach out to young adults? The answer is: Yes, and you need to do more. Prices of events, decorations, and social media are a great start but more can always be achieved and experienced by participants.

Reframe the question: It is not about *how* to engage young adults, but rather, *why* do we want to engage young adults? What is motivating your organization to reach out to this cohort? In what ways is the organization willing to make the Next Gen a part of the work you do? The goal is to build partnerships, not just get people in the door. Generation Me is not just about self-service. The "Me" of this generation is also about belonging. We do not want just a cheaper ticket to party. We want to feel invested in, heard, and counted. It is about meeting us where we are and creating a joint vision moving forward. It is time to look around the community and bring young leaders to the table to help articulate/participate in these conversations in meaningful ways. Young leaders can offer valuable advice about catching the attention of their peers.

My personal desire to find new ways to engage my cohorts, give back to the regional community, and provide pathways for Jews of all ages to become culture seekers led to the development of a new initiative called NuART Projects. While the initial idea for NuART Projects was my brainchild, I understood this effort could not be achieved alone. I quickly turned to trusted colleagues and fellow graduates of the USC Roski School of Fine Arts Public Art Studies program, Daniella Gold and Kim Newstadt. Together we combined our knowledge of the Jewish art and culture community to develop, launch, and grow this project. From the beginning, the founders wanted to emphasize that NuART Projects is about community. This was deeply embedded in our efforts.

Using NuART as a case study, I will explain our model, share our successes, and offer lessons learned. In conclusion, our model will enumerate tips for engaging young adults in meaningful ways using culture as a convening method.

NuART Projects [Insert Jewish Culture Here] Case Study

NuART [Insert Jewish Culture Here] is a project dedicated to increasing Jewish cultural appreciation through well-crafted participatory experiences. NuART founders recognized the need to create a new initiative that goes directly to where people are congregating and living. Thus, NuART uses mobile or "pop-up" experiences to engage Angelenos with quality Jewish contemporary culture. NuART encounters our audience where they are and pulls them into cultural happenings that expose Jewish concepts to a broad audience. Our effectiveness is amplified by using art as an innovative way to engage participants and transport Jewish culture to wherever Angelenos are congregating. Our current programming includes the SEDER Art Micro-Grant Initiative and *Halomot* (Dreams)—Through the Looking Glass. Among our projects under development is the NuART Mobile Gallery.

We are engaging the community with the SEDER Art Micro-Grant Initiative, which is a series of community meals committed to exploring how Jewish culture is financed and experienced communally. During these public events, all funds raised in exchange for a meal become a micro-grant awarded to an artist at the end of the event. Rather than gathering to retell an ancient story, this SEDER convenes attendees quarterly to actively participate in creating the next chapter of modern Jewish culture. Those attending the SEDER directly fund new, creative, and uniquely Jewish artistic or community-led projects meant to invigorate the Los Angeles community.

In our fast-paced society, there are an increasing variety of ways to identify as a Jew, especially for the growing number who do not affiliate with the established Jewish community. A recent study concluded, "The Los Angeles Jewish community is very spread out . . . Because of traffic and perceived cultural differences and geographic barriers, Jews in some areas rarely visit others. While there is a downtown area that serves as a hub for some cultural events (theater, orchestral music, etc.), there is no central area that serves as a hub for Jewish life."[1] SEDER seeks to bridge this geographic disconnect by bringing Jews from all over the city together in their mutual support of the arts.

Since launching in February 2011, the SEDER Art Micro-Grant Initiative has awarded over $3,000 in funds to four regional artists with plans for several large-scale events during 2012. We are committed to raising awareness in Los Angeles and beyond regarding the value of art in Jewish life. Our effectiveness is amplified by using art as an innovative way to engage participants. Our programming allows Jews of all ages the ability to explore, engage, and foster an increased appreciation of Jewish culture. The use of ballots to vote reflects our crowd-sourced fund-raising method. The ballots used during a SEDER event include a summary of each cultural project and a short participant survey. The survey includes questions about price of admission and the quality of the presentations. For example, was it clear how each project was Jewish and how it would benefit the community? The data collected from the survey at the first four events was very valuable. It showed that 98 percent of respondents connected to both the cultural aspects of the event and to the idea that they were helping the Jewish community.

The SEDER Art Grant is based on two secular models, Brooklyn's FEAST (Funding Emerging Artists with Sustainable Tactics) and Chicago's Sunday Soup program begun by InCUBATE. I first learned about both projects from The Creative Time Summit: Revolutions in Public Practice held on Saturday, October 9th, 2010. The Creative Time Summit is a conference that brings together cultural producers—including artists, critics, writers, and curators—to discuss how their work engages pressing issues affecting our world. The conference is broadcast live and I tuned in to the 2010 Summit. During a session featuring Brooklyn's FEAST and Chicago's Sunday Soup, I began to think how their models could be adapted for the Jewish community. Having worked in the Los Angeles secular and Jewish art community for seven years, I was deeply aware of the need to increase support for artist projects. Artists often struggle to find funding to produce work. Grants available to artists and arts organizations are often restrictive regarding who can apply and how the funds can be used. For example, many government and private foundations will not grant to individual artists and many exclude religious or spiritual work. Thus, Jewish artists often struggle to find funds that will help launch projects or produce small-scale initiatives. Micro-grants are a great way to help artists create new projects focused on Jewish culture. Thus, many of the reasons FEAST and Sunday Soup turned to community-driven fund-raising for the arts are mirrored in the SEDER Art Micro-Grant.

SEDER understands that community participation in the grant-funding and selection process is key. Applying for a SEDER grant is intentionally simple and unbureaucratic in order to encourage broad participation. This enables SEDER to stimulate and promote experimental, critical, and imaginative practices that may not be eligible for formal funding. As a nonartist participant in the SEDER, you are choosing to join an experience that engages directly with art and community projects. Each SEDER event reminds the planning team that this process is powerful for those gathered. Young adults are looking for ways to connect and NuART believes SEDER provides a unique alternative to current cultural programming for Jews in their twenties and thirties in Los Angeles. As one young adult remarked, SEDER was the "most incredible Jewish event" she had ever attended.

Most importantly, NuART is creating a community of Jewish art patrons! Each event begins with an explanation of how the participant's generous gift of $18 (or more) combines with the other attendees to support the advancement of Jewish culture. Traditionally, one might think to be a patron of the arts you must be part of a foundation or a private donor placing your name on the wing of an art museum. However, anyone can fund and join in the continuation of Jewish culture. Each artist or organization vying for the funds must explain to the SEDER participants how their project will affect the regional Jewish community. This aspect has led to interesting presentations and interactive elements at each SEDER Art Micro-Grant dinner. This feeling of community and giving back inspired the first SEDER Grant winner, Will Deutsch, to join our planning team after receiving his award. The exciting element is that as our project continues to grow, so does our community. We now have participants who have been to several events, thus funding multiple works by Jewish artists. We estimate over two hundred adults have participated in our first four events. Each event excites, inspires, and reminds the participants that Jewish culture is a powerful convener of community.

Another program is *Halomot* (Dreams)—Through the Looking Glass. In Hebrew, the difference between the word for windows (*holonot*) and dreams (*halomot*) is one letter. This seems to suggest a link between these concepts. Art can expand this view. It can expose us to new worlds and uncharted landscapes. When we provide artists a chance to dream and place to experiment, anything is possible. The *Halomot* (Dreams)—Through the Looking Glass project in partnership with retail spaces, nonprofits, and private residences offers regional Jewish artists a chance to create culturally relevant and site specific work. Each display (or installation) is temporary and will be on display for two to four weeks. This project is in its pilot year. We have interest from several venues. It will launch at the Silverlake Independent JCC in East Los Angeles during the fall of 2012.

NuART is currently exploring a project we believe will reach a wide range of the LA Jewish community. As conceptualized, the NuART Mobile Gallery will be a fully functional exhibition and educational space set up inside an altered recreational vehicle (RV). This mobile art space would house installations, soundpieces, performances, paintings, sketches, and videos. The NuART Gallery would create programming that extends beyond the visual arts including theatrical performances, dance pieces, poetry or literature readings, concerts, cooking demonstrations, and onetime happenings. You might find the NuART Mobile Gallery at a Jewish day school, a Jewish Community Center, the Jewish Federation, your campus Hillel, your local farmer's market, the beach, a community garden, an outdoor movie screening, or your next neighborhood gathering. This would be the first Jewish mobile arts laboratory to hit U.S. streets. We believe this effort can be duplicated with similar programs in other cities.

To learn more about NuART Projects visit our website, www.nuartprojects.com. Using NuART as a model, I would like to offer suggestions for engaging young adults with *kavanah* (intention). We have been successful, in part, because our model is deeply influenced by the following strategies:

1. **Identify and Cultivate Several Key Young Leaders in Your Region**
   Regardless of your overall young adult strategy, take a lesson from Jim Collins, author of *From Good to Great,* and Malcolm Gladwell, author of *The Tipping Point*. Make sure you have the

right young adult leadership in place before launching any efforts at broadening attendance. It is very important that these leaders be "tipping point" people. These people should be the connectors, the young socially savvy adults who are gatekeepers to large networks. When they endorse an event, group, or initiative, these adults give an organization immediate clout. Next Geners do not just want a crafted experience that guesses at what each of them is looking for as individuals. They want to have a part in shaping events that are an authentic reflection of what excites them about the world today.

Do not plan an ambitious series of young adult events without creating a committee or getting buy-in and planning ideas from your target demographic. Young professionals should be engaged in these conversations. In many cases, the young adult staff will be the ones actualizing these projects; therefore, they should have clear buy-in. However, turning to your youngest employees at a JCC, synagogue, or museum is not a way to ensure success. You also need to include lay leaders. The involvement of young professionals already employed in your organization should not negate the cultivation of additional leaders.

Investing in young leadership means they can offer a sense of regional support. You are creating ambassadors for your projects who will give the event, series, or initiative legitimacy among their social networks. Many managers and executives have vented about how to engage young adult leadership with statements, such as, "My organization is small and we cannot afford to create a young adult board." This way of thinking places roadblocks preventing success. Many organizations are small or regional in scope and still have successfully engaged young adults. They think out of the box. If your institution is small and you cannot have a separate young adult board, then add a young adult position/representative to your main board. The twenty- or thirty-something perspective could energize your board activities. If adding a young leadership position to your board is not doable, then look to your extended community as highlighted below in number 2.

2. It Takes a Village—Network and Collaborate!

If your community has a Federation and synagogue, chances are it also has at least one, if not more, Jewish young adult groups. Find and nurture these partnerships. They have a budget to engage young professionals. You have a venue. If you collaborate with these groups, the possibilities for exciting programming are endless.

Beyond temples and the Federated system, there are several growing networks engaging Jewish young adults. ROI, Presen-

Tense, Reboot, Six Points Fellowship for Emerging Jewish Artists, Birthright NEXT, *Slingshot: A Resource Guide to Jewish Innovation*, the Dorot Fellowship, Moishe House, Joshua Venture, and the Natan Fund are organizations that largely support a younger Jewish demographic (twenties to forties) through micro-grants, educational conferences, professional development, and major funding opportunities. Alumni of these programs are spread across the globe. They are found in small towns in the south, major cities on the East Coast, throughout Middle America, and all along the West Coast. They are entrepreneurial start-ups, often working on innovative projects that are culturally motivated. Collaborating with this caliber of Jewish young leadership can create several strategic alliances for both parties. In many cases, the opportunity to work with a museum, national university, temple museum, or gallery is exciting. The Contemporary Jewish Museum in San Francisco has collaborated on several exhibitions with Josh Kun, professor and cofounder of The Idelsohn Society for Musical Preservation, and Roger Bennett, cofounder of Reboot and The Idelsohn Society. The Jewish Museum of Maryland used their *Chosen Food: Cuisine, Culture, and American Jewish Identity* exhibition as a way to collaborate with Kayam Farm at Pearlstone, the most active Jewish community farm in North America. Kayam engages a large network of young Jews interested in sustainability and the environment. These partnerships extended the reach of museum exhibitions to participants who would be interested in the core topic and may not have known about the museum.

Consider working with the new kids on the block! There are a growing number of independent organizations and projects led by young Jewish culture creators targeting their cohorts. The leaders of these initiatives know how to attract their peers. They are proving their social impact, and start-ups or first-stage organizations serve as perfect program partners. They are naturally innovative, attracting thought and culture seekers. Tap into their enthusiasm, creativity, and networks. Offering a venue and chance to partner can lead to exciting possibilities. Examples include: G-dcast.com; Haggadot.com; Jewish Art Now, NYC; NuART Projects and the SEDER Arts Micro-Grant, Los Angeles; East Side Jews, Los Angeles; JDub Records (archive of musicians), NYC; Bible Raps, Philadelphia; Bibliyoga, Los Angeles and the UK; Jewish Chicks Rock, Brooklyn, NY; Jewish Rock Radio (JRR), Chesterfield, MO; *Punk Jews: The Documentary*, NYC; Yiddish Farm, New Hampton, NY; Jewish Rock Records, Gersham Y, Philadelphia; Hebrew Mamita, NYC; First Fruits Festival, Portland, OR; Zshuk Jewish Art

Initiative, NYC; KFAR Jewish Arts Center, Chicago; Art Kibbutz, NYC; A Member of Two Tribes, Los Angeles; Shemspeed and the Sepharidic Music Festival, NYC and Los Angeles. International examples of culture producers include: Socalled, Montreal, Quebec; Marom, Budapest; El Toratron, Buenos Aries; Jewish Salons, Amsterdam; Oleh! Records, Tel Aviv; Look to Learn, UK; Kol HaOt, Jerusalem; and JewishCultureUK.com.

3. Mobility—Take Your Message to the Streets

Robert Putnam, author of *Bowling Alone,* found that every ten minutes of commuting time reduces the likelihood of event attendance by 10 percent. People are more programmed now than ever before. We are more likely to skip events that require navigating traffic. If you want to get your message heard, you must go to where people are congregating. The days of waiting for participants to walk through the doors of museums, galleries, and cultural institutions and even our synagogues are waning. Repeat cultural consumers at Jewish museums is, on average, 15 percent lower than their secular counterparts. It is time to learn from secular art and cultural ventures and be willing to leave the confines of our institutional homes. Secular museums and curatorial collectives have been making their message mobile for decades. There are several innovative models available including using online technology to reach international audiences (streaming events live, creating secondary websites that expand exhibition content, or creating mobile apps), using a vehicle in order to make your collection or arts programming mobile, and creating pop-up exhibitions and events. Amazing examples of art vehicles include the Walker Art Museum on Wheels, Mobile Mural Lab in Los Angeles, and Camper Contemporary. A few examples of secular projects exploring pop-up exhibitions and happenings include InCubate, Chicago; Fallen Fruit, Los Angeles; and Phantom Galleries, Los Angeles. An ongoing exhibition of particular note is *Folk Art Everywhere,* which was organized by the Craft and Folk Museum (CAFAM), a small regional museum in Los Angeles. The exhibition as explained by CAFAM, "promotes the unique cultural and artistic landscape of Los Angeles by bringing art into unexpected spaces and celebrating all folk." They have placed objects from their collection in secure cases at restaurants, markets, community centers, coffee shops, bookstores, and other places where people naturally gather. The museum produced a map, events, and labels that connect each object to a chosen location. Consider how incredible it would be if Jewish museums or synagogue museums/collections partnered with local shop owners, Jewish businesses, Federations, JCCs, delis, and other gathering areas and linked items from their collection with each space. It could be a citywide effort to place Jewish ritual and material culture back into the community with exciting programming and endless opportunities for collaboration. There are several examples of Jewish organizations exploring mobile and transitory experiences. Rachel Jarman, director of the Museum of the Southern Jewish Experience, created a wonderful interactive traveling trunk project. As explained, "The Museum of the Southern Jewish Experience Traveling Trunk is a hands-on educational opportunity containing artifacts, photographs, maps and three lesson plans to teach Mississippi students about nineteenth century European immigration to the American South and how these Jewish immigrants made an impact on their communities."

4. Social Media and Branding

If you want to catch the attention of a younger crowd, your branding needs to feel contemporary. Check out hip designs by Br&.ish (http://brand-ish.co/) for ideas. Most organizations are now on Facebook and Twitter. Make sure to keep these accounts active and post events on both outlets.

Also, consider old school media used in contemporary ways. If you are trying to reach the unaffiliated, try creating posters that can be placed in regional hotspots including cafes, bars, or music venues. Leave stickers or postcards in similar areas. For the very brave, create a stencil or sticker that can be applied to the area surrounding your venue. Check out the Contemporary Museum in Raleigh, North Carolina, and their sticker project.

Conclusion

Generation Y (Millennials), Echo Boomers, and Xers might desire individualized approaches regarding community involvement, fund-raising, and affiliation with religious organizations. However, Facebook and other social media sites prove that adults in their twenties through forties want to feel connected, they also want to feel that they are part of a community! Remember, "It is not what you know but who you know." In an era of social networks containing thousands of "friends," who we know and how we connect to members of our network/community matter. NuART, and our programming including the SEDER Art events, is successful because a group of young Jews adapted a proven secular model, capitalized on our personal networks, and gathered other key people with large spheres of social influence. Most importantly, we literally and metaphorically welcome people into our community, provide a low barrier for inclusion ($18), give them a seat at our table, and ask participants to actively engage in creating a shared vision. There is always an extra seat at our table for anyone interested in eating a meal and supporting Jewish art!

Note

1. Sarah Bunin Benor, "Young Jewish Leaders in Los Angeles: Strengthening the Jewish People in Conventional and Unconventional Ways," The Avi Chai Foundation, 2010.

The New Authentics: Artists of a Post-Jewish Generation

Yael Rooks-Rapport

When the Spertus Museum in Chicago opened its inaugural art exhibition of 2007 its patrons were shocked and scandalized from the moment they walked through the gleaming glass doors. The exhibit was called *The New Authentics: Artists of a Post-Jewish Generation* and featured the contemporary work of sixteen carefully chosen North American Jewish artists. It was the title itself that caused such a fuss. Though exhibits of contemporary Jewish art, both ritual and secular, have become fairly normative in a variety of museums (whether "Jewish museums," "art museums," or both), the term "post-Jewish" had never been heard in this context. What were the implications of this phrase? Was the Spertus Museum trying to suggest that Judaism had come and gone?

Curator Staci Boris had purposefully chosen this provocative title to incite just such a conversation. But, "the end of Jewish art" was not the definition that she meant to imply; to her, "post-Jewish" means much more. "In the simplest terms, post-Jewish means that 'Jewish' has many interpretations and that it is difficult to define exactly what Jewish is and how people engage with their Jewishness . . . Post-Jewish identity is idiosyncratic, open-ended, and personally determined."[1] What Boris had effectively accomplished in creating and naming *The New Authentics* gave voice to a new and rising generation in a way they had never before been heard: through their art.

YAEL ROOKS-RAPPORT is in her third year of rabbinical school at HUC-JIR/NY. Her article comes out of research conducted for her cross-departmental honors thesis in Near Eastern and Judaic Studies and Art History at Brandeis University, where she graduated in 2009.

The Contemporary Post-Ethnic Art Movement

As postmodern identity politics become increasingly diffused and nuanced, cultural institutions have risen to the occasion showcasing programs, initiatives, and exhibitions, attempting to explore this complicated landscape. The Spertus takes its place alongside several other prominent museums that had recently curated shows dealing with issues of post-ethnicity, including the Museum of Modern Art's 2006 exhibition *Seventeen Ways of Looking,* dubbed "post-Islamic," and El Museo del Barrio's *The (S) Files/The Selected Files 2005,* which pioneered the title of "post-Chicano." The first use of any such term was in reference to *Freestyle,* the 2001 exhibition at the Studio Museum in Harlem, which applied the term "post-black" to describe the work of its twenty-eight emerging African American artists whose works were included in the show.[2] Boris pointed out, "These uses of "post" did not mean to reject ethnicity or blackness, they intended to go beyond it, complicate it, indicate that something was new about it."[3]

The *Artists of a Post-Jewish Generation* exhibit provided itself with a very thorough mission statement:

> *The New Authentics* exhibition and publication include artists of a specific place and time, representing the wide contours of both American Jewish identity and American art now, while posing the following questions: How do contemporary Jewish artists operate within a larger relational context? If an artist chooses to incorporate a Jewish subject, a Jewish image, or a Jewish symbol, how and why does she do it and what can it mean? What are today's Jewish artists' particular perspectives and obsessions, and, given their diversity, can they all be called "authentic"?[4]

These *New Authentics* sought to create work that was informed by their Jewish heritage, but not purely defined or limited by it. Their art concerns itself with Jewish issues as well as human issues such as family, gender, politics, and personality with which any viewer can empathize, whether or not they identify with the artist's specific culture. But in seeing any of the work from any of these artists, a viewer may be struck whether or not to read the piece within its Jewish identity construct.

For instance, Shoshanna Weinberger's contribution to the exhibit, entitled *All of Me* from 2005,[5] is a piece that demands to be read on multiple levels. *All of Me* is a printed work on paper, depicting an exuberant crown of hair created from all types of tresses entwined together. This mane is beaded and dreaded, curled and straightened, and changes color from a black that is almost brown to a brown that is almost blonde. To further highlight the differences in texture, the dreadlocks are drawn in ink, while the rest of the styles are painted in gouache. But the face, which should be surrounded by this thick mass of hair, is nothing more than an empty void, with no features or even outlines. Though her hair may be a clear indicator of her ancestry, the artist's face and true identity is a mystery to the viewer, and maybe even to the artist herself.

This piece can be understood as being by a woman artist, an American artist, a Caribbean artist, a Jewish artist, an artist of mixed heritage, but more accurately as several of these descriptions at once. Each reading of the artist's background and intentions has the potential to bring multiple understandings to the work, in addition to whatever cultural insight the viewers bring with them when they personally experience the piece. *All of Me* would lose much of its visual and cultural impact if any aspects of its creator's multifaceted identity were not taken into consideration. With complex contributions like this one from each of the *New Authentics*, the Spertus Museum had created an exhibit that placed it on the cutting edge in the art world as a museum that dealt with the complex politics of identity through art.

The Notion of "Post-Ethnicity"

Though this choice of exhibition was both innovative and challenging, it did not materialize miraculously. By choosing this title, Boris intended to conjure a host of art-historical implications and legacies: "I also meant to have it sound contemporary and be aligned with postmodernism, both chronologically and conceptually, as a phenomenon that questions its very definition without ever really intending to answer it concretely."[6] The content followed in the footsteps of the contemporary "post-ethnic" art movement, which according to historian David Hollinger, author of *Postethnic America,* could be described as an art form that would not reject the past outright, but would welcome adaptation and refinement. But in an age where many abstract nouns are prefaced with the term "post" to bring the concept up to date, "post-ethnicity" sought a slightly different connotation from that norm. "'Posting' is often a way of repudiating a preceding episode rather than building upon it and critically refining its contributions...Instead, postethnicity is more respectful of ethnicity."[7] This conscious deference to the movement that came before, alluded to by this term, was an important aspect to Boris as well:

> The term is not meant to suggest that Jews or Jewishness is gone, rather it is meant to suggest nuance and complexity to the notion of Jewishness. This is really not a totally new idea as the character of the Jewish population, at least for the last century if not longer, has never been monolithic and has continually evolved or changed . . . Since the exhibition was meant to explore contemporary notions of Jewish identity and how that manifested itself in these artists' works or how we could explore Jewish identity by looking at this group of artists' work, I felt the title of the exhibition needed to reflect that. I didn't want to deny or ignore the fact that though this exhibition had a broader scope and referred to identity in general, at its core it was about contemporary Jewish identity.[8]

The North American Jewish community's boundaries are particularly fluid and depend very much upon self-affiliation. The prevailing opinion until now on the subject of identity was best expressed by Horace Kallan when he said: "Men may change their clothes, their politics, their wives, their religions, their philosophies, to a greater or less extent; they cannot change their grandfathers."[9] However, for the *New Authentics* and those of their generation, this adage may no longer be true. More specifically, since Jewish identity is now held as an in-group responsibility for identifying themselves and their families as Jewish rather than an outsider-imposed appellation, every American Jew now has the ability to decide to what degree (if at all) they choose to identify with this community and what practices and beliefs they choose to hold regardless of familial origin or descent. For Hollinger, this option of "revocable descent," and specifically those individuals who decide not to take it, are the key to post-ethnicity itself:

> Instead of simply asserting a new amalgam identity, it is possible for a multiracial or multiethnic person to identify at one and the

> same time as both Irish and Italian, or both black and white, or even Jew and Christian. That is, in place of a new, monolithic identity to take the place of the ethnic or racial identities that make it up, one could imagine multiple identities held simultaneously and chosen as much as inherited. To put it in Horace Kallan's terms, we may not be able to choose our grandparents, but we can choose the extent to which we affirm our connection to this or that grandparent.[10]

Though Jews in North America are blessed with many freedoms, this particular personal entitlement comes with the heavy burden of individual responsibility. In order to be a Jew in this day and age, any given person must consciously and consistently make that choice. If we view this artist collective as they purport themselves to be, as cultural representatives for their generation, those of us invested in the continuity and changing nature of Jewish identity should take notice of their creative representation. Each of the artists who make up the *New Authentics* has purposely chosen to become, remain, and continue to be Jewish in some capacity. They may have chosen to subscribe to Judaism as either a culture or a religion, or they have made efforts to splice Judaism into their lives in addition to their other cultural identities. Some only maintain the choice that was made for them at birth by their families, some might have actively chosen to become Jewish in their adulthood, and some make that same choice for their children. They all made the choice to include the implications of this cultural identity in their work, and all of them agreed to have this work shown in this post-Jewish context, thereby choosing this particular label for at least a part of their identity, as well as their artistic output.

The New Authentics

The New Authentics themselves represent a wide array of Jewishly identified individuals. Of the sixteen artists included in the show, one is Canadian and the other fifteen are from the United States. All the artists are born in the 1960s and 1970s and belong roughly within the same era of Generation X. Their shared histories include Watergate, the Iran Contra Affair, the war on drugs, the beginnings of the AIDS crisis, and soaring divorce rates. Their formative years were spent in an intensely media-saturated environment, and they grew up to possess more than a healthy amount of skepticism towards any established institution.[11] All sixteen artists identify themselves as Jewish as a base definition, but each in their own way. They affiliate with many different movements within the Jewish community, and all have differing levels of practice. Most claim not to identify themselves primarily as Jews, and many do not regularly feature identifiably Jewish themes in their work. A few have experienced formal religious education, a few were raised in highly observant households, several are of mixed heritage, and one converted during adulthood.[12]

Boris approached each artist included in the show, the majority with whom she had already established relationships. Some who were unknown to her had been recommended by other artists, and some she sought out specifically and visited their galleries. As a result, Boris's curatorial vision, and indeed, Boris herself, were instrumental in the pioneering of this new moniker. "I wanted a culturally diverse group of artists to show the changing character of the Jewish population. I also wanted some artists who had partial Jewish backgrounds and who converted to be included, if I could find them," she said. "The show was meant to be inclusive, which is indicative of our new museum's mission."[13]

Though each of the artists indicated to Boris both their interest in being involved with the show and their understanding of its aims and themes, every one of them possesses a highly individualized and differentiated understanding of what being a "post-Jewish artist" means to them. The artist Joel Tauber could be described as being on the very engaged end of the spectrum. Even so he says, "I am happy to be categorized as a 'post-Jewish' artist, so long as the term is accompanied with a certain amount of discussion…I view myself as Jewish, but it is not the dominant element of my identity (at least from my perspective). I think being categorized as a post-Jewish artist is accurate, because I am an artist who is Jewish, who makes work about lots of things, and sometimes some of those things point to my Jewish identity. And, other times they do not."[14] Tauber grew up in an Orthodox home and creates works that illustrate his desire for meaningful personal practice. His contribution to the *New Authentics* was a twenty-four-minute video entitled *Seven Attempts to Make a Ritual,* a one-year project he worked on from 2000 to 2001, that tapes seven separate experiments in which the artist digs a hole large enough to immerse his body, or finds a natural alternative such as a cave, and sits inside observing the landscape or meditating.[15] While Tauber very much identifies with certain aspects and attributes of Judaism, he needed to look outside of its typical practices to create his own, private form of ritual. This calling on a connection for individual spirituality is a quality that ties Tauber to much of the rest of the post-Jewish generation.

Johanna Bresnick, the creator of a life-sized sculpture of herself astride the actual "flying carpet" her grandparents brought out of Germany, does not identify herself with Jewish faith, but as purely a "cultural Jew." She is a bit more cautious about her association with this label: "Part of me says 'what is a post-jewish[16] artist again?' But the 'post' part allows for an identity beyond a strict, discreet [*sic*], definitive one. So, to that I might say 'sure, whatever.' I'm a lot of things but I would never introduce myself in an artists' talk as, 'Hi, I'm a post-jewish artist.'"[17] Her work is titled *Ohne Lebensraum*, a reference to one component of Nazi political ideology or "living space" for the burgeoning Aryan population. She signifies her family's exclusion from the greater Germany by adding the prefix *ohne* (without). While *lebensraum* for most Germans meant freedom, privilege, and literally "space," for the Bresnicks it meant persecution, discrimination, and eventual expulsion—a loss of whatever space they had previously possessed. To Johanna Bresnick, it seems her Jewish identity itself can be symbolized by the rug that holds such a central place in this work. For her, Jewishness can be described as an inheritance, something that was passed down to her that she did not choose but cannot imagine throwing away because of all the sentimental meaning that is attached to it. It is filled with stories and memories, it travels with her wherever she goes, but it stays in the home sphere—her private domain. Her Judaism informs her past and her present, but plays only a symbolic role in her deciding her future.

Fawn Krieger, however, is adamantly opposed to this as well as any other attempts to institutionally isolate her work:

> I don't consider myself to be a Jewish artist, so I wouldn't consider myself to be a Post-Jewish artist. I also don't consider myself to be a white artist. I feel less aversion to being called an American artist, since it can be used simply to define geographical and pedagogical/critical backgrounds and contexts. And I do call myself a woman artist, since there are particularities in this field that pertain specifically to women—all women, whatever

> their cultural, ethnic, or religious backgrounds may be. As a rule, I steer away from defining myself as part of any institution…One of my responsibilities as an artist is to stand outside of institutions. I'm not sure my responses could be trusted, and I'm not sure I'd be fully accountable to my audience if I didn't adhere to this ethical structure. But I also understand that as an artist, I need to move through institutional structures, and to establish within them ruptures for human experience. I also understand that I come from things . . . I have a history, and I've inherited that history. Jewishness is very much a part of where I come from and how I've learned who I am, what I need to do, and the ways that I can do it in the world.[18]

Krieger's contribution to the *New Authentics* is just as thoughtful and controversial as her artist's statement. She produced a series of digital drawings from 2004, grouped as a collection called *Treyf.* These twenty ink-jet prints are simple compositions, drawn in a cartoonish hand. One shows a mountain of shrimp capped with slabs of bacon. Another depicts sirloin steaks sitting side by side with cartons of milk. Her assemblages break all the rules when it comes to keeping kashrut in such thorough detail that only an observant practitioner would be able to recognize the many myriad permutations; yet, they are explicit enough in their irreverence that even a cultural outsider could recognize that ritual lines have been crossed. In an ironic fashion, Krieger's artistic transgressions show the impressive level of her commitment and her cultural competency better than a thousand words ever could.

Though some artists, like Krieger, may have had personal misgivings about the classification of "post-Jewish," or any other classification for that matter, each of them recognized some affinity they and their art had to such a grouping. According to Boris, all of the artists were very much involved in the process of creating this exhibition, making post-Jewish art not only a curator-validated contemporary movement, but an artist-validated one as well.[19]

Conclusion

The Jewish world might view itself as a whole made up of many smaller parts. We may wish to ensure that "recognizing and responding to the connection between personal action and communal well-being are accepted as fundamental necessities to ensure the continuity of the Jewish people and therefore are incumbent upon all Jews."[20] But, the art world has more often been concerned with the expression of the individual as a representative for their time. The *New Authentics* gives us as committed Jewish professionals the opportunity to gain insight into the intersection of these two mentalities by investigating each artist's individual Jewish journey, how their religion and upbringing has affected the way they see the world, and what they want us, as the viewers, to see with them.

Each artist has a different and highly personalized reason for identifying with just such a description. For some, this inspiration is featured centrally in the pieces they contributed to the show, and for others the motivation is more ephemeral, its implications more abstract. This ambiguity is by no means unexpected. After all:

> The question of how one's being Jewish is understood, defined, and expressed in American society is not easily answered. For many, their Jewish identity is shaped by the experience of the Holocaust and what it symbolizes—namely, persecution for no other reason than that they are Jewish . . . For religious observant Jews, Jewish identity is defined in their observance. For many others there is no particular meaning they can cite as the source of the center of their Jewish identity. Rather it is just there, a part of them. They *feel* Jewish.[21]

These individuals have created their own cultural identities much in the same way they create their art by using creative processes to both exorcise and enlighten their views on issues of great personal import. In this case, issues of import that figure into the construction of their Jewish identities such as ancestry, hybridity, gender, cultural history, and personal practice are now the ones in question. We have made it our practice to recognize that when it comes to owned Jewish identity, "there will be many paths by which persons connect. To this extent, the process is closest to that of creative development, and each person can be thought of as an artist who must construct his or her own Jewish identity."[22] How can we and our institutions better support this creative process to nurture confident and thoughtful Jewish individuals and Jewish families?

These brief vignettes suggest that post-Judaism is not a paradigm shift to be feared or one that stands counter to the contemporary goals of institutional American Judaism. Rather, like postmodernism, it should be described as a movement that is introspective and self-aware. It is hybrid in nature, balancing a number of often opposing cultural identities while conscientiously giving voice to each one. It makes room for the implications of feminism and is mindful of gender's changing role in contemporary society. It is conscious of the events of history and seeks methods of giving meaning to the past, though it grows ever farther removed. It unhesitatingly questions the meaning of common and institutional practice and looks for methods that will increase individual connection. It is highly personalized, specified, and self-determined. It is both hopeful and skeptical, critical yet idealistic. In this postmodern age, meaning is a result of a completely individualized search for an answer—and what else is Judaism's goal than to aid its people in their search for meaning in their own lives and in life itself? Post-Judaism is no different in this regard, and from both a Judaic and an artistic standpoint, if an individual discovers an avenue for meaning or understanding in their own practice, I would deem this, conveniently, as a "new authentic": a version of authenticity that is as highly personalized as any other aspect of a post-Jewish identity.

Notes

1. Staci Boris, e-mail message to author, October 27, 2008.
2. Staci Boris, *The New Authentics: Artists of a Post-Jewish Generation: Exhibition, November 30, 2007–April 13, 2008, Spertus Museum, Chicago* (Chicago: Spertus Press, 2007), 20.
3. Staci Boris, e-mail message to author, October 27, 2008.
4. Boris, *New Authentics*, 23.
5. Ibid., 127.
6. Ibid.
7. Ibid., 4–5.
8. Staci Boris, e-mail message to author, October 27, 2008.
9. David Biale, "The Melting Pot and Beyond: Jews and the Politics of American Identity," in *Insider/Outsider American Jews and Multiculturalism*, ed. David Biale, Michael Galchinsky, and Susan Heschel (Berkeley: University of California, 1998), 25.
10. Ibid., 30.
11. Boris, *New Authentics*, 22.
12. Ibid., 23.
13. Staci Boris, e-mail message to author, October 27, 2008.
14. Joel Tauber, e-mail message to author, January 22, 2009.

15. Boris, *New Authentics*, 37.
16. Artist's use of lower-case letters preserved
17. Johanna Bresnick, e-mail message to author, December 12, 2008.
18. Fawn Krieger, e-mail message to author, December 28, 2008.
19. Staci Boris, e-mail message to author, October 27, 2008.
20. Roberta R. Farber and Chaim I. Waxman, "Postmodernity and the Jews: Identity, Identification, and Community," in *Jews in America: A Contemporary Reader*, ed. Roberta R. Farber and Chaim I. Waxman (Hanover, NH: Brandeis University Press/University Press of New England, 1999), 400.
21. Roberta R. Farber, "Creative Decision Making and the Construction of a Modern Jewish Identity," *Jews in America*, 298
22. Roberta R. Farber and Chaim I. Waxman, "Constructing a Modern Jewish Identity," *Jews in America*, 191

Towards a Taxonomy of the "Cultural Jew"

Richard A. Siegel

I am a "Cultural Jew." I am more engaged by what artists have to say—whether in words, paints, movements, or sounds—than by most rabbinic sermons today (except those of my wife).[1] I am moved more by Steve Reich's *Tehillim* than by what passes for *Hallel* in most shuls. I am more disturbed by Donald Margulies's play *Sight Unseen* than by most Yom HaShoah commemorations. Paul Taylor's choreography in *Klezmer Bluegrass* is a more resonant and joyous image of Jewish life in America than that encountered in most of the Jewish media.

Because of this, I found that one of the most interesting questions and unanalyzed findings in the 1990 National Jewish Population Study related to the respondent's perception of what being Jewish means:

> When you think of what it means to be a Jew in America, would you say it means being a member of:
>
> a) A religious group
> b) An ethnic group
> c) A cultural group
> d) A nationality

Respondents could choose more than one.

Putting aside the curious and imbalanced wording of the question, 70 percent said "cultural group," 57 percent said "ethnic group," 49 percent said "religious group," and 42 percent said "nationality." Even more, the official report on the study observed:

RICHARD A. SIEGEL is currently the director of the HUC School of Jewish Nonprofit Management in Los Angeles. He was with the National Foundation for Jewish Culture (now the Foundation for Jewish Culture) for twenty-six years, fifteen as executive director.

A"Further analysis shows that less than 5 percent of all respondents consider being Jewish solely in terms of being a member of a religious group, whereas 90 percent define being Jewish as being a member of a cultural or ethnic group."[2]

As far as I could tell, these responses were only analyzed as a comment on the weakening hold of religion on American Jewish identity. But the cultural implications of the numbers were not even considered. It seems that, absent some means of determining what people actually meant by belonging to a "cultural group," it was safer to assume that this term was a stand-in for "secular" or "just Jewish," and therefore unimportant in terms of learning anything more interesting about the psyche of American Jews. I question that assumption and would be interested in knowing how many people chose "cultural group" affirmatively, as in "This term describes how I am as a Jew." Unfortunately, there were no follow-up questions in the 1990 study that could help shed any light on the issue.

In the 2000 National Jewish Population Survey, there were a couple more questions aimed at better understanding this category. However, these were mostly about behaviors,[3] and although these generated some intriguing results indicating that "Jewish cultural engagement provides an important link to Jewish life for the intermarried, the geographically remote, the unmarried, and the unaffiliated,"[4] it still left the central question unasked or unexplored. Is there a positive paradigm of the Cultural Jew?

I believe that Cultural Jew can be an affirmative identity, although there has not yet been a demographic survey designed to test my assertion. In trying to describe it, we can safely agree that the term "Cultural Jew" does not have a single definition any more than the term "Religious Jew" does. The term embraces a spectrum of attitudes, behaviors, and perspectives ranging from the most unconsciously indifferent to the most consciously engaged. The relevant question, then, is where and when on the spectrum does the Cultural Jew move from being an indifferent Jew to an engaged Jew? Where and when does the Cultural Jew enter into the "Jewish conversation"? It is at this point when Cultural Jew becomes an affirmative identity.

On the lowest level, in terms of the hierarchy of cultural identity, is the "Nominal Jew," the person who says "I'm Jewish, but . . . ." For instance: "I'm Jewish, but I'm not religious." "I'm Jewish, but

I don't contribute to Jewish causes." "I'm Jewish, but I'm not really interested in Israel." For this one, "cultural" means identifying with what's left after religion, ethnicity, and nationality are dismissed. Like the Evil Son in the Haggadah, they have taken themselves out of the Jewish conversation. The ones on this level cannot articulate a positive identity structure around it; they may be Jewishly conscious and even proud, but they are not all that interested. They choose "Cultural Jew" both because the term has a positive valence and because the choice does not impose any demands. It is a nominal Jewish cultural identity, the exact opposite of a dominant Jewish cultural identity discussed later on. I suspect that there are a lot of Cultural Jews of this kind.

The next category is the "Audience." These are the Jews who attend arts and culture events, be they films or lectures or concerts; these are the Jews who show up.[5] This is the group who the 2000 National Jewish Population Survey was targeting. These are the ones who bought Jonathan Safran Foer and Nathan Englander's *New American Haggadah* or downloaded a Matisyahu recording or watched the film *Footnote* at the local multiplex. The Audience is *amcha* (the community of intellectually or emotionally engaged Jews).

Within this stage, however, there's also a spectrum of identity. For instance, there is a significant difference between those who attend reluctantly and those who attend avidly, between those who attend occasionally and those who attend frequently, and between those who watch and those who participate. The real distinction, what differentiates the Audience from the Nominal Jew is that they have joined the Jewish conversation, or at least they are eavesdropping. They have entered into the larger Jewish discourse going on simultaneously across the globe, even if they are not yet contributing to it.

On the most literal level, the Audience tends to talk about the Jewish cultural experience that they have participated in, whether it's an episode of *Mad Men* or the cantor's singing of *El Malei Rachamim*. On a more significant level, attending Jewish cultural activities has at least two corollaries that reinforce the attendee's communal perception/perspective. First, these events are most often attended with others, whether family or friends. Having a Jewish social network is a positive marker of engaged Jewish identity. Second, this encounter, particularly in the secular or larger

American society, is a constant reminder of the interpenetration of American and Jewish culture. When Jewish creativity is presented on or through the major stages of American arts and letters, the result is American Jewish culture and, with it, American Jewish cultural identity. While it still may not be the dominant identity of these Cultural Jews, neither is it minimal as in the previous group.

The third level is the "Cultured Jew." This person does not just listen in on the Jewish conversation; he or she contributes to it, adds to it, and is a virtual partner in its vibrancy. What constitutes being a Cultured Jew, as opposed to being an Audience? Does it mean being familiar with the Jewish canon? Does it mean knowing Modern Hebrew? Does it mean following Jewish blogs? Yes and no.

I prefer to see the Cultured Jew in a more Kaplanian frame, someone who is consciously engaged in and by the Jewish civilization and its various components, namely "a land; a language and literature; mores, laws and folkways; folk sanctions; folk arts; and social structure."[6] The Cultured Jew is finally a dominant identity; it is a primary lens through which to see the world.

The Cultured Jew reads Jewish books (whether Psalms or Philip Roth), listens to Jewish music (whether *chazanut* or Noa), watches Jewish films (whether *The Jazz Singer* or *A Serious Man*), visits Jewish museums (whether art or Holocaust), and participates in other types of Jewish intellectual and creative activities. But at its essence, it is not the participating that matters. What matters is the individual's response to the experience. What new thoughts does it raise or ideas does it inspire? Is it "good for the Jews" or is it a challenge to a Jewish sacred cow? The Cultured Jew commands a prime and active seat at the table where the Jewish conversation is going on. And inevitably, those who are most active in the Jewish conversation are the ones who end up shaping it, and with it, the Jewish future.

There is yet another level above this, however, and that is the "Cultural Innovator." These are more than participants; these are the actors themselves, the ones who generate the action. This could be the artist or scholar, but it could also be the producer, the curator, the collector, the critic, the patron, anyone involved in the complex process through which culture is created. The Cultural Innovator is almost by definition the smallest cohort within the typology of Cultural Jew. However, its impact on the collective should not be underestimated/cannot be overstated.

Together the Cultured Jew and the Cultural Innovator make up the Jewish "Creative Class" (as Richard Florida describes it).[7] These are the ones who provide the substance of the conversation. In a living community, the Creative Class is indispensable. These are the ones through whom the civilization evolves. Without them, there is literally nothing to talk about.

In 2002, in celebration of the fortieth anniversary of the National Foundation for Jewish Culture (NFJC, now just the Foundation for Jewish Culture), I edited a "Report on the Future of Jewish Culture in America" extracted from interviews with thirty-two artists, scholars, intellectuals, and leaders of Jewish cultural, communal, and religious institutions. Some of the responses touched on the meaning and value of both the Cultural Innovator and the Creative Class to the larger Jewish community:

R. B. Kitaj, *z"l*, renowned visual artist, painter:

For many years, I have been obsessed with something called Jewish Art, unlike my Jewish artist friends, who just want to be very good artists. I do too, but I want both, and I like the term Jewish Art, which a lot of folks reject. All good painters of the Jewish Diaspora have been deeply influenced by the host-culture. I had to coin a new word, Diasporist, in order to begin to think about a new Jewish Art for myself . . . The very complex, controversial idea of Jewish Art is a game I like to play and defend. It is not very popular. I feel it in my bones and in my mind's eye. If there can be a controversial Jewish State, I believe there can be a controversial Jewish Art.

Liz Lerman, MacArthur Award winning choreographer:

My experiences have ultimately taught me that if I had measured myself on my Jewish knowledge or if the Jewish community decided to measure me based on my Jewish knowledge, I and they would have been very disappointed. But if they measured me on what I know as a person, as a human being and as an artist, I know a lot and I know how to combine what I know with Jewish knowledge to create incredible things.

Tony Kushner, Pulitzer and Tony award winning playwright:

Whatever you have got packed inside your soul comes out as you write, that's the danger and the excitement about writing. More than you know will come out, and there is more in you than you ever know and you can't control it completely. There are a lot of people, a lot of entities holding that pen. Writing *Angels in America* I expected it to be a gay play; I didn't expect it to be a Jewish play, but it turned into one. It turned into this very Jewish as well as gay as well as American play. That surprised me.

Art Spiegelman, Pulitzer Prize winning graphic comics artist:

What made me interested in Jewish culture was my glomming onto comic books at an early age and finding that everything I needed to learn was there. All of my art appreciation, all of my moral teaching came from the comics, were available through this popular culture that turns out to have been a Jewish secular American culture. And you know like I'm definitely shaped by the founding fathers, not Abraham and Isaac, but Harvey (Kurtzman) and Jack (Kirby) and Will (Eisner). And Tom and Jerry. The comic book world is a kind of secular Jewish culture.

Joan Rosenbaum, former director of The Jewish Museum (NY):

With any show of 20th century art or even 19th century art, you have to confront the issue of modernity and the tremendous changes that it made for Jewish identity in the world. We have had some terrific shows over the years relating to Jewish identity. One of them, "Too Jewish?" was young contemporary artists doing Jewish identity issues, especially as they are reflected in popular culture, popular culture reconsidered by the artist. Many of the young Jewish people who wrote in the comment books said, "You are finally speaking to me. I think this is my show, this is my life story, this is who I am." They see themselves connected to a contemporary world of popular culture and reflected images of Jewishness.

Ilan Stavans, a noted writer and scholar of contemporary Jewish culture:

It is a task of our generation to be aware that if every generation chooses its own memory, then we have the responsibility of making new ones. That's the role of the critic or the intellectual, of the educator and the writer . . . The role of the writer is to be a reflective voice that tries to understand the time we're living in either through fiction, non-fiction, through memoirs. If we as individuals have a need to find our place within a particular society, I think ideas need to find a place in society, and it's the role of the intellectual to explain how ideas fit.

The Creative Class brings innovation into the community, keeps it from becoming just a "survival" community, and allows it to keep breathing fresh air. Without the Creative Class, Judaism would eventually become ancestor worship. This then is the positive paradigm of the Cultural Jew and of "Jewish cultural identity."

There is an irony, however, in regard to the Cultural Jew, in general, and of the Creative Class, in particular. The identity of Cultural Jew is very difficult to pass down. Jewish cultural identity does not have a set of rules to obey or texts to study or rituals to observe, as does Jewish religious identity. The cultural perspective is a combination of sensory, emotional, and cerebral experiences; and these are, by definition, personal, idiosyncratic, and nontransferable. Even the Yiddish secularists, who had their own language and a well-developed worldview, could not sustain attachment to Yiddish culture, literally "Jewish" culture, beyond a couple of generations. Ironically, those who shape the texture of Jewish life through the arts and humanities leave a rich legacy, but no heirs.

Passing down culture is not the same as passing down religion, nationality, or ethnicity. In each of those cases, respectively, the transmission is inherited, born into, or ingested. Culture, on the other hand, is as much about breaking with the past, as it is about revering it. Each new generation must hope that it has its own Creative Class who, both as innovators and as critics, will stimulate the community's imagination and keep the Jewish conversation going. Cultural Jews cannot sustain Judaism or the Jewish people. But without Cultural Jews, neither Judaism nor the Jewish people will be able to retain their vibrancy for very long.

It would seem to me, then, that a prominent question for community planners should be: "How to nurture the Creative Class, that amalgam of Cultured Jew and Cultural Innovator? Since cultural identity cannot generate its inheritors, it must be constantly created anew. Can we, as a community, encourage the ongoing replenishment of the Creative Class? And if so, how?" Articulating a full agenda would require at least another article, but certainly a simple step would be to encourage more creative interactions of the Jewish and the American experiences. Both the Skirball Cultural Center in Los Angeles and the 92nd Street Y in New York, among other institutions in cities across the country, attest to how the interaction of American and Jewish cultures generates energy, creativity, audiences, and revenues.[8]

That this arena garners so little communal attention, not only from planners, but from researchers, funders, Federations, rabbis, and others who have the ability to actually do something to remedy this situation, is further confounded by how relatively easy—and inexpensive—it is to do. Little investment is actually needed to nourish the Cultural Innovator, because a little goes a long way. The communal impact of our most creative talents, whether in the arts or humanities, is significantly greater than either their numbers or the size of the Jewish communal input. Think Maurice Sendak, who died while this article was being written. Or Debbie Friedman, who died last year.

Shortly before I left the NFJC in 2006,[9] we had developed the plan, secured the funding, and put in place the major players for the Six Points Fellowship. This ambitious project, cosponsored by the NFJC, Avodah Arts, and JDub Records (*alav hashalom*), with visionary funding from the UJA-Federation of New York, created a mechanism to identify and then support creative artists who were pushing new combinations of the Jewish DNA. The dozen artists chosen were given substantial financial stipends, as well as incalculable networking, learning, production, and marketing assistance. This has proven to be an immensely successful program, now with its second New York cohort and a new one underway in Los Angeles. Social scientist, Bethamie Horowitz, in her evaluative report, "Cultivating Art, Artists, and Audiences," observes:

> Each of the Six Points events can be viewed as a magnet for attracting a number of audiences or subcultures. If culture is conceptualized as practice, engagement and interaction, then anything you do to encourage this kind of interchange occasioned by artists' performances and exhibits adds to the conversation. The important thing is to seed the growing subculture of artists and their audiences.[10]

The Six Points Fellowship and other institutions and initiatives working to stimulate new Jewish creativity in the arts and humanities merit the serious attention and support of the Jewish community: Jewish foundations, Federations, philanthropists, rabbis, and other communal leaders. These Cultural Innovators are refilling the wells of Jewish creativity; they are fueling the Jewish conversation. We, as a community, are foolish and short-sighted to ignore them.

To answer the question I asked at the beginning, then, "Yes, there is a positive paradigm for the Cultural Jew." There are, in fact, several dimensions of the Cultural Jew, most of which reflect an active and distinct Jewish identity. On the upper levels, these Jews are critical to the further evolution of the Jewish civilization. I would hope that future Jewish population surveys try to investigate this phenomenon more fully. We would benefit enormously as a community if we took our Cultural Jews more seriously and understood them better.

Notes

1. Laura Geller, senior rabbi of Temple Emanuel of Beverly Hills.
2. Barry Kosmin et al., "Highlights of the 1990 CJF National Jewish Population Survey" (Council of Jewish Federations, 1991).
3. "During the past year, did you . . .
   - Listen to a tape, CD, or record because it had Jewish content?
   - See a movie or rent a video because it had Jewish content?
   - Read a book other than the Bible because it had Jewish content?"
4. Steven M. Cohen and Ari Y. Kelman, *Cultural Events & Jewish Identities: Young Adult Jews in New York* (National Foundation for Jewish Culture, 2005). Coincidently, this is a large and highly desirable demographic from the perspective of the organized Jewish community.
5. While in this article, I am referring to activities within the "arts and culture" arena, this perspective can be seen in other arenas, as well. For instance, many Jews look at services, particularly on the High Holy Days, with essentially a cultural lens . . . the quality of the rabbi's sermon, the cantor's chanting, the choir's harmonies, the wardrobes of the other congregants.
6. Mordecai M. Kaplan, *Judaism as a Civilization: Toward a Reconstruction of American-Jewish Life* (New York: Schocken Books, 1967), 186.
7. Richard Florida, *The Rise of the Creative Class*, and the recently published *The Great Reset*.
8. The Skirball's *Noah's Ark* is one of the most successful children's exhibits ever mounted. The 92nd Street Y's lecture series has set the bar both for Jewish and general cultural institutions in North America.
9. I was executive director from 1991–2006 and am now the executive director emeritus of the renamed Foundation for Jewish Culture.
10. See Bethamie Horowitz, "Cultivating Art, Artists, and Audiences: An Evaluation of the Six Points Fellowship for Emerging Jewish Artists—Executive Summary" (Six Points Fellowship for Emerging Jewish Artists, October 2009), 5.

Choosing Art for the Jewish Chapel at the U.S. Air Force Academy

Joel Schwartzman

I was stationed as Jewish chaplain at the U.S. Air Force Academy from the summer of 1983 until the summer of 1986. Being rabbi to a meager forty cadets of a total student body of four thousand, I found myself with time on my hands as I entered the second year of this assignment, devoting my first one to learning how the Academy operated. It was a system that, in many ways, reflected other Air Force bases. However, the Air Force Academy did have its significant differences especially as it regarded garnering cadet time, and it was critical that I mastered these if I were to be successful with the Jewish program.

Serendipitously, in my second year, a Jewish major general named Robert A. Rosenberg arrived at Space Command as vice commander. His offices were located at Peterson Air Force Base, not more than twenty-five or so miles from the Air Force Academy. Over the course of the general's attending my services, he, his wife, Marge, and I made a verbal pact to renovate the beautiful, intimate Jewish chapel that, along with the Catholic and All Faiths' chapels, was located in the basement of the iconic Air Force Academy's Cadet Chapel.

It was as part of this rather stimulating cabal that I had occasion to commission nine pieces of artwork that still grace two-thirds of the circular walls that comprise this chapel. What follows is the story of how this commissioning came to be.

RABBI JOEL SCHWARTZMAN, having dedicated nearly a quarter century to serving the military of the United States, and having served a year with Denver's Temple Sinai and another decade with URJ Congregation B'nai Chaim in Morrison, Colorado, is now retired and is enjoying being husband to Ziva, father to Dr. Micah and Rabbi Ilana and their respective spouses, Dr. Leslie and Art, and grandfather to Solly and Abie Schwartzman and his soon-to-be-born brother.

First, there is a critical detail I need to explicate about how this "art project" came about. It concerns the Academy's having liaison officers (LOs) in every state in the Union. Their responsibilities include identifying outstanding high school students, explaining to them the benefits of attending the Air Force Academy, and helping them in the not uncomplicated process of making application. One particular LO was a fellow by the name of Ken Klotzkin. His domain was the state of New York. But being an LO wasn't Ken Klotzkin's only useful role to the Academy. He was also a tax expert, and, with his knowledge of tax law, he played go-between, connecting big, successful corporations with nonprofits and opening opportunities for them to gain tax deductions through making sizable contributions to organizations that were probably thrilled to be selected.

Lieutenant Colonel Klotzkin showed up unannounced at a Shabbat dinner on Parents Weekend of 1984. Because my wife, Ziva, was doing the majority of the cooking for well over one hundred people that night, I did not take well to anyone we hadn't counted on crashing the party. In fact, if memory serves, I think that I was rather rude to Mr. Klotzkin. Sometime later, I remember explaining the reception I had given him and apologizing for it. Nonetheless, I thought that we had gotten off to a poor start. Ken didn't hold it against me; for, some months later, he phoned me and said, "Rabbi, if ever you should need a large gift for the Jewish program there at the Academy, just let me know." I told him on the spot that I needed three thousand dollars for new pulpit chairs. Klotzkin responded that I surely wasn't hearing him, and he reiterated that he was talking about a BIG donation. I filed that information away in the back of my mind, disappointed that I couldn't deliver the money MG Rosenberg and I were pursuing to buy the needed chairs.

It was in the spring of 1985 that Ziva, our kids, and I were able to attend the CCAR convention, which was being held in Minneapolis, Minnesota. One of the major draws for this conference was that my father, Dr. Sylvan D. Schwartzman, *z"l*, and Rabbi Allan H. Schwartzman (his brother, my uncle) would be there. It was, indeed, rare that the three of us were ever able to see one another together.

At these occasions various vendors and salespersons of Jewish items would come and set up booths we attendees could peruse and from which we often made purchases. There were those who sold mezuzot and books; there were travel agencies whose goal it was to attract groups to Israel; and there were informational booths. At one particular booth was an art dealer who was displaying the portfolio of an Israeli artist whose work he handled. The dealer's name was Jacob Adler. His artist was an Israeli, Shlomo Katz.

Now, truth be told, I knew only slightly more about art than I did about how the Air Force ordered carpet or upholstery. I knew what I liked when I saw it. I also knew some about the world's great artists including, of course, Marc Chagall and Amedeo Modigliani. My wife and I had purchased serigraphs by Mordecai Ardon and Edward Ben Avram; and we were enamored of Yaakov Agam's work and that of Shmuel Katz. But when I first looked at what lay before me, Shlomo Katz's Passover portfolio, what struck me weren't so much thoughts of like or dislike, but rather, that this man's style of painting might work in the Academy's Jewish chapel.

Katz was drawing exaggerated, elongated figures with a distinctive style. Most important was that he was working with a Judaic theme. The Jewish chapel had a ceiling that was at least twenty feet above the floor. Nothing diminutive on those walls would work. No painting that depicted only smallish figures could succeed either. The images would be lost to people sitting at the opposite section of the sanctuary. Then too, I needed to concern myself with the Jewish prohibition against making images. The Cadet Chapel was a prime tourist destination for people of all faiths including Orthodox Jews. Katz's work answered both concerns. His technique, which incorporated oils painted on gold leaf giving an iconic effect, and particularly, the size of his figures, which did not directly represent the human figure but rather made caricatures of it, all clicked instantly in my head. I turned to Ziva and said, "You know? While I'm not instantly in love with what I'm seeing, this fellow, Katz, could work in the chapel."

After we returned to the Air Force Academy, I set about contacting Ken Klotzkin. When I got him on the phone, I reminded him of the offer he had made: "Ken, remember when you said that if ever I want a BIG donation for the Jewish chapel I should call you? Well, I have something in mind." I explained how I had been attending the CCAR convention and had seen Shlomo Katz's work and thought that it might work on the walls of the Jewish chapel.

We both concurred that while Katz's work did not immediately or exactly endear itself to us personally, we could see that his art would be terrific for the space involved. Klotzkin said that he would contact Adler to begin the project, but I stopped him before he could close the deal with me or end the call. I told him: "Ken, I am willing to be project officer for this endeavor on one condition. I do not ever want to know about the monetary arrangements. I intend to leave all that up to you. I want nothing whatsoever to do with money." Again, Ken Klotzkin agreed and that arrangement has held until this day.

While I was sanguine about my role in renovating and beautifying the Academy's Jewish chapel, I was way out of my element when it came to tax law and to the deals that Klotzkin was putting together. As an Air Force officer, I knew enough about what I could and could not receive in gifts and remunerations to understand that it was all a huge potential minefield, and I wanted no part of that side of things.

It was in the summer of 1985 that Jacob Adler came to the Academy, and we met in the Jewish chapel one warm afternoon. As I had come from my office in Sijan Hall to the Jewish chapel, I remember waiting for Mr. Adler in the sanctuary. Suddenly he was there. He reintroduced himself and we immediately got to work: "What do you want Shlomo to paint?" he asked somewhat brusquely. Not having thought much past my telephone call with Klotzkin to get the ball rolling, I was taken a bit off guard. "Well," I fumbled. "I really don't know; except I do know one thing: the bimah"—I pointed to the front of the chapel at what comprised one third of the circular sanctuary—"is off limits." As I swept my arm around to the remaining two-thirds, I said: "The rest of this space is fair game." "Yes," Adler said, indicating that he understood, "but what do you propose for this space?" I reiterated my uncertainty, feeling a sense of panic at my being pinned down to something I wasn't prepared for. I remember thinking about the foci of the Air Force Academy: space and flight. But Jacob interrupted my nervous, mental scramble nearly jumping as he bolted toward the northern portion of the sanctuary wall. He said, "Let me suggest that there be three sections with three paintings per section. They ought to have themes that Shlomo can draw from the *Tanach*. They can be five feet by four feet." (That threw me because I didn't understand if he meant five feet long by four feet high or vice versa. But I didn't interrupt him because what he was proposing thus far made much, much more sense than my being caught flatfooted, having little as yet to offer.) I grew excited by the concept, and my mind began to contemplate possible biblical sources for Katz's work. "Well certainly, one theme that comes to mind for anyone painting for the Air Force Academy would be space and flight," I offered. Adler and I immediately looked skeptically at each other because we both knew that there were only a limited number of instances that anything having to do with space and flight occurred in the Bible. There was King Solomon's perplexity in Proverbs over the "how" of the flight of the eagle. There was the scene of Elijah being lifted alive into heaven in a fiery chariot. Then, there was Ezekiel's vision of the four winged beasts, which were comprised of screws, wheels, and springs. These creatures surrounded God. Apart from those, we both drew blanks. Yet these three were enough to compromise the back wall, which faced the bimah.

Knowing that the Academy operated by an honor code that states, "We shall not lie, cheat, or steal or tolerate any among us who do," I knew that a Wall of Justice would resonate well with everyone at the institution. Tentatively, I offered this as an idea for the northern third of the chapel wall. I began by suggesting "Abraham's confronting God on behalf of the inhabitants of Sodom and Gomorrah" as one possible subject. Adler then continued with the idea of a second painting to be based on Solomon's judgment to split the disputed baby. I then suggested a third idea to be based on Deuteronomy 16:18: "Judges and officers you shall put at your gates." If memory serves, I was teaching that very portion at that time to a bat mitzvah student. But I also knew that those words were reflected at the Academy by the Honor Committee and by both the fine officers who taught there and the excellent students, who graduated each year, pinned at that ceremony with the rank of second lieutenants.

Having nailed down the Wall of Justice, and looking for some inspiration, I picked up a copy of the siddur, *Likrat Shabbat*, because I remembered a responsive reading that, quoting the *Tanach*, had given voice in me to a possible third theme. I leafed through the pages and finally came upon what I was looking for on page 136: "The call to justice and brotherhood." Therein were lines based on Isaiah 58:7: "Is it not to share *your bread* with the *hungry*, and that you bring the poor that are *cast* out to *your* house? when you see the naked, that you cover him. . . ." These words reflected a social responsibility whose message I thought appropriate to challenge every cadet, Jewish or not.

Then, too, there was the theme of love that was so beautifully depicted in the Book of Ruth. It is embodied by Boaz and Ruth, and watched over with blessing by Ruth's mother-in-law, Naomi. This became the second painting on the southern third of the chapel's walls. The ninth and final painting was one that I, for a very particular reason, ardently requested. It was Jacob's wrestling with the angel. This is a theme that I believed all college students ought to see, be confronted by, and understand as they contemplate their relationship with God and struggle to define it.

Just exactly how Shlomo Katz would draw these different biblical set pieces, I did not know. After the paintings were completed and hung, I learned about which ones gave the artist the most trouble in translating their subjects to canvas. I also learned just how helpful Katz's wife, Mickey, was in suggesting to him how he might bring them to concrete expression. Two of the paintings, in fact, carry a small inscription, "Mickey's Painting," which is not all that hard to find. But off Adler went with what we had concluded that July afternoon. I was not to hear from him again until later that winter of 1985 when he and the artist himself came to the Academy one snowy, freezing day to deliver the first five of the works.

It is instructive now in retrospect to say a few words about some of the intimate details of the nine paintings that Katz produced for the Jewish cadet chapel. After delivering his final four works in May 1986, Katz offered that he had never worked under such pressure and so quickly in his life as he had to finish this set of nine paintings. Knowing that I had an assignment and would be leaving the Academy, I had set a spring deadline to complete all the projects the Rosenbergs and I had undertaken so that I might be able to dedicate the renovated chapel and the magnificent paintings before my departure. This included re-carpeting the sanctuary, reupholstering the congregational chairs, having Torah mantels woven to match the original Ludwig Wolpert accoutrements (Wolpert being the premier American artisan in Judaica throughout the mid-twentieth century), and finishing the high-backed pulpit chairs that were to replace the original, orange colored, broken 1950s models.

In the winter, when Katz and Adler delivered the first five works, they immediately set about opening their crates and walking the paintings, one at a time, down to the chapel. I remember thinking to myself, "If this art works, no one will ever remember who I am or the part I played in getting them here. But if it doesn't, they'll never forget the fool who commissioned all this!" I felt like King David when he accompanied the Ark to Jerusalem, dancing with all his might to bring the holy to its rightful place.

As each painting entered the chapel, I didn't know what to think. But the dear friends I had invited to this special event were so enthusiastic that I was soon swept up in their exuberance. There was *Solomon's Vision* and *Elijah's Ascendance*. Then, too, came *Abraham's Challenge to God* and *Solomon's Judgment*. Last to arrive was *Cast Your Bread*.

We set about mounting the works, which were curved in their light colored, pine frames, shaped to fit the curved walls that were to be their homes. I remember Katz taking me aside at one point during this process, presenting me a project that was to test me for many years to come. He said, "I've created these paintings and their frames. It's your job from this point forward to see that they are properly lit." Although Katz was absolutely correct, I came to perceive that difficult task in the often underfunded chaplain career field as a mild curse. It wasn't until the year 2000 that I actually succeeded in fulfilling Katz's challenge. It was in that year, having retired to Colorado, that I discovered a new lighting technology with fixtures that could be recessed into the Chapel's ceiling. Raising the funds for this project turned out to be rather easy.

Shlomo Katz spoke about each painting as we mounted and fastened them to the walls. He was surprised to realize some very poignant coincidences that had arisen between the environs of Colorado and his work. For example, in the Elijah painting, Katz had drawn some rugged mountains. When he arrived in Colorado Springs, he had the time to visit the Garden of the Gods. He now perceived a direct parallel to these peaks in not one but two of his works. He also saw that the thistle plant was common to both places, Colorado and Israel.

It was only some months after Elijah's arrival that someone pointed out to me the epilogue from *Out of the Whirlwind*, wherein Elijah represents the Jews of Europe rising to heaven in the flames of the Nazi death camps. To that point, I had not seen this painting, whose fiery horses when lit nearly came flying off the canvas at the viewer in a profound, almost 3-D effect, as a depiction of the Holocaust. Since reading that powerful piece, I have never again seen the painting in the innocent way I had viewed it upon its arrival.

Another discovery I made both for myself and for the artist arose from the Ruth and Boaz love scene in which Naomi watches over this couple with obvious approval. Naomi peers out from a grapevine. Upon closer inspection, I realized that Naomi had no feet. They were entirely covered by and contained within the vine. I remember saying to the artist: "Naomi isn't only standing in this grapevine; she is the vine. For, as we hear so often in our High Holy Day liturgy, just as Israel (Naomi) is the vine, God is the vineyard keeper." Katz smiled approvingly, not agreeing or disagreeing with my interpretation.

There were other discoveries and interpretations that arose as the Katz paintings settled into the consciousness of us who utilized the Jewish cadet chapel. Truly these paintings, rich in color and theme, demanded illumination, losing their impact when they were unlit. As with all great works of art, each painting spoke differently to people and did so as much reflecting the season of the year as the mood and knowledge of the viewer.

Whether anyone recognizes that Ezekiel's vision has its roots, so to speak, in Raphael's work depends upon their knowledge of the world of art. Whether they recognize Jacob's family standing on the side as the patriarch struggles with the form of a man-angel may depend upon their knowledge of that story. Some point out the Oak of Mamre in the painting where Abraham pleads for the inhabitants of Sodom and Gomorrah. Others see in that same work the suggestive, flailing arms and legs emanating from the buildings, the ominous, dark clouds filled with brimstone overhanging the same structures, and the sadistic smile on a horse that is chasing down a terrified, fleeing woman; and they immediately understand what they are seeing.

In the years since the dedication of the Shlomo Katz paintings on May 23, 1986, the paintings have been depicted in many ways. Adler and Katz published sets of lithographs and published a beautiful, desktop book called *The Way of the Eagle in the Air*. Then, too, there were a set of postcards and a brochure. Jacob Adler even had the paintings woven into tapestries, a fact I was to learn at Adler's URJ convention display not so many years ago.

Just prior to the dedication ceremony, I had tried to work through the Academy's Office of Public Affairs to have a national magazine like *Life*, *Newsweek*, or *Time* come and do a piece on Katz's work. The best I was able to accomplish was to have Denver's *Intermountain Jewish News* do an article, although when they published slides of Katz's paintings, they did so backwards! Since then, I have entertained the idea of having what I have now come to believe are true masterpieces published as U.S. postal stamps. However, since Katz was not a U.S. citizen, his work falls outside Postal Service rules. To my mind, this is too bad because Katz's creations have become national treasures. They deserve national and international recognition.

The nine Katz paintings have toured once, as far as I know. They are on permanent loan to the Air Force Academy from the Falcon Foundation, the nonprofit organization through which Ken Klotzkin labored to secure these works for an institution we both honored with our respective energies and labors.

Leviticus/Vayikra: *Artists' Voices*

Just as *Adonai* had commanded Moses, so the Israelites had done all the work.

(Exod. 39:42)

Art and Prayer

Isaac Brynjegard-Bialik

"I found myself experiencing something new: the sensation of being engaged in prayer—of finding that the work of creating these prayers out of paper was in many ways akin to a prayer experience itself."

"I always start studying text when working, but there was something different about studying prayers and creating my own interpretations of them. Making the prayers became, for me, an act of prayer itself. And that thoughtful engagement—the intention of studying and interpreting and expressing these prayers—was integral to the [creative] process."

"In my arena, the acts of art creation and prayer merged into—at times—a singular experience. If art is an arena, for me it became as well a place of worship."

ISAAC BRYNJEGARD-BIALIK lives in Southern California with his wife, who is a rabbi in the Reform Movement, and three daughters. He has been cutting paper for twenty years and reading comics for about twice as long; more of his work can be seen online at www.NiceJewishArtist.com.

Engaging Community

Mark Hurvitz

"Each [Jewish lapel button] is a tiny public billboard using text and imagery, often from popular culture, produced and worn to call attention to an issue."

"It is as though the button presents an additional face to the world."

RABBI MARK HURVITZ (C78) is the creator of davka.org, a weaving together of fringes of Jewish life. He collects artifacts and ephemera that depict the values and the acceptance of Jewish life in America. His collection of Judaic lapel buttons has been displayed in synagogues, JCCs, and libraries around the United States.

Collaboration and Participation

Flora Rosefsky

Jewish visual artists bring their unique perspectives in how to interpret Judaism through their work. Rather than the written word, or through music, it is the visual artist who sees the world in a different way, stretching the boundaries of the past while inspiring those they teach to find the creative spirit within. Starting a dialogue of conversation and hands-on activities with a contemporary Judaic artist can be the beginning of a journey for a congregation, while leaving behind a community Judaic arts project to be appreciated and enjoyed for the present and the future.

Rabbi Marc Berkson, in speaking about the seven Torah covers created by members of Congregation Emanu-El B'ne Jeshurun in Milwaukee has stated, "I marveled at how Nancy [Nancy Katz, artist] took members of our congregation—members of all ages—and taught and guided them in the creation of new mantles for our *sifrei Torah*. Nancy taught, surely; more important, Nancy helped build community in the process of engaging in *hidur mitzvah*.

FLORA ROSEFSKY, noted for her Judaic inspired paper cutouts, mixed-media, illustration, stained glass, and Judaic needlework designs, has been a teaching artist for more than forty years. She has been an artist in residence and conducted workshops in Upstate New York, Atlanta, New York City, and other areas, where her popular Drawing with Scissors program has reached thousands of children, teens, and adults. She has also developed museum collection–related curricula and led the Sunday Studio family workshop program at Atlanta's High Museum of Art from 1996 to 2008.

Transformative Experience

Peretz Wolf-Prusan

In the 1970s at UAHC Camp Swig, the camp community was completely committed to the task of the transmission of Jewish culture, history, and thought. Imaginative people bonded the integration of art, education, culture, and love. After volunteering in Israel from 1973 to 1974, I came to the San Francisco Bay Area to teach art at UAHC Camp Swig and study at the San Francisco Art Institute.

As a result of this early initiative, the artistic depth of the camp began to deepen and broaden, eventually to include music, dance, drama, and printmaking. My job was to build a printmaking workshop. My challenge was to emulate the creative leaders who preceded me and to create a printmaking workshop that was artistically productive and advanced the educational effort. Each session of camp had a learning plan, skillfully implemented by the staff. There was also meta-consciousness that the camp was a source of fundamental learning and experience for young teens and that this experience would influence their West Coast communities. I had used screen-printing to make posters for the Free Soviet Jewry Movement. It struck me as a perfect technique for the camp setting. We would teach Hebrew lettering, find Hebrew text associated with a session theme, and create poster art. Each camper would be sent home with a pile of posters, filled with text and images.

Two of my favorite posters were created by the young artist, Lisa Sloane, who was in the workshop in 1975 and 1976. The art, craft, and message stood the test of time. I found her on Facebook, now a multimedia artist living near me in Northern California. I invited her to share her thoughts with me, just as we shared the printmaking workshop long ago.

Lisa Sloane

"Peretz provided so much more than just a great technical learning experience about artistic process for me. These workshops were really a conduit to expressing and processing the experiences around me, the information I was taking in, and, most importantly, my emotions, feelings, and beliefs about them. They stand out in my mind as my first experiences in what continues to be a driving factor in my artistic vision today—conveying an emotion, experience, or message through my art."

PERETZ WOLF-PRUSAN (C90), master teacher and winner of a Covenant Award, served for two decades at Congregation Emanu-El in San Francisco. He has been a senior rabbinic fellow at the renowned Shalom Hartman Institute in Jerusalem and currently serves as rabbi and senior educator at Lehrhaus Judaica.

LISA SLOANE is a graduate of Rhode Island School of Design (BFA) and New York University (MA). She has exhibited her work in New York, New Jersey, New Mexico, Ohio, Rhode Island, and Paris, France. She is also a graphic and web designer

Spiritual Journey

Yehudis Barmatz-Harris

"Jewish Mysticism incorporated into visual arts is a concept rooted in earlier centuries . . . Forming mystical symbols was a process to reflect upon and connect to God."

"The conflict between the physicality of art and the spirituality of process is one not only felt amongst the American Jewish artists, rather [it] seems to be a common Jewish theme."

YEHUDIS BARMATZ-HARRIS was born in Boston and is currently practicing art, working towards an Art Therapy degree in Tel Aviv. She teaches art and gives workshops to a variety of populations. She believes that the process and achievements in creative arts can provide confidence and healing.

The Passion of a Rabbi and Artist

Josh Plaut

Each and every Jew, in each and every generation, holds the Torah in a unique way. As a rabbi, I have been able to connect Jews to their heritage, inspiring them to discover their own unique Jewish pathway. I am a teacher. I am an active transmitter of tradition. I am an emissary. I try to bring near the Divine Presence—to release God's holy sparks in the seemingly simple moments of each day. I am a storyteller of Jewish life, far and near. As a photo-ethnographer and artist, I narrate the stories of Jewish life. I have always viewed the world through a Jewish lens and encourage fellow Jews to do the same. As a cultural anthropologist and folklorist, recounting new stories born of our own time and telling sacred stories from days gone by, I both impart the historical narrative and am shaped by it. From today's vantage point, thirty years and counting, I have used my camera to create compelling artistic, visual portraits, adding a new documentary layer in Jewish history.

This dualism, as a rabbi and as a photographer, as a folklorist and as an artist, is intrinsic to my soul.

Jewish history teaches us about the forces of dispersion, whether voluntary or imposed. The hallmark of dispersion is an active absorption of knowledge and culture from the host society, while simultaneously enhancing the host culture with Jewish values and traditions. The emphasis of my work is to document the diversity that is the Jewish world. My lens has captured the historic exodus of Jews from Uzbekistan in the Soviet Union in the early 1990s; the haunting old neighborhoods of Marrakesh in Morocco; the alleyways of Jerusalem's color-saturated fruit and vegetable stalls in Machane Yehudah, the outdoor market; the fading street signs of former Jewish dry goods stores in small towns across Arkansas and Mississippi, which remarkably resemble the disappearing Jewish storefronts in Greece, Turkey, New Zealand, and Manhattan's Lower East Side; and the similarities in the faces of Jewish men, women, and children throughout the world. I have recorded contemporary visual life histories of Jews in Samarkand and Auckland, Salonika and Istanbul, Jerusalem and New York. My emphasis recently has shifted to capturing the renewal of Jewish life in America.

Immersed in the life of the cultures I visit, my photographs convey images of Jews and Jewish life in places that at first glance may seem unfamiliar, but reflect the thread of a shared destiny. My photography represents a cultural and spiritual vision of people, of life, of scenes from every day, and the world that I inhabit and have been blessed to explore. I leave the interpretation to the viewer, knowing they will discover a familiar connection with places and people who share a portable and proud heritage. Perhaps, some will even realize that each one of us is capable of holding the Torah in our own way and in our own time.

RABBI JOSHUA ELI PLAUT, Ph.D. (C86) is the executive director of the American Friends of Rabin Medical Center. He is the author of *Greek Jewry in the Twentieth Century, 1913–1983* (Fairleigh Dickinson University Press, 1996) and *A Kosher Christmas: 'Tis the Season to Be Jewish* (Rutgers University Press, 2012). His ten photography exhibitions have been displayed at museums and galleries the world over from 1983–2012 and are part of major collections in archives and museums.

An Artists' *Beit Midrash*

Words of Introduction

Leon A. Morris

> The Eternal is my strength and song, and has become my salvation. This is my God, whom I will glorify, my father's God, whom I will exalt.
>
> (Exod. 15:2)

What does it mean to glorify God, asks one of the *Tannaim* in a *baraita* from the Babylonian Talmud (*Shabbat* 133b): "Glorify yourself before God in the mitzvot. Make for yourself a beautiful sukkah, a beautiful *lulav*, a beautiful shofar, beautiful tzitzit, a beautiful *sefer Torah* and write it in the finest ink, with a fine reed, and fine penmanship, and wrap it in fine silks."

While serving as a textual basis for the concept of *hidur mitzvah*, this passage also speaks more broadly to the value of visual aesthetics in Jewish life. To suggest that God can be glorified through artistic creativity may be surprising given the Torah's repeated warnings about the seductive danger of the eyes leading one astray (see Num. 15:39) and the inherent connection that exists between idolatry and the visual. The *baraita* does something additionally noteworthy. While explicating the notion of what it means to glorify God, its answer is about how to glorify ourselves before God: Be glorified (*hitnaeh*) before God through mitzvot. What initially appears to confuse or conflate the object of glorification may offer us something new. When visual beauty is applied to the service of bringing honor to God or to the mitzvot, there is an additional result in our own glorification.

The way in which the arts can represent this interplay between the enhancement of Jewish life and the enhancement of the self has been demonstrated repeatedly in the experience of the Artists' *Beit Midrash*, established more than eleven years ago at the Skirball Center for Adult Jewish Learning at Temple Emanu-El in

---

RABBI LEON A. MORRIS founded the Artists' *Beit Midrash* together with Tobi Kahn in 2002 and served as the executive director of the Skirball Center for Adult Jewish Learning at Temple Emanu-El for ten years. He is now the rabbi of Temple Adas Israel in Sag Harbor, New York.

Manhattan. The goals of the program include fostering a deeper relationship between Jewish artists and classic Jewish texts, allowing Jewish study to impact on the creative life of the artists involved, and enabling new visual commentaries to emerge as a result. The group of artists is diverse, comprised of various ages, different levels of artistic ability, and a wide range of Jewish backgrounds and affiliations. The group meets weekly for two hours. One broad theme is developed over the course of an entire year. The first hour is devoted to text study, while the second hour is an opportunity to share artwork (finalized and in-progress) that was inspired by the study of previous weeks, as well as to discuss and highlight current gallery shows and museum exhibitions that relate to our theme.

The group is led by two teachers: one with expertise in classic Jewish texts, and the other an artist. Since its inception, Tobi Kahn, a renowned painter, sculptor, and ceremonial artist, and a teacher at the School of Visual Arts, has been our resident art teacher.

At the conclusion of each year, the Artists' *Beit Midrash* exhibits its work at a curated and professionally installed show, drawing well over one hundred visitors at a gallery opening and dozens more in the weeks that follow. This show enables participants to share their individual, unique experiences of art and text with the greater Skirball Center community, as well as the larger community. In addition to sharing their creations, the participants explain how their art serves as a kind of visual commentary on a set of texts.

The effect on the artists is immeasurable, both in terms of their personal deepened relationship to Jewish text study as well as their growth as artists. The Artists' *Beit Midrash* exposes both experienced and novice Jewish learners to texts that are turned over and over and renewed as students explore them. The students, inspired by texts about sameness and difference, about dreamers, about hiddenness, or about revelation, turn back to their art, refreshed and full of new ideas and inspiration. The body of their artistic work, too, is renewed and altered through Jewish study.

The success of this program, which has been replicated and adapted by other communities and congregations, expands the educational methodologies for adult learners. It presents yet another way to integrate the arts into the life of congregations and communities.

However, the largest impact of the Artists' *Beit Midrash* is felt far beyond the students who participate in the program and the communities that convene such opportunities. A small group of artists, actively engaged in creating new commentaries on our people's most ancient texts, demonstrates the continued relevance these texts have to our contemporary lives and the unlimited (and often untapped) creative potential that exists in them.

What follows are the words from four participants in the Skirball Center's Artists' *Beit Midrash*, capturing their own personal reflections.

The Artists' Words

My first experience trying to make meaning of Jewish texts came somewhat late in life. It occurred when Rabbi Leon Morris asked a group of artists and writers to respond to the famous Talmudic *sugya* about how the destruction of Jerusalem was the result of a mix-up between a man named Kamtza and another named Bar Kamtza. I had read Jewish texts before but never tried to understand their underlying meanings. In trying to understand the many levels of meaning to this story I explored many sources and found the exposure to ancient writings a wonderful experience.

I had been a "seeker" in Judaism starting in the first grade of Sunday School. I can still picture my teacher and the thrill of winning a book of Jewish children's stories. Since I grew up in a classical Reform Jewish home in the 1940s it was hard to find much Jewish material to draw from. The Reform Jews in my suburban town were shedding their Jewishness while I was trying to explore mine. I continued to seek and became connected to the Hillel in college where I realized for the first time how little I knew. Midwestern girls from small towns in northern Wisconsin seemed to know more than I did. I raised my children in a Jewish home where we lit Shabbat candles, observed holidays, and went to synagogue. My children became *b'nei mitzvah* and were confirmed, and I am happy to say that today they each connect to Judaism and have taught their children accordingly. But the Judaism that we knew ignored the great Jewish texts. When I moved to Manhattan after my children were grown I started studying Yiddish, and then Hebrew, and eventually had an adult bat mitzvah.

At the same time as I was searching for a deeper connection to Judaism, I was always involved in creating art—painting, jewelry, photography, and enameling. I sometimes made ritual objects that had a Jewish connection. I collaged images using photographs combined with text and paint and often turned to Jewish imagery.

So ten years ago when studying that complex text about why Jerusalem was destroyed, I felt as though I had finally found my Jewish artistic home. For me, combining art and Jewish study was a match made in heaven. I have been a member of this group from the first year when we were just a handful of students. Since that time, we have studied many texts dealing with themes such as life and death, creation, prophecy, sacrifice, and liminality. In trying to create art based on these texts, I learned much about Jewish practices, rituals, and beliefs.

In addition to being a supportive environment for studying Jewish concepts, the group is a supportive source for many of us personally. One of my great experiences was inspired by a member of the class who used black-and-white photos printed on fabric. I then created a white woolen tallit covered with images of my entire family including images of my parents, my children, and my children's great grandparents before they left Europe. My grandchildren helped me make the tzitzit and attached them to the tallit.

Creating art inspired by texts is a wonderful way to re-experience Judaism. It makes me feel connected to something very deep and inexplicable. The art that I create is often not directly related to the actual text but emerges from the feelings that the text inspires from something deep within me. I feel it connects me with a Jewish spirit that influences how I work. It is not the same as drawing an image that represents certain characters. It is just that my artistic imagery is based on who I am becoming through this study.

BARBARA FREEDMAN, after retiring from many years as a clinical social worker, rediscovered her artistic interests and combined them with her longstanding involvement with Jewish Studies. She lives in Manhattan and Sag Harbor, New York.

Before I joined the Skirball Center's Artists' *Beit Midrash* five years ago, I could never have imagined the alchemical power of joining Torah with art. From the start, the *Beit Midrash* engaged my creativity in ways that would change my relationship to Judaism, my art practice, and my spiritual self.

Our *Beit Midrash* has a different theme every year and the theme for my first year was Sacrifice. Bringing animals and first fruits to be burned up on the Temple altar had always seemed to me a primitive rite we were well rid of. But now, when we read the Rabbinic statement that a sacrifice returned to God what had been God's all along, I made a connection I hadn't made before: the loss of my breast to cancer had been a sacrifice in which I returned a part of my body to its creator.

This shift in perspective healed a grief that I didn't know I was still carrying and led to my creating a piece of art unlike anything I'd done before. I found a large glass form reminiscent of a *Kiddush* cup, calligraphed the words "*El na refana lah*" (God please heal her) around the outside in gold paint, and filled it to overflowing with fabric breasts of different patterns and dimensions. I titled the piece *Where Do the Breasts Go?* When Tobi Kahn, our beloved teacher saw it, he told me I'd taken my painful experience and lifted it up; "You made it holy," he said.

For this past year's *Beit Midrash*, the theme introduced by our new rabbi co-facilitator, Rabbi Yael Shmilovitz, was Hu v'He (He and She). Living far outside the strict gender roles of Judaism, I found myself offering my lesbian perspective, which was welcomed by the facilitators and my colleagues. Despite their openness, before long I was again in a narrow place with Leviticus 18:22, "Thou shalt not lie with mankind as with womankind; it is abomination." After years of study and discussion, I thought I was done with this biblical abhorrence and all the condemnation of homosexuality that has followed in its wake.

When it caught me up this time, though, I had a new idea: to make an art installation about the impact of this curse on myself and other gay people. Because being *toeivah* (an abomination) made me feel dead, I printed the Talmud page (*Sanhedrin* 54b) where the Rabbis first argued about this passage on white fabric from which I constructed shrouds like those used in a traditional Jewish burial. Then I donned the shrouds and in collaboration with art photographer Trix Rosen, we explored the physical and emotional dynamics of being enclosed in such garments. I titled the installation *Abomination: Wrestling with Leviticus 18:22*.

The impulse to make art of this painful legacy and the visceral connection to the shame, anger, claustrophobia, and sadness I found inside the shrouds brought a healing I didn't know I needed.

And an empowerment: I was now part of the discussion, as the images we'd created represented their own commentary on *toeivah*. Through this process, I transformed and transcended the pain of that word.

Finally, I wondered: What should become of these shrouds printed with such painful text? I'd never found a satisfying way to handle the words of this Torah verse. Now that I had actual garments to deal with, a new answer occurred to me: *genizah* (our traditional repository for sacred texts and objects that have outlived their ritual use).

SUSAN KAPLOW is an artist and student of Torah in New York City. She's a member of the Jewish Art Salon and a frequent participant in the *beit midrash* at Drisha Institute.

What defines a work of art is something that displaces me and brings me to a place I have never been before. The Torah represents a timeless piece of poetry that fulfills and meets my personal definition of art. As a photographer, I struggle with how one transforms the written word and language into a significant visual translation.

This past year, the Skirball Center's Artists' *Beit Midrash*, focused on gender roles and responsibilities attributable to male and female, concepts of beauty and sexuality. In addition to the Torah, readings based on Rabbinic sources and midrash were introduced and used in our discussions. We studied concepts of beauty and how the Torah defines and describes beauty. How does the Torah apply these attributes to males and females within its stories? Are an individual's internal characteristics and qualities included within the Torah's definition of beauty? Perhaps the Torah portrays beauty as a metaphor for an entirely different purpose. How is homosexuality dealt with? What are specific sexual criteria that define and differentiate male and female? In biblical times did issues of transgender even arise? What do the words within the Torah mean, what are the messages within those words, and what are the issues that the Torah is dealing with? No question went unasked.

In our discussions we considered how as artists we might interpret and translate written language into meaningful visual imagery and what inherent challenges arise within this process. As a Jew participating in an Artists' *Beit Midrash*, an unexpected idea arose within me. Just as the Rabbis debated these issues centuries ago, we as modern Jews were debating similar concepts today. I began to ask myself, as a twenty-first-century Western Jewish male, how do I incorporate these ongoing issues into my own beliefs within Judaism? My own feelings regarding my religion is that it should include, rather then exclude, any individual who wishes to practice Judaism. Through our weekly dialogue, interchange, and sharing of ideas, feelings, and personal interpretation, I was being exposed to a whole different way of thinking and seeing. The group dynamics afforded me the opportunity to approach the issues from a completely new perspective and to formulate my own definition of what beauty, sexuality, homosexuality, and transgender mean. Judaism must embrace, respect, and value any individual and allow them the freedom to follow their beliefs within Judaism. However, I recognize that the beauty of our religion allows us the freedom and encourages us to have these open dialogues. Whatever one's personal feelings are on these issues, we must deal with them as a united Jewish community and in a respectful and constructive manner. Our Artists' *Beit Midrash* served as the crucible and incubator for the formulation of these new personal realizations. I feel that, through our art, we artists offer new definitions and altered perspectives as to how Judaism might be able to adapt to and incorporate these difficult issues in order that it may fulfill the needs of its constituents.

During the year, I began to incorporate these new feelings into my photographs. What was most difficult for me was to alter the written language and ideas I was studying into visual imagery. I asked myself how my photographs convey concepts and ideas that were being discussed within our group. My first forays were complete failures, and I was becoming quite frustrated. Then I realized I was trying to create an image as an outsider looking in. I was not portraying my internal feelings. Once I figured out how to integrate Jewish text, prayer, and objects into my work from an internal source, I began to feel more successful in creating the work. Art has always been a very important aspect of my life. After this year I felt I was able to finally portray and express my Jewish identity, origins, culture, religion, and beliefs into visual imagery.

LARRY FRANKEL received an MA in Art from NYU's joint program with the International Center of Photography. He works with the Hudson River Museum and teaches photography in the Yonkers school system.

One aspect of being an artist is that I spend a lot of time alone. All the hours working in my studio, sitting at the sewing machine, or standing at the ironing board are a solitary pursuit. The Artists' *Beit Midrash* has created a community where once a week I have the opportunity to study, discuss, critique, disagree, support, and nurture myself, my work, and the work of my fellow artists. The Artists' *Beit Midrash* is also a laboratory where I can experiment with new ideas, new mediums, and new ways of working. It is a nourishing and supportive artistic environment in a Jewish setting—a rare opportunity.

I have always been interested in studying Jewish texts but it wasn't until I joined the Artists' *Beit Midrash* that it became such a central part of my life. I have spent the last ten years studying in the same environment with many of the same people, and it only gets better year after year. Being in the Artists' *Beit Midrash* has made me a more curious, focused, and interested Jew. Studying in a communal setting has allowed me to listen to many voices and many opinions about the texts. It has influenced the way I approach texts and the way I look at Judaism today.

My art and Jewish life are woven together so tightly that at this point I don't think one could exist without the other. Judaism influences my art by being an inspiration and a catalyst for ideas. My art affects how I look at, celebrate, and understand Judaism. One way I experience Judaism is through the visual images in my mind and the objects I create through my hands. My knowledge of Judaism makes my art more meaningful and my work as an artist makes my Judaism deeper and more satisfying. The Artists' *Beit Midrash* is what supports both parts of my life. It is like a sacred well of water that follows and sustains me on my journey.

RACHEL KANTER is a fiber artist who creates new Jewish ritual objects using traditional quilting, sewing, and embroidery techniques. Her work is in the permanent collection of the Jewish Museum and she is on the executive board of the Jewish Art Salon.

Bezalel's Legacy

Parashat Ki Tisa (Exod. 30:11–34:35)

Richard McBee

Bezalel, oh Bezalel, what company you keep! Your *parashah, Ki Tisa,* takes us from humble devotion to God's commandments to the utter collapse of Israel's faith. God-inspired creativity morphs into pernicious communal idolatry that expressed gnawing doubt and a desperate need for the mechanics of *t'shuvah.* Yet in the midst of tragedy, drama, and redemption, one quiet man and his assistant, Bezalel and Oholiab, were chosen by God to become the alleged ancestors of all Jewish artists.

So, let's get one thing straight. Bezalel and Oholiab are NOT the first Jewish artists. As the Torah describes Bezalel, he was a craftsman filled with God-given wisdom to learn from others, understanding of his own, and knowledge of divine inspiration (Rashi) whom God directed to create the objects of the Tabernacle. So far, he sounds like an ideal artist. But the catch is that neither of them made art. They were inspired Jewish craftsmen who made objects that had specific functions and uses. True, there can be great artistry involved in the beauty, design, and cleverness of functional objects. But it's not art. So what we need to address is the nature of art and, more specifically, Jewish art.

Art by its nature is contemplative and contentious. Its primary purpose is to stimulate the viewer to think about something beyond the art object itself. Art is a medium to pass through. This is true of narrative representations and even abstract and conceptual works that evoke emotions and stimulate intellectual engagement. Craft is different.

A beautiful *Kiddush* cup is a wonder in itself, determined to call attention to the object and its ritual use. The same was true of the objects Bezalel made for the *Mishkan*: the physical structure, the *Aron*, the showbread table, the menorah, and even the priestly garments. From architecture to sacred fashion these ritual objects

---

RICHARD MCBEE is a painter and writer on Jewish art.

were participants in the *avodah* whose primary meaning rested in the ritual, not in what was used to perform it. As central to the worship of God they took on an aspect of sanctity unimaginable for an art object. So it is true with the objects of Jewish craft that we use today. A Torah mantle or ark curtain has sanctity in themselves by virtue of their use and proximity to the Torah scroll. Once worn out or damaged they must be buried with the same respect as a Torah. Art has another agenda. Art is artifice that directs one to an entirely different realm.

Art does not come naturally to Judaism, rather it is almost certainly adopted from the Greco-Roman world. The decorations in early synagogues evidenced by the Dura Europos murals (235 C.E.) or the Beit Alpha mosaics (518 C.E.) are cultural imports. But as such they were totally Judaized. The images produced are obsessed with meaning and not ritual. And while initially decorative they refer to the undercurrent of textual commentary, midrashim that were forever heard in the background and that always informed our sacred texts. They are gateways into more intense textual analysis and emotional involvement in narrative and meaning. The images of Jewish art are not expressions of the will of God, rather they are our attempt to understand the complexities and contradictions of divine command. Jewish art in this context is *talmud Torah,* a visual midrash whose purpose is to pose questions and raise issues. Ritual and its beautiful artistic objects must provide certainty.

Nonetheless, there is much to be learned from *Ki Tisa* about Jewish art. The ideal ethical and spiritual qualities of Jewish art and Jewish craft are identical because we hope for equal refinement and intention in our ritual objects and our art. We want the best whether the purpose is to worship or study. Since the Torah knows this, why should it juxtapose the elevated mission of Bezalel with the most grievous sin of the Golden Calf? There's the rub.

The warning that *Ki Tisa* presents concerns the nature of objects, ritual objects that we invest with too much meaning, in fact fall in love with and forget the ultimate incorporeal reality of our God. When we doubt the verity of divine promise and command we second guess the existence of our Creator. And the first thing we make is an alternative ritual object as a way to serve the transcendental God concretely. Our desire for God to be manifest became an idol in the form of the Golden Calf. We fashioned it as a way to certainty. And looking for an assurance of faith, a comfort of that which is substantive, we err, in fact we sin. It becomes Bezalel perverted. It is the sin of the object.

As Rashi tells us (Exod. 31:18), there is no necessary chronology in the Torah, and actually the incident of the Golden Calf preceded the work of the Tabernacle done by Bezalel. Therefore God's command to Bezalel can be seen as a response to our deep need for some kind of objective certainty. Make ritual objects that will be used to serve Me, says God. Similarly, doubt about the absent God (and his servant Moshe) that provoked the creation of the Golden Calf was answered in the Thirteen Attributes of Mercy that God gave us as Moses ascended the mountain a second time. Each attribute is an insight into the mysterious nature of the unseen God. Our God demands faith and yet provides us with precious concrete hints as to how to serve Him and how to know Him. Jewish craft and Jewish art have a hand in both.

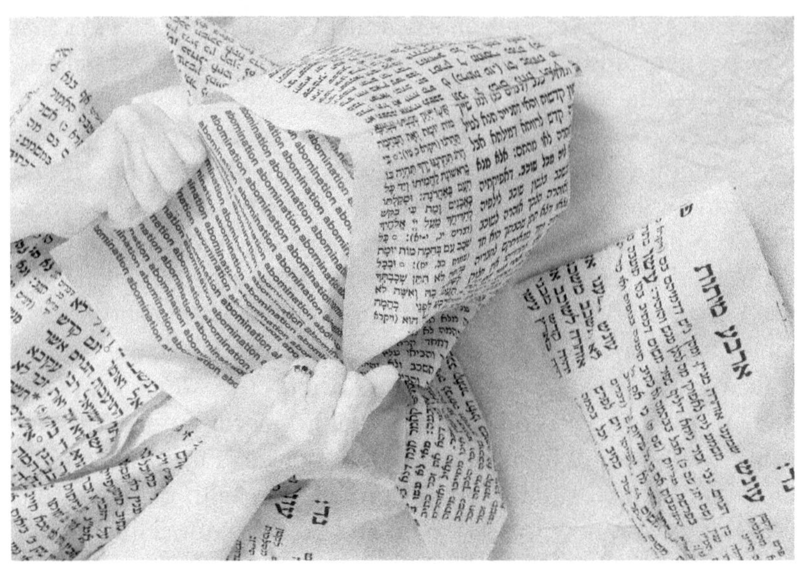

Abomination: Wrestling with Leviticus 18:22 by Susan Kaplow
Photography copyright by Trix Rosen, 2012

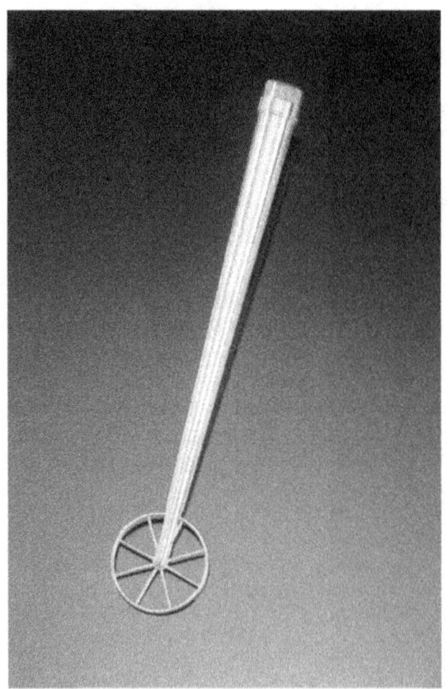

Anika Smulovitz
Untitled (Wheel/Perambulator/Torah Pointer
Sterling silver, 18k gold, sand, glass; 8¾″ × 1½ × ¾″
Photographed by Doug Yaple

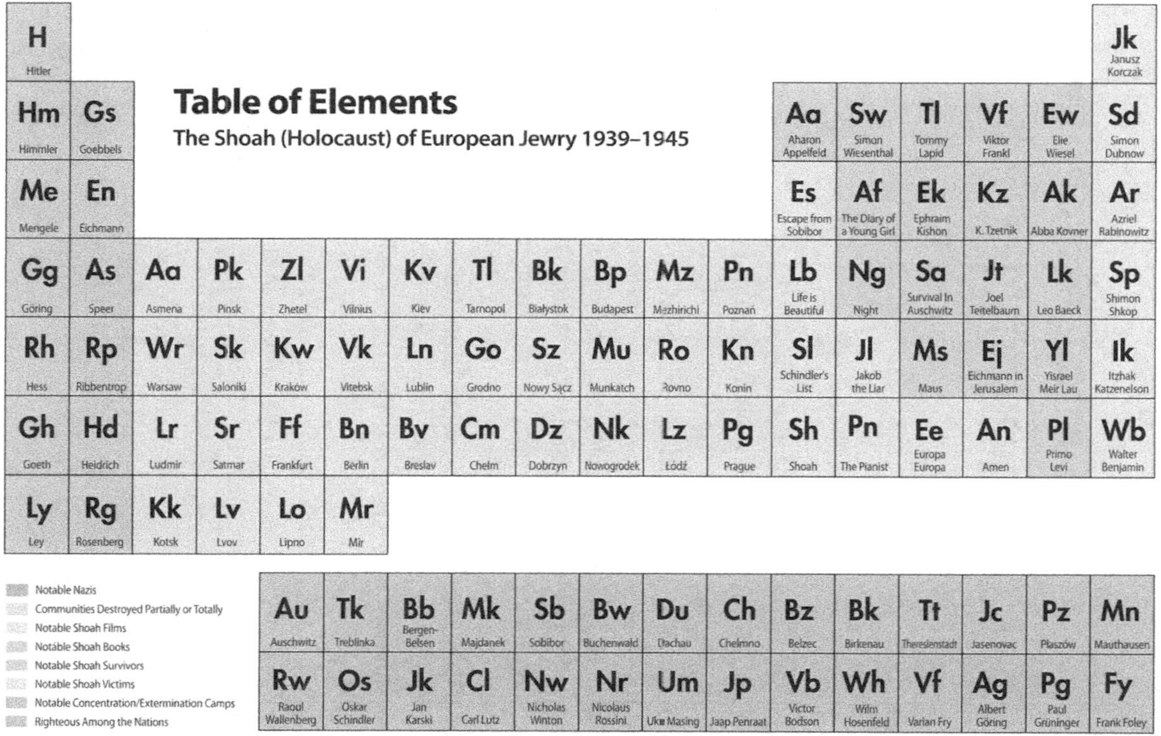

Table of Elements

The Shoah (Holocaust) of European Jewry 1939–1945

H Hitler																	Jk Janusz Korczak
Hm Himmler	Gs Goebbels											Aa Aharon Appelfeld	Sw Simon Wiesenthal	Tl Tommy Lapid	Vf Viktor Frankl	Ew Elie Wiesel	Sd Simon Dubnow
Me Mengele	En Eichmann											Es Escape from Sobibor	Af The Diary of a Young Girl	Ek Ephraim Kishon	Kz K. Tzetnik	Ak Abba Kovner	Ar Azriel Rabinowitz
Gg Göring	As Speer	Aa Asmena	Pk Pinsk	Zl Zhetel	Vi Vilnius	Kv Kiev	Tl Tarnopol	Bk Białystok	Bp Budapest	Mz Mezhirichi	Pn Poznań	Lb Life is Beautiful	Ng Night	Sa Survival In Auschwitz	Jt Joel Teitelbaum	Lk Leo Baeck	Sp Shimon Shkop
Rh Hess	Rp Ribbentrop	Wr Warsaw	Sk Saloniki	Kw Kraków	Vk Vitebsk	Ln Lublin	Go Grodno	Sz Nowy Sącz	Mu Munkatch	Ro Rovno	Kn Konin	Sl Schindler's List	Jl Jakob the Liar	Ms Maus	Ej Eichmann in Jerusalem	Yl Yisrael Meir Lau	Ik Itzhak Katzenelson
Gh Goeth	Hd Heidrich	Lr Ludmir	Sr Satmar	Ff Frankfurt	Bn Berlin	Bv Breslav	Cm Chelm	Dz Dobrzyn	Nk Nowogrodek	Lz Łódź	Pg Prague	Sh Shoah	Pn The Pianist	Ee Europa Europa	An Amen	Pl Primo Levi	Wb Walter Benjamin
Ly Ley	Rg Rosenberg	Kk Kotsk	Lv Lvov	Lo Lipno	Mr Mir												

Au Auschwitz	Tk Treblinka	Bb Bergen-Belsen	Mk Majdanek	Sb Sobibor	Bw Buchenwald	Du Dachau	Ch Chelmno	Bz Belzec	Bk Birkenau	Tt Theresienstadt	Jc Jasenovac	Pz Płaszów	Mn Mauthausen
Rw Raoul Wallenberg	Os Oskar Schindler	Jk Jan Karski	Cl Carl Lutz	Nw Nicholas Winton	Nr Nicolaus Rossini	Um Uku Masing	Jp Jaap Penraat	Vb Victor Bodson	Wh Wilm Hosenfeld	Vf Varian Fry	Ag Albert Göring	Pg Paul Grüninger	Fy Frank Foley

- Notable Nazis
- Communities Destroyed Partially or Totally
- Notable Shoah Films
- Notable Shoah Books
- Notable Shoah Survivors
- Notable Shoah Victims
- Notable Concentration/Extermination Camps
- Righteous Among the Nations

Dov Abramson
Shoah: A Table of Elements, 2007
Print on Paper, 1000 × 700 cm

לזכר משפחת אמי, מוילנא, שנספתה כמעט כולה.

Numbers/B'midbar: *Challenge and Perspective*

Text and Commentary: Contemporary Jewish Art

Ori Z. Soltes

Questions and Categories

The ultimate Jewish art is that of asking questions. Like all humans, Jews prefer ideas to fit into neat definitional boxes; more than most groups, our history is one of embracing ones that do not—just consider the Rabbinic discussion of property possession that begins in *Bava M'tzia*. The question of "Jewish art," not surprisingly, is one that does not. It begins with *multiple* questions. What defines "Jewish"—conceptually and historically? Is Judaism a religion, a nation, an ethnic group, a people, a civilization? Since Abraham was a Hebrew, Moses and Solomon were Israelites, and Queen Esther a Judaean, would art associated with the periods in which they lived be called "Jewish"—or should it be called "Hebrew," "Israelite," "Judaean"?

Through most of history, art has served to portray divinity or to visualize its relationship with humanity—from Egyptian images of Amon-Ra to Christian images of Jesus. The Second Commandment worries that Israelites and their spiritual descendants might do that. How does "Jewish art" manage to be art without abrogating that commandment—or portraying God? Do we base our discussion on the *artwork*—its subject? symbols? style? purpose?—or on the *artist*? In that case: the artist's biologically Jewish birth?

ORI Z. SOLTES teaches theology and art history at Georgetown University and is the former director and curator of the B'nai B'rith Klutznick National Jewish Museum. He has curated dozens of exhibitions and written scores of articles and catalogue essays on aspects of contemporary Jewish art, and is the author of the forthcoming book, *Tradition and Transformation: A Conceptual History of Jewish Art*.

convictions? intentions? What of an artist who converts into or out of Judaism?

So one must define one's criteria of definition. And these will change as focus changes from one medium and era to another. An ancient mosaic synagogue floor, a medieval spice box for *Havdalah*, a Renaissance-era illuminated manuscript, a timber synagogue from Lithuania—all offer different angles of approaching the question. They all, in turn, offer different starting points for discussion from, say, *Sabbath Afternoon* by Moritz Oppenheim or an impressionist landscape painting by Camille Pissarro. A portrait by Amedeo Modigliani or a cubist sculpture by Jacques Lifschitz will further change the mode of addressing the question, as will—still further—a chromatic abstract expressionist painting by Mark Rothko a decade after the Holocaust.

The shifting of questions within the question is in part related to internal developments within the Jewish community, which has always been a dispersed community of communities, with diverse approaches to liturgy and customs. In part the shift relates to how these communities have responded to the shifting pagan, Christian, Muslim, and other seas in which Jews have been a complex archipelago of islands throughout history. How Jews and Judaism are defined, how visual art is defined, and how the Second Commandment is understood has varied, and the pace of variation has sped up in the last two centuries.

"Where do 'Jewish art' and 'Jewish artists' fit in?" becomes still more complicated through the twentieth century, with the trauma of the Holocaust and the birth of Israel, and with the expanding interest in spirituality and ethnic identity reflected particularly in Jewish America of the past forty years or so. What *is* "Holocaust art"? Is the work of non-Jewish Holocaust artists "Jewish"? Where does Israeli art fit into "Jewish" art? Do women artists alter the shape of the overall inquiry?

There are more questions than answers. But this has made visual self-expression in the contemporary Jewish world dynamic in range and variety. Jewish artists have been subject to an accumulation of issues and ideas and forced to consider their own self-definition, and have responded with energy and imagination. The sheer mass of them in the past generation makes it impossible to be comprehensive in discussing their contributions to transformative thought. Their work, more often than not, refuses to fit into comfortable definitional boxes, as they cover diverse territories of subject, style, and medium. What they nearly all share is an interest in exploring and commenting on the varied aspects of being Jewish and artists in the contemporary world.

That exploration and commentary can lead and has led others —both Jews and non-Jews—to rethink even fundamental definitional categories. For instance, not only has the shaping of ritual objects proliferated, but new categories of ritual have been created. The cup of Miriam has, in the past nearly two decades, found its way onto the Passover seder table of many households. Filled with water, it "balances" the Elijah goblet and brings the sister of Moses back into the narrative, alluding to the well of water found in the wilderness "for the merits of the prophetess Miriam" (See, e.g., *B'Midbar Rabbah* 1:2).

Often not only this object but more traditional ceremonial pieces are nontraditional in their visual conception—eroding the line between "fine art" and "functional craft." For example, Alan Wexler's 2000 *Gardening Sukkah* looks like a wooden gardening shed on wheels. But inside, the ceiling is open (as halachah requires for a sukkah) and shelves offer implements that allude both to the harvest and to the *Kiddush* and festival meal: a pitchfork and a fork, a shovel and a spoon, and wine goblets and place settings.

Tobi Kahn redefines the ritual category from a different angle. He began producing ceremonial objects in the 1980s—and still does—from small objects like *etrog* boxes, spice boxes, and *chanukiyot* to chairs for baby-naming and circumcision ceremonies, a Holy Ark, and a chuppah. Like his paintings and sculptures, his ceremonial objects have "names," made up (sometimes but not always, of Hebrew elements) that evoke but don't quite settle on recognizable subjects and meanings.

Most of these objects could easily be mistaken for abstract sculptures by the untutored eye—and in turn also relate to his paintings. On the other hand, many of his sculptures—"shrines"—suggest liturgical art without being liturgical, and simultaneously evoke Greco-Roman aedicula, Christian reliquaries, and—not least of all—the *Mishkan*. These are thought-demanding works that bridge ceremonial and abstract contemporary art: looking at one of his "shrines" one asks what it is, and into which art/craft category it fits, forcing one's mind outside a simple definitional box.

What we may recognize is that artists like these are engaged in double text study, but with images, not words. They are wrestling both with the question of what art and craft are and with what Jewish ritual is—and what the underlying multiple meanings of its ceremonial components are. Occasionally the work itself completely rearticulates the ceremony, as in the emphatically egalitarian, "curated" wedding of Melissa Schiff to Louis Kaplan—and the videotaping of the ceremony as the centerpiece of a 2006 exhibition at the Jewish Museum of Prague entitled "Reframing Ritual: Postmodern Jewish Wedding. *Featuring Melissa Schiff as the Bride and Louis Kaplan as the Groom*," that "offered the acknowledgment that what we were doing in terms of reinventing the rite and mediating ritual would have a larger audience outside of the private and personal domains."

Visual exploration has become an important part of the directions being taken by contemporary Jewish thought and its modes of dialogue: it is part of the ongoing question of how to conserve Jewish essentials and yet to reform them in accordance with needs provoked by a changing world.

The Holocaust

No question has exercised Jewish thinking in the last two generations more than the Holocaust and its theological and anthropological implications. A surprising number of Jews who perished during the Holocaust left visual records—from professionals like Felix Nussbaum to prodigies like Charlotte Salomon to inexperienced amateurs desperate to record the horrific events around them. Post-war, the Holocaust has gradually moved toward the center of overt Jewish artistic focus since the 1950s. Those responding to the cataclysm at that time included Barnett Newman and Mark Rothko, albeit they were not recognized by critics as doing so. But Newman's *The Name II*, a 1950 white "triptych," for example, circumlocutionarily asks the question of God's absence/presence with his use of that colorless/all-color hue.

By the 1970s artists who were themselves Holocaust survivors began to exhume their painful memories and wrestle them onto the canvas. Alice Lok Cahane, in a series, *Ashes from the Rainbow*, did that, combining blacks and whites and sometimes burnt paper and sand with bright pigments. Within that series, *Jacob's Ladder* puns between the image of a ladder and train tracks—and on the semiabstract angels hovering along the ladder as the souls of the dead, rising as colorful flecks of ash from the tracks leading to the crematoria.

Kitty Klaidman didn't turn her brush back toward childhood memories until 1989. In her *Hidden Memories* series, the crawlspace between attic and second floor of a Slovakian farmhouse in which she and her family spent over a year becomes transformed in monumentally sized triptychs. This form, borrowed from Christian art with its Trinitarian symbolism, implies a question: where were the adherents of the Christian God of mercy when Jewish children were being systematically destroyed?—and an answer: in her case, Christian friends and their friends assured the survival of her family. The paintings reflect a process of healing: personal *tikkun*. They are semiabstract and airy—without knowing her story one would not guess at their subject.

Not surprisingly, offspring of survivors offer another group of artists addressing this topic. Kitty's daughter, Elyse, grew up and became an artist—but with interests different from those of her mother, until that same 1989 trip that brought the family to Slovakia to seek out the family that had once hidden Kitty and her family. Returning home, Elyse found the old black-and-white photographs of relatives, living and dead, offering new meaning. In a strident, expressionist style very different from her mother's, she turned these into large paintings—such as the one of her two great aunts as teenagers, arms around each other, one of whom survived and one of whom did not—with blood-red pigment, dripping down the canvas, as part of its ground color.

Sooner or later, it seems that nearly every Jewish artist, even if only briefly, has come to feel the *need* to address the Holocaust. For an artist like Vienna-born Diane Kurz, the far-reaching array of family members who perished are the main focus of her intricate triptychs begun in the 1990s—complete with predella scenes, often of culturally or historically rich sites (like the *Stadtpark*) with ugly associations for Viennese Jews. Differently, Geraldine Fiskus has, since 1995, approached the Holocaust obliquely—with a series, *Reclaiming a Legacy*, focused largely on details from Eastern European gravestones and their imagery. She underpaints not with the usual white gesso but with black—and yet her paintings have a paradoxical luminescence to them.

So: people, objects, and for Sherry Zvares Sanabria, spaces. Sanabria applied her general interest in walls and doorways and windows and hallways to four concentration camps in the 1990s. These large-format paintings offer a silent eloquence. A long Mat-thausen hallway with well-polished floors, a bright-lit window at its end and multiple doors along its walls: can one look and not wonder what happened behind those doors—whether if the walls could speak they'd scream?

Art Spiegelman's pathbreaking 1986 *Maus* combines a very personal Holocaust narrative—his father's story and his own questions regarding his father—with issues broad and specific. Turning Nazis into cats and Jews into mice (and other groups into other animals) he plays both with the issue of stereotyping and with the wider question of what humans are as a species—we who commit "inhuman" acts that *only* humans commit. Placing them all within the format of a graphic novel—that accords equal weight to image and text—he addresses the question of how the People of the Book can also be a People of the Image.

Text and Image

The graphic novel as a particularly appropriate "Jewish" art form (but not only Jews use this format) precedes Spiegelman's epic—it begins with Will Eisner's *Contract with God* (1978)—and continues to this day, from James Strum's *The Golem's Mighty Swing* (2001) to JT Waldman's *Megillat Esther* (2006). The first of this pair is a story set in the America of the 1920s with its unresolved racial and religious prejudices, and plays on the theme of Judah Loew's creature in late sixteenth-century Prague; the other is a visually dynamic, midrash-laden retelling of that problematic biblical tale that never mentions God.

But the graphic novel isn't the only answer to the "Book vs. Image" question, and a growing army of Jewish artists has looked directly to texts—the Bible, Talmud, midrash, Kabbalah—for inspiration. Certainly nobody has wrestled with Jewish books—by way of images that are brash, coloristically bold, and intensely emotive—more fiercely or midrashically than Archie Rand. Rand never looked back after he overran the walls of the B'nai Yosef synagogue in Brooklyn in 1974–1977 with a painting cycle of a sort not seen since that at Dura Europos on the Euphrates in the 250s C.E.—or rather, in pushing forward he has continuously looked back: a double future-past vision endemic to Jewish thinking. In 1989 he did a series called *The Chapter Paintings*—a large visual midrash for every Torah *parashah.* His 2008 *The 613* offers one painting for each of the mitzvot delineated in the Torah, the totality of which is both visually and cognitively breathtaking: one could hardly be more textually grounded than this!

Scores of contemporary Jewish artists, emulating their Christian counterparts over the centuries, have addressed particular biblical moments like the *Akeidah.* If an obvious question for Jewish artists of the past two centuries is "where do I fit into Western art that has been so profoundly Christian for the past seventeen centuries?" then addressing shared biblical subjects offers one mode of answering that question.

Howard Lerner's 1998 *Binding of Isaac* is in part inspired by an early sixteenth-century French relief sculpture from Perigord, in which the ram stands, as if quietly grazing, by the altar. Lerner places an opening in the wall of that towering structure. A green tree and its roots are discernible through the opening, which tree, in turn, grows through and up and out of Isaac's belly. Thus the *Tree of Jesse*—which, in Christian art, offers Jesus' genealogy as a tree growing from the belly of King David's father—has been refocused. The Jewish understanding of Isaac as the first in an ongoing tree of covenantal transmission has been connected to the Christian understanding, which makes Isaac's self-sacrifice the forerunner of the Crucifixion—with some irony. For the opening through which we see the base of the tree is recognizable as the oft-repeated, Auschwitz oven opening.

These works are visual midrashim that interweave examination of a particular text with diverse historical, theological, or psychological issues. Carol Barsha's 1997 triptych, *The Love That Binds,* presents Isaac floating in "a limbo of love and oblivion" (her words). He is caught between realms in being *tied* by this event to his father's God—he is next in line as prophetic intermediary between human and divine realms—and he therefore hovers between earth and heaven. His hovering is born of the oblivion of meaninglessness (faith as complete unreason—expressed by his father's irrational faith-prompted act, who awakens him before dawn and leads him on a nightmare journey that culminates with his being bound by that father standing over him with an upraised knife). It is also born of *love* in the most ambiguous way: his father's love of God, his own love of his father—and in the end, with his redemption and his consequent initiation into the covenant, his father's love for him.

Textual intensity also connects kabbalistic thought to images. Jane Logemann's various series since the early 1990s endlessly repeat letters or entire words or phrases. At times the implication is triple: obsessive kabbalistic (Abulafian) repetition intertwined with thematic repetition familiar from contemporary classical music such as that of Philip Glass—and also with implicit political midrash, as when "Coexistence" is repeated again and again and again, in Hebrew on one side of the image and in Arabic on the other side.

Dutch-born Yona Verwer connects mysticism to other issues textlessly. Her 2005–2010 *Kabbalah of Bling* series comments on the commercialization of Kabbalah—from pop Kabbalah centers to the industry of Kabbalah-based candles and incense. Canvases shaped as large-scale modern "amulets"—hung on chains and "ready to wear"—explore the faux spirituality (like faux bling jewelry) of worshiping objects for themselves; in depicting guns they "protect" the "wearer" from gunshot injury.

Where does Anselm Kiefer fit into this definitional discussion? His huge works focusing on kabbalistic concepts, particularly Lurianic thought—like his large multimedia 1989 canvas, "*Zim Zum*," or his 1990 installation, *Breaking of the Vessels*—are invariably also connected to the Holocaust. The subjects could not be more "Jewish," but the artist is a German Christian who grew up in an environment that recognized no responsibility for the Holocaust, and he has spent twenty years addressing that issue, most often through kabbalistic ideas.

Cynthia Madansky's 2000 installation *On the Jewish Question* combines Jewish/non-Jewish definitional with text/image definitional complications. It centers on the words of the 1843–1844 essays by Karl Marx—Jewish-born but converted to Christianity at age six through his father's upwardly mobile hopes—beaten, letter by letter, into metal panels that are illegible, scarred, and distorted. The result is both, and neither, text and/or image—and the panels look remarkably like plates used to print paper money; they shimmer like giant square coins. Madansky reflects on "Jewish" art and religion by reflecting on Marx's identity confusion, resonating in essays interpreted both as defending Jews and as anti-Jewish—in which he reduces Judaism's God to money.

Israel

Fifty years before the birth of Israel, Martin Buber and Boris Schatz were theorizing (Buber) or trying to actualize (Schatz) "Jewish national art." What eventuated as Israeli art is a vast story—there are more (Jewish and non-Jewish) visual artists per capita in Israel than in any country on the planet—that must be mostly reserved for another definitional discussion. Complications include the fact that many Israeli artists have ended up between Israel and elsewhere. Kinetic and Op art pioneer Yaacov Agam (b. 1928), for example—whose work often plays both on esoteric Hebrew terminology and on the issue of seeing what cannot be seen—lives primarily in Paris. Holocaust survivor Samuel Bak (b. 1933), who grew up in Israel—and whose classically detailed paintings often complexly interweave Kabbalah-based ideas, like the concept of *PaRDeS*, with questions evoked by the Holocaust regarding both God and humankind—has lived for years in Massachusetts. Is he Lithuanian, Israeli, American?

Conversely, Dafna Kaffeman has spent a good deal of time studying in Holland and the United States, but still lives in Israel, heading the Glass department at the Bezalel Arts Academy. Her work since 2006—exhibited in 2011 in America—mixes glass with fiber, embroidered with Hebrew and Arabic, often focusing directly or obliquely on the Israel-Palestine conflict. So, too, Jewish American artists have focused on Israel in some of their work. Fay Grajower's 1996 *Jerusalem Encounters* is a lush acrylic, oil, sand, and paper painting on canvas that translates the stones of the sacred city, its passageways and arches, into a light brown hue laced with nuggets of bright pigment: darkness and light—distant (biblical) pasts and more recent (diasporic) pasts contend with each other and with questions (Orthodoxy and secularism, Israelis and Palestinians) of present and future.

J. Barry Zeiger's found-objects installation, *Seder Table* (2000) bursts with Israel-embracing continuity: birch boughs thrust through it, from floor to ceiling. The table is covered with diverse candlesticks—their whispy flames symbolic of souls now gone, historically and due to the Holocaust—and crockery, together with myriad other evocative objects—the flotsam and jetsam of diasporic existence—most of it broken, as the table itself is broken. But the table is broken by trees, symbols of spring and rebirth. Light blue cloth (the color of the sky, of the tallit, of the stripes and star of Israel's flag—in short, of hope) flutters from the wall, illuminated by bulbs framed by blunted Stars of David. The installation articulates the tension between wholeness and breakage, continuity and interruption—and, one might say, between the Holocaust and Israel in the Jewish (particularly the Jewish American) psyche.

Sociopolitical Commentary

Israeli artists can hardly avoid sociopolitical commentary: In such a small, intense community, even to veer away from it into pure aesthetics becomes a political statement. Jewish American artists have certainly exhibited a taste for social and political commentary, from Ben Shahn and Jack Levine to Philip Guston and Mimi Gross. It is a visual response to the demand for *tikkun olam* imposed on Jews by the Rabbinic and Lurianic traditions. Judy Chicago first became known for her bold mixed-media commentary on the gender-laced history of culture, *The Dinner Party* (1974–1979), in which place settings focus on 39 historical and mythological women—and another 999 women are honored on the white floor tiles.

Her turn toward overtly Jewish subjects came when she and her husband, Donald Woodman, turned to an ambitious *The Holocaust Project: From Darkness into Light* (1985–1993)—a mixed-media work emphatic in its engagement of the broad (and not merely Jewish) implications of the catastrophe. Marcia Annenberg's 2010 *News/No News* pop-style painting series, in fact, suggests the comfort with which Jewish artists often offer unabashed commentary on far-reaching aspects of the world around them. Her strident visual review of history, art, the environment, economics, and politics addresses their increasingly disturbing tangle within the web of American democracy.

A review of this discussion will make it clear that among the important features of Jewish visual productivity in the past generation is the dominant role of women. Moreover, some Jewish women artists have asked: "where do I fit in as a Jewish woman artist in a dual tradition (art and Judaism) that for so long virtually excluded or liturgically limited women?" *Hygiene* (2000), a small installation in which Rachel Giladi (an Israeli living in New York) has placed tampons in a toothbrush-holder and painted it all black, reflects on the male association between the monthly flow of female blood and uncleanliness. Christianity associates birth blood with Original Sin; for traditional Judaism, menstrual blood is an impurity. But these male-made associations reflect male fear at women's ability to bleed and yet not die, month by month.

Canadian Devorah Neumark's 2000 installation *Harrei At Mutteret . . . (Behold You Are Released . . .)* wryly comments on traditional divorce and its male-governed limitations. Her installation presents the female passage between marriage and nonmarriage as a metaphor for the passage between entitlement and nonentitlement. A minyan of photo boxes with illustrations depicting Jewish weddings are surmounted by wine goblets, alluding to the ceremonial breaking of the wineglass—but seven of the goblets (the number of wedding blessings and the bridal transits around the groom) are inscribed with the Hebrew words of release.

Among Helene Aylon's array of mixed-media commentaries—beginning with her 1996 *The Liberation of G-d*, which highlighted passages (in pink) in each book of the Torah where women were rejected, excluded, or hidden—her 2007 *All Rise: An Installation of a Beit Din as a "House" of Three Women* transforms that traditional male bastion into a question that interweaves *Sanhedrin* and *Nashim*: "isn't it time for female judges to serve in a *beit din*?" she asks.

Some male Jewish artists ask parallel questions. Geoffrey Laurence's vertical 2000 triptych, *T'fillah,* depicts three discontinuous parts of a woman's body. Around each is wrapped a *T'fillin* strap—worn by men whose prayers include thanking God "that He did not make me a woman." The issue of women as commodities (soulless body parts) and woman-exclusion and woman-negativity in aspects of Jewish ritual are interwoven with the suggestion of contemporary sexual mores: the nipple ring offers a pun between "binding it" and bondage.

Diversity and *Tikkun Olam*

In works like Siona Benjamin's *Fereshteh* ("angels" in Urdu) series, from the late 1990s to today, female figures are blue-skinned, like the Hindu god Krishna (and others), and like the sky shared by all peoples. Born into the Bene Israel community of Mumbai, surrounded by Hindus and Muslims, sent to Catholic and Zoroastrian schools, she immigrated to an America with its own still-unresolved issues of religion and race. Siona's images, often with embedded words and texts—in Hebrew, Urdu, and English—synthesize the Hindu idea of *Ardhanareshwara* (a being both male and female) to the kabbalistic idea of the *Shechinah* (the female aspect of the genderless God potentially within all of us).

Moreover, Benjamin has noted how "even well-intentioned Western feminists often direct a Eurocentric gaze at sexual practices and politics elsewhere in the world . . . I have . . . experienced myself . . . [how] assumptions are made before [non-Western women] open our mouths: . . . 'Are you educated?' 'Do you have our level of sophistication?'" Her work, combining Indian, Muslim, Persian, Rajput, and Moghul styles and Jewish and feminist subjects assaults the very concept of definition. Her universalist goal is simply *tikkun*.

High-quality work by Jewish artists today is as varied as it is far-flung—from coast to coast. The Southern California–based Jewish Artist Initiative overflows with significant artists, as does the Jewish Art Salon in New York. Many artists explore a particular time or place, wrapping layers of past around the present—like Joyce Ellen Weinstein's *Lithuanian Timber Synagogue* series, or Robert Kirschbaum's rigorously abstract series devoted to the Temple. In the 2010 *Dura Europos Project* two artists, Richard McBee and Joel Silverstein, who are principals in the Jewish Art Salon, asked four dozen artists to respond, each in a 12"x12" work, to any scene from the Dura synagogue wall paintings. The result was stunning: images in an endless diversity of subject, style, symbol, color, texture, medium—endless engagement. Endless questions.

Rabbinic literature offers multiple answers—and no answers—to its questions. Contemporary "Jewish art" offers an important aspect of the Jewish urge toward questions with myriad and nonexistent answers. Visual images are transforming Judaism's dynamic tension between conserving and reshaping traditions across shifting conditions. "Jewish art" involves studying, thinking, debating, asking, answering—and not answering—as part of the varied, obligatory process of *tikkun olam.* Even as many of these artists begin with text study, their work—often with words and phrases embedded within it—become texts that in turn invite our commentary, pushing us to look at (and thus to think about) things in new ways, intensifying the ongoing process of discussing and defining what it means to be a Jew in the world.

Jew as (German) Product: Rubber Ducks and Other Commodifications of Jewish Identity

Michal S. Friedlander

In the small circles of the German intellectual and cultural elite, Jews are clearly present. The first violin (Konzertmeister) of the Berlin Philharmonic orchestra is Jewish and plays Christmas concerts, postdoctoral Israelis are sitting in the libraries and labs of the Max Planck Institute, and several Jewish artists have been elected as members of the Akademie der Künste. Home-grown German Jews are back, even if they are not perceived or acknowledged as such. However, is there a specifically Jewish popular culture that reaches the German mainstream? Are there mass-produced, three-dimensional "Jewish" objects for Jewish and non-Jewish consumption? What can a plastic bath duck reveal about twenty-first-century perceptions of Jewish identity in Germany?

These questions need to be placed in a comparative context by looking at other nations with Jewish populations. A Jewish presence is firmly established in today's North American mass media, in both the intellectual and popular cultural landscape. It has gradually been woven into the huge cultural tapestry of the United States with widespread, if sometimes grudging, acceptance.

There are approximately 6.5 million Jews living in North American, the majority of whom are not traditionally observant. As long as there have been Jews in the United States, there has been a demand for traditional ritual objects. In recent years, however, there has been a massive increase in the production and consumption

---

MICHAL S. FRIEDLANDER has worked in a curatorial capacity at Jewish museums in New York, Los Angeles, and Berkeley. She has curated numerous exhibitions and published extensively on a variety of Jewish themes. Since 2001, she has served as Curator of Judaica and Applied Arts at the Jewish Museum Berlin.

An earlier version of this article appeared in the *JMB Journal*, no. 4 (2011): 68–75.

of superfluous Jewish kitsch objects—often of dubious taste and quality—manufactured in China. Their widespread existence is a powerful expression of cultural self-confidence. One might imagine that a Jewish household that maintains some level of ritual observance would need a *Kiddush* cup and a *kippah*, but which Jewish home requires an inflatable matzah ball, "Mazel Tov" flip-flops, a "Nice Jewish Guys" photo calendar, and a Lego mezuzah? Through these internal cultural gags, Jews can enjoy shared reference points and laugh together at themselves. Many non-Jews laugh along with them at these familiar references and so Jews become part of an American multicultural mainstream, where ethnic diversity is promoted.

Jews living in Israel form part of a completely different cultural context, with its own challenges. In Israel, young people are forced to confront questions of personal identity and national politics at a relatively young age. Are they religious or secular, politically to the left or right, and just how should the Israeli-Palestinian conflict be resolved? After years of regimented army service they need a break from the daily confrontation with fast-paced, stressful, Israeli discourse. Many follow well-trodden Israeli paths to India, Tibet, and South America, looking for an alternative way of life, where they can just be themselves rather than being just Israelis. Those who return to Israel may express their varied Jewish Israeli identities, ranging from the patriotic to an ironic distancing from the Zionist creed, through the invention or reinvention of objects. One example is the kaffiyeh, a headdress for protection against the harsh sun and desert sand, worn by Semitic peoples from ancient times. The black-and-white cotton version of the scarf became a symbol of Palestinian nationalism and Yasser Arafat's trademark. It is now worn as a sign of solidarity with the Palestinian people, or for those not in the know, as a fashion accessory/blunder. A blue-and-white kaffiyeh woven with a Star of David motif is now being produced in Israel. Other creations include the most basic signifiers of identity: Star of David necklaces are being updated in neon-colored plastic, and even the iconic heroes of Israel's modern history—Theodor Herzl, Golda Meir, and David Ben-Gurion—become visual commodities when mass-reproduced on pop-art drink coasters.

Sixty-seven years after the end of World War II, can one find popular "Jewish" cultural products in Germany and, if so, who are the makers? Current estimations of the Jewish population in Germany lie at around one hundred thousand, according to the number of people registered with the official Jewish communities. The numbers were boosted by a large influx of Jews from the former Soviet Union, but there are thousands more nonaffiliated Jews and these numbers are swelling due to the recent flood of young Israeli émigrés (estimates run to fifteen thousand and beyond).

Despite the considerable rise in the number of Jews living in Germany, an extreme uneasiness exists and great caution is exercised when criticizing, praising, or finding humor in "Jewish issues." When Michel Friedman, a Jewish leader and television personality, fell from grace in a very public, cocaine-laced fall, the media lampooning was notably restrained. The legacy of guilt relating to historic events still lingers, as does an underlying resentment against the particular attention paid to Jewish life in Germany. In the rare instances when non-Jews do choose the volatile path of making humorous representations of Jews, they have a good chance of offending someone. One example is a "Jewish" rubber duck that recently entered the German market. Another is the popular caricaturization of the leading German Jewish book critic, Marcel Reich-Ranicki.

Marcel Reich-Ranicki is known to a broad public through a literary talk show on the German television station ZDF in the late 1980s until 2000, when he was at the height of his fame and became a cult figure. Non-Jewish designers warped his "Semitic" nose and lips into various collectibles: a Reich-Ranicki bookend; a gift bag for books, which squawks a credible version of his voice when the bag is opened; quite apart from the numerous caricatured drawings of him in the media. With a marked absence of linguistic self-reflection, he is often referred to as the irrefutable Pope of Literature ("Literaturpapst"). These responses to Reich-Ranicki's public persona show an apparent insensitivity to his Jewish identity. Now aged ninety-two, his autobiography was published in 1999, where he details his experiences in the Warsaw ghetto. The book was filmed for television and various biographical documentaries have been made about his life.

Has his Jewish identity simply been ignored or has German society reached a state of ease with its history and Jewish co-citizens ("jüdische Mitbürger") that such jokes and objects are now permissible? This is doubtful. Is Reich-Ranicki counted among the untouchable German Jewish superstars, Einstein and Freud, who are reproduced and affectionately collected in the form of plastic action figures? Perhaps. As with Einstein and Freud, Reich-Ranicki's rise to fame was based on his intellectual merits, rather than his personal Jewish history. It seems to be simply irrelevant to the broad general public if Reich-Ranicki is Jewish or not, and the morphing of his pliable features, which indeed play with anti-Semitic clichés, serve to sell the Reich-Ranicki brand.[1] One could even surmise that the German designers were not familiar with the anti-Semitic visual canon and the intellectual discourse on representations of "the other."

In Germany today, there is fortunately always a minority of people whose radars are fine-tuned to any anti-Semitic representations of Jews. Yet in 2012, there is a growing and pervasive blind ignorance about Jews and Jewish culture in the population at large. The topics are difficult and irrelevant to the lives of the average German who has a meager chance of meeting a living Jew, and should it actually happen, they most likely would feel helpless and uncomfortable in conversation. In 2009, Michael Wuliger published *Der koschere Knigge*,[2] a satirical, humorous book written as an authoritative guide to behavior when meeting Jews. He gives basic tips: don't assume that all Jews are Israelis, rich, clever, religious, or that they can absolve guilt feelings for a family's Nazi past. His examples of encounters between Germans and Jewish Germans still, sadly, mirror the experience of German Jews and his text may be amusing for Jewish readers, but it is also used in seminars to teach about anti-Semitism.

The theme of uncomfortable German Jewish/non-Jewish interface is the basis of Oliver Polak's brash, largely autobiographical, comedy. A thirty-something Jewish man who grew up in the only Jewish family in the backwaters of Papenburg, Polak is a Jew making fun about Jews and even using the Holocaust as comedic material. Is the audience permitted to laugh? In his semi-autographical book entitled *I'm Allowed, I'm Jewish* Polak states: "Let's be easy on each other . . . I'll forget the Holocaust thing—and you forgive us for Michel Friedman."[3]

Polak seems to have hit a nerve. There is laughter, relief, and shock on the part of his non-Jewish audiences, the curious few who have grown up mostly in a Jewish vacuum. On his MySpace comedy website Polak has marketed "I ♥ Jews" buttons (which completely sold out) and "Ich darf das" ("I'm allowed") T-shirts. Some German Jews empathize with Polak's provocative stance, which relates to their own experience. As a second-generation insider, Polak has the prerogative to get away with the unmentionable, and he knows it. Will his comedic talent and topic of choice lead him to become a national celebrity, a cult figure, or a forgotten one-man attempt at Jewish self-assertion?

Polak's humor is closer to German Jews than American or Israeli Jewish kitsch products, which are regarded with amused disdain. The weekly national newspaper *Die Jüdische Allgemeine* dedicates a large photograph on its back page to their "Schlock Shop" feature. Here, the charms of Chagall matroshka nesting dolls, a bagel card game called "Schmear," and a cuddly shofar ("recycled from leftover teddy bear legs") are often firmly dismissed.

Jewish Americans have developed shared cultural reference points and a tremendous confidence, bolstered by their numbers; Israelis have common bonds based on nationality, language, history, and military involvement. Jews living in Germany have such diverse historical, cultural, linguistic, and religious backgrounds and experiences that they are somehow unable to unify and forge a shared Jewish identity, quite apart from a specifically German Jewish identity. Over time, this may ultimately lead to a loss of Jewish identity altogether. The sensitive issue of living in Germany does not seem to allow for much humor beyond the Jewish fold. This also means that Jews in Germany have not produced any Jewish rubber ducks.

The classic bright yellow rubber duck, sporting an orange bill, was once the sole domain of children. It has been the inspiration for an endless variety of themed ducks, from fairy and biker to dentist, which are now sought out by eager adult collectors. In the United States several Jewish models exist, including Chanukah ducks, which carry a dreidel or Chanukah gelt, or wear a Star of David necklace. There is also a duck wearing a *kippah* and tallit. These "cute gifts" are not perceived as politically incorrect as they do not utilize gross cultural stereotypes (although the Moses and Pope ducks, with human faces, are up for discussion). In 2010, Cedon, the gift shop situated in the Jewish Museum Berlin, decided to follow the market trend and commissioned a Jewish duck, with no provocative intent. The shop's proprietors are not Jewish and brought out a cheerful yellow duck, dressed as a Chasidic Jew. He wears a white shirt, black outerwear, and a flat hat; he has a beard, sidelocks (*peiot*), and heavy-rimmed round black glasses. In a moment of conceptual reflection, the duck's squeak mechanism was removed, in case a *squeaking* Jew duck might be going just a little too far. For whom was this duck created? Reactions are divided, but it is the non-Jewish visitors who tend to buy this silent yet jolly souvenir item. Many Jewish visitors are just offended.

The Cedon duck perpetuates a stereotypical tradition and the Jew-costume makes the duck identifiably Jewish through an outdated and inappropriate visual code, historically loaded with negative connotations and still used in anti-Semitic cartoons today. One could argue that the Jewish Museum gift shop is not an anti-Semitic context, but why perpetuate this Jewish stereotype, rather than reflect Jewish diversity today?

The lack of a homogenous Jewish identity and an unspoken decision to keep a low, Jewish profile makes it impossible for Jews in Germany to produce indigenous, self-ironic products for mass consumption. The fear of stimulating controversy and a negative backlash is indeed understandable. Despite the growth of some religious German communities, there is not enough demand for ritual objects to a keep a single Judaica silversmith in business—the need is served by imports from Israel and elsewhere. There is no critical mass of confident Jews, lighting Brandenburg Gate Chanukah lamps and wearing "Super Jew" T-shirts, although a few, lone individuals have tried to raise the flag of German Jewish pride. Members of the general German public are largely ignorant of their parents' or grandparents' history, which is as remote to them as the Thirty Years' War. Even the expression "Never forget!" has largely been forgotten. It is likely that uninformed, popular representations of Jews, by non-Jews, will continue to be manufactured and albeit unintentionally, old stereotypes will be revived. Where can these stereotypes and simplified conceptions lead, except to the further stigmatization and exclusion of those who do not meet the "German norms"?

The big-nosed, "who-cares-if-he's-Jewish" literary Pope, Marcel Reich-Ranicki, holds up books on the shelves of non-Jewish homes. His new neighbor, wearing matching thick-rimmed glasses, is the myopic German Chasidic duck who will also gather dust. This unlikely pair makes evident the general absence of sensitivity and knowledge about Jewish questions in Germany. In 2006, following the launch of a competition by an Iranian newspaper for cartoons about the Holocaust, an Israeli cartoonist from an Israeli newspaper successfully solicited anti-Semitic caricatures by Jews. He wanted to fight fire with humor and self-reflection. The authentic and provocative Jewish cultural product venture, recently initiated by Oliver Polak in Germany, has little chance of taking off. Let's be realistic, Jew or non-Jew, who in Germany today would wear an "I ♥ Jews" button in public? Would you?

Notes

1. Although the Reich-Ranicki bookend was still advertised on the German Amazon website in January 2011, it is essentially off the market. The gift bag was widely available in German shops during the Christmas period of 2010 and is still available online in 2012. In 2007, a version of the bag appeared with the caricature removed but Reich-Ranicki's unmistakable voice was kept.
2. "Knigge" refers to the German author, Adolph Knigge and his most famous publication *Über dem Umgang mit Menschen* (*On Human Relations*) which first appeared in 1788. This didactic work was actually intended as a sociological and philosophical treatise rather than an etiquette handbook. However, over time, the word "Knigge" became a German idiom that is synonymous with rules of social conduct.
3. "*Lassen Sie uns ganz unverkrampft miteinander umgehen . . . Ich vergesse die Sache mit dem* Holocaust—*und Sie verzeihen uns* Michel Friedman." Oliver Polak, *Ich darf das, ich bin Jude* (Köln: Verlag Kiepenheuer & Witsch, 2008), 11.

The Presence of What Is Absent: Art as Inquiry into Jewish Text

Adina Allen and Pat Allen

Introduction

Like the natural world, Torah too may contain entire dimensions that are not yet apparent to us. These may disclose themselves to us through new interpretive tools, or by fresh new uses of the old ways of reading... We should strive to remain open to learning on as many levels, and by as many methods, as we are able to. In this way, Torah will become for us, as it was for earlier generations, a way to navigate those mysterious channels of existence.[1]

Adina:

Growing up as the daughter of an art therapist, spending time in the studio and engaging with art materials was a part of my daily life. Often when I faced a problem that I did not know how to solve on my own, my mother would advise me to go into the studio and to make art about my question. I was brought up with the notion that creative exploration via art and writing is a way to tap into one's own unconscious and into God as the Creative Source in order to access information that had previously been concealed.

As a rabbinical student my days are spent immersed in learning, analyzing, discussing, and teaching the foundational texts of our tradition. Traditional commentaries have become codified and

---

ADINA ALLEN is a fourth-year rabbinical student at Hebrew College and a Wexner Graduate Fellow. She envisioned and curated the multimedia art exhibit *Emunah V'Omanut: Creative Responses to an Ancient Tradition*, and has facilitated the Studio Process in diverse Jewish settings.

PAT ALLEN is an artist, registered art therapist, and author of *Art Is a Way of Knowing* (Shambhala, 1995) and *Art Is a Spiritual Path* (Shambhala, 2005). She is the cocreator of the Studio Process and has taught the method in settings throughout the world. She served as a member of the art therapy faculty of the School of the Art Institute of Chicago for over twenty years and is the cofounder of the Open Studio Project in Evanston, Illinois.

they provide the foundation for serious text study. Because of the sheer genius of our Rabbinic ancestors, we rarely consider that there is space or need for us to receive new information about our texts. We often fail to see that we, too, have the capacity and even the responsibility, to not just *learn* Rashi, but to emulate him as exegetes in our own right.

In every era, commentators have brought the tools and historical circumstances of the current time period to bear on the text, yielding new and diverse interpretations that were needed for people at that time. For example, Rambam worked systematically to reinterpret Jewish tradition in light of Aristotelian thought. As a result, his commentaries rendered the Jewish canon relevant to his generation and beyond. Our texts can still speak to contemporary issues if new and diverse voices continue to engage with these texts, catalyzing those ideas that are needed to come into existence at the present time.

Pat:

The process Adina grew up observing and engaging with, the Studio Process used in our work described here, has a long history. While an art student at the Boston Museum School of Fine Arts in the mid-1970s I studied with Margaret Naumburg, one of the founders and chief theorists of the then nascent field of art therapy. Naumburg was a pioneer in applying the understanding that dreams and fantasies appear to us primarily in images and that the unconscious is a repository of information stored in imaginal form, which can be accessed through art making.[2] Like other early art therapists, she underwent both a Freudian and a Jungian psychoanalysis, essentially a deep study of her own unconscious. Like Freud, Naumburg regarded the unconscious warily and considered that art therapy was a way to retrieve repressed personal information that, once understood, might free the person from neurotic behaviors.

I became fascinated with the work of Carl Jung while a graduate student in art therapy, and through my own Jungian analysis as well as deep study of Jung's work I have made a lifelong use of his technique of active imagination.[3] It is upon this foundation that the Studio Process is based. Jung had a more positive view of the unconscious as holding all creative potential, not merely the unacceptable or taboo, but all that is as yet unknown, both personally and collectively. He himself made extensive study of his own dreams and spontaneous images through active imagination, which he described as "dreaming the dream onward." In other words, taking the dream image, which is often fragmentary, becoming relaxed and receptive, and simply observing as the mind unfurls the image into a story. What Jung discovered, and what my own work and that of the hundreds of participants in the Studio Process supports, is the existence of a strata of the unconscious that contains collective as well as personal material. The images of all cultures and religions are richly varied expressions of the human history we all share.

Like Jung I believe that access to this realm is our birthright as humans and is also a manifestation of *b'tzelem Elohim*, the way in which we are both made in the image of God and are makers of images ourselves, a way in which we dialogue with the Divine. In the recently published *Red Book*[4] the full transcript of Jung's journey and his writings about his images—closely guarded in his lifetime for fear his colleagues might think him mad—is finally made available to us. Jung's material in the *Red Book* demonstrates that the basis of his psychology lies in his personal imaginal work with his own understanding of religious symbols and myths of his time; in his case, the Christian story of the death and resurrection of the Christ. Joseph Campbell, the famous scholar of myth, continued this work in his four-volume series *The Masks of God*,[5] confronting the universal source material from which human beings make unique meaning and then codify it into shared religious beliefs and practices to guide their lives in cultures throughout the world.

My contribution to the field of art therapy has been creating a method, the Studio Process, through which ordinary individuals who are not necessarily artists nor psychologically sophisticated can access their own connection to both the personal and collective realm of imagery as a practice of self-exploration and meaning making in their lives without an intermediary professional, either religious or therapeutic. In 1995, with two partners, I founded the Open Studio Project, which became and remains both a laboratory for exploring active imagination and a teaching and now training center for what evolved into the Studio Process.[6] I went on to found a second studio, Studio Pardes, in 2000 to further pursue the spiritual and religious themes that I found emerging in my own work.[7]

The Studio Process consists of three steps: stating an intention, making images, and witnessing, which is writing in response to those images and reading the writing aloud, usually in the company of others.[8] The technique of intention, by defining and limiting what one is asking to receive from the infinite well of the Creative Source, serves as a structured way for individuals to invite onto the page imagery from what is commonly called the unconscious but in spiritual traditions referred to as the void, the dreamtime, the Creative Source. While the first layer of this work often accesses personal material, it is common for religious symbols from one's own background as well as universal symbols to emerge. In the work described here, Adina and I crafted very specific intentions that allowed us to "dream the dream" of the Exodus story onward and to surface unheard voices.

Jung believed that this work was not about making up stories but rather that the stories and images have a life of their own and remain waiting for willing individuals to help them unfold further. The purpose of giving the images form through art making is to provide both a way for the images to manifest that can be shared with others and also to serve as a means to allow transit into unconscious realms while remaining anchored in concrete reality. The use of one's hands, mixing of color, and making marks on paper provide a form of grounding so that what comes through does not overwhelm or destabilize the person. The witness writing also allows a safe return to ordinary reality by gradually returning us to the space of the studio and the company of others through the physical act of writing. When we read the witness aloud our return continues and we have the witness or verification of another person that we are understood and acknowledged. What may feel strange when read to ourselves evokes resonance when heard by others.

Adina:

During my third year of study at Hebrew College I took a yearlong class on Exodus. We were encouraged to think creatively—both in methodology and in content—about our final project for the course. Spending the year immersed in traditional Rabbinic commentary, midrash, and scholarly interpretations on the book of

Exodus, I was exposed to the true genius of the Jewish enterprise. It is unique to Judaism to have many, often contradictory, commentaries on a particular verse held side by side together on the page, as in *Sh'mot Rabbah*. Likewise, other forms of innovation are about creating and holding the tension of multiple understandings, allowing these to continue to yield new possibilities, meanings, and stories. Through my studies, I felt excited by new interpretations of verses I thought I had fully understood. I felt a curiosity and sometimes a sadness about portions of the story that had not been commented on, and those neglected or obscure parts of the story called me to join the exegetical enterprise.

Faced with the opportunity of this project I sought to discover how I could best bring my unique self into conversation with the text. During college I had collaborated with my mother to see how the Studio Process that she had developed could be used to integrate the emotional component of the intellectual learning I was doing in school. Since starting rabbinical school I have found multiple ways to meld our different fields of knowledge and expertise. The Exodus project offered us the chance to work together to see if the Studio Process could be used as a means of close scriptural interpretation.

Pat:

When Adina proposed working together on her Exodus project I was excited to continue what we had begun when she was in college. In that project I functioned as a guide to the Studio Process, a consultant about materials and art methods, and a witness to Adina's process so that she could recover, express, and integrate the emotions that had arisen during challenging academic work exploring global climate change and resource depletion. As with much intellectual work, no time was made for students to share the grief and fear they felt as they awakened to the perils of ecological disaster facing the earth. These actions, embodied in the physical presence of someone trustworthy, allows the seeker to relax conscious control and let the images arise. This role constitutes "holding the space" in all forms of expressive arts work. The Exodus project allows us to participate together as *chevruta*, sharing our different backgrounds and insights while engaging side by side in the study of the text through art making and writing, witnessing together what would emerge. This form married both of our skills in a deep and intimate way.

Process

> *Bible stories do not flatter or fascinate like Homer's; they do not give us something artfully rendered; they force readers to become interpreters and to find the presence of what is absent in the fraught background, the densely layered narrative . . . The accreted, promissory narrative we call Scripture is composed of tokens that demand the continuous and precarious intervention of successive generations of interpreters who must keep the words as well as the faith.*[9]

We looked at three sections of chapters 1–2 of Exodus. We began our process by reading through the biblical text together, in typical *chevruta* fashion: out loud, in English and Hebrew. As we read we listened until we felt a natural stopping place in the narrative and broke our sections there. Next, we shared commentaries, questions, reflections, and analyses about that section of text. We noted themes that we were curious about or that were becoming newly apparent to us and asked questions of the text related to these themes.

As we worked together we noted seeming contradictions in the text that raised many questions for us. For example, in Exodus 2:1–10, Why does Pharaoh's daughter defy her father's edict and pay for Moses to be raised as opposed to having him killed? Why does Moses' mother leave him without any apparent longing or regret, especially after having hid him for three months because of his beauty? Were Pharaoh's daughter and her maidens scanning the riverbed for babies to save? If not, why did Pharaoh's daughter insist on going down to the Nile to bathe? What does it mean that water, a symbol of the feminine, is such a part of Moses' story (e.g., he is found in the Nile, parts the Sea, and smashes the rock to draw forth water)? After reflecting on our brainstorm we realized that there was a single question that was clear to both of us that needed further analysis: Where is the perspective of the women who are so prominent in this story? At the conclusion of our brainstorming, we transcribed the ideas, which would become the creative context for our collaboration.

We then followed the steps of the Studio Process. First, we each set an intention. In this context an intention is a statement of what one would like to receive from the Creative Source at a particular moment. Intentions are worded clearly, in the present tense, without using the word "want."[10] For Exodus 2:1–2:10, Adina's intention was, "I illustrate an image of the scene of the women at the riverbed." Pat's intention was, "I open to an image that helps to clarify the emerging story of the women." We then set our intentions aside, releasing them to the universe like prayers that had already been answered.

Next, we began the art making stage of the work. Often in the Studio Process there is a wide range of materials available. For this project we chose to work with watercolor paper, watercolors, and pen and ink. We agreed upon a specific paper size knowing that the project would be collated together when finished. To begin, we each chose a brush and color that attracted us and started by putting marks on the page without a particular image or desired outcome in mind. The goal at this stage is to follow pleasure and to let the intellectual mind, and even the intention, recede in order to create the spaciousness into which the answers to our questions could arise. We typically worked for three hours, broke for lunch, and resumed for three more hours in the afternoon.

We then turned to the next stage of the process: witnessing. First, we sat in front of our piece quietly and noticed its look and feel. Then we described in writing what we saw as fully as possible without coming to any conclusions. We wrote down any feelings or thoughts, including judgments and seemingly extraneous tangents that came up. Finally, we reread our intention and asked the image how it related to our intention. In the Studio Process, the image is understood to have a life of its own, having arrived from the Creative Source, and so we address it as such. The image is something one receives, not something one makes.

The witness writing creates a transition from the art making to discussion and reflection. This step extends the liminal immersion in color and form of the art making and, therefore, functions like the period between sleep and wakefulness, the time when we often remember our dreams. The witness writing mediates the energy that comes during the creative act. To the degree that we are able, we remain in that relaxed state with our discerning capacities quieted, while gradually returning to the here and now where we can receive what was given in the art.

The information that came through in these writings bears traces of our current life, thoughts, studies, and preoccupations.

In addition to the specific subject matter of the text, the witness is a record of an intimate moment between each of us and our soul.[11] In preparing this work to share with a larger audience we resisted the urge to edit. Through this process we noticed that the witness writings exhibit the same ambiguous and multivalent qualities as the Exodus text itself.

An excerpt of Adina's witness on the image *Women at the Nile* painted in response to Exodus 2:1–2:10:

> Mounds formed around the grove of trees. The trees seem protective for the women, perhaps sister trees of the Asherot they once worshiped. The mounds reflect the shape of the pyramids. The mounds between which the women took the men and forced them to have sex in order to keep life going, new generations coming.[12] "The more they oppressed them, the more they increased."[13] Nature is everywhere in this image: the grove, the mounds, the protective reeds, the bush concealing Miriam, the tree under which the mother sits, the flowing stream.
>
> Pharaoh's daughter in the middle of the dividing line. She jumps into the Nile, the waters flowing around her body, a *mikveh* of sorts, perhaps. She is cleansed of the disgrace of her father's decrees and can see clearly. Her senses receptive, she immediately spies the basket. Miriam looks very masculine and sort of Egyptian. Maybe it's not Miriam; maybe it's Pharaoh, watching the whole scene. He often goes to the Nile "early in the morning."[14] His heart later hardens because his own daughter has betrayed him. He is powerless in the height of his power. That water changes Pharaoh's daughter; the water changes slavery to freedom.
>
> Pharaoh's daughter can you speak? Who are you, character in blue? You look like a hieroglyph. Fist in air? Frozen in time. Stiff and stationary or strong and grounded? Moses' mother, relaxed, attentive, protected by the tree. Now the figure looks like Miriam again. In the background, checking on the scene, she knows she is not the one to play the leading role but rather to orchestrate behind the scenes. She is ready to take the stage next, to bring the baby to his mother to nurse. The slave girl is bent over like the slave men in the background, but bent towards redeeming life from death.

Adina:

In my witness writing I noticed threads of many of the texts we had been studying in class coming through. These separate commentaries and verses began to weave together a new understanding of the biblical text.

An excerpt of Pat's witness on the image *Moses Is Found* painted in response to Exodus 2:1–2:10:

> Only Pharaoh's daughter, Moses, and Miriam appear in the scene, amid the lush reeds and flowing Nile. A vast space separates them from the distant labors of the pyramids and the enslavement of the people. Moses is surrounded by female energy active on his behalf. For Pharaoh's daughter he seems to represent a chance at redemption. She recognizes that her mother's and her own bodily narrowness represent the restricted and effete culture that has grown up in Egypt focusing on denying and controlling death rather than celebrating and living life. She looks older than a young daughter here; perhaps child bearing has in fact passed her by. Both she and Miriam reach toward Moses, both are united in an effort to support and nurture a more robust masculine energy, one that will be restored to acting justly. Miriam's devotion to her brother recalls the relationship of the Egyptian stories of Isis and Osiris, so they strike a special chord in Pharaoh's daughter.
>
> **Pat:** Can anyone speak?
>
> **Pharaoh's daughter:** I've longed for a child! I can't bear the Egyptian men, they are weak and spineless but also I couldn't risk my life and health. If I too were lost my father would go mad and murder the people, not just enslave them. We have become a culture obsessed with death because we dishonor life. This boy will be my act of reparation, my chance to turn my misfortune to good.
>
> **Miriam:** Thank you for your grace and kindness and for saving my brother.
>
> **Reeds:** We live in the swamp edge where the most fertility lives, we create a magical space where change can be grown and nurtured in almost invisible ways, we filter the evil waste that Pharaoh dumps in the Nile in his mad plans to conquer death.

Pat:

I recognized familiar concerns—the balance of masculine and feminine energy—that have been apparent in my artwork for decades.

Even though I know and believe that the images arise from the place of infinite possibility that is the core and basic home of every person, I was surprised to find a new story emerging about Pharaoh's daughter's motivation for saving Moses.

After reading our witnesses out loud to one another we noticed midrashic elements appearing in our writing. We decided to amplify this emergence and add a new step to the Studio Process: midrashic writing. Through the course of actively engaging with this work for a full week, we had increased our capacity to remain in the liminal stage with the words and to receive stories rather than construct them. As Martin Buber wrote in his seminal work, *I and Thou*:

> This is the eternal origin of art that a human being confronts a form that wants to become a work through him. Not a figment of his soul, but something that appears to the soul and demands the soul's creative power. What is required is a deed that a man does with his whole being: if he commits it and speaks with his being the basic word to the form that appears, then the creative power is released and the work comes into being.[15]

It became clear that engaging with these characters is a relational experience: they have an ongoing energy and new information for us to glean if we are willing to receive them.

An excerpt of Adina's midrash on Exodus 2:1–2:10:

> This midrash is in the voice of a female Hebrew slave who tells how many women, Hebrew and Egyptian alike, were creating a counterbalancing force to the enslavement that was also the reality of the time:
>
> > We women knew different. So, we took the liberty of paving the way for the change we saw coming, the change we were dedicated to helping bring about. We set up clinics, camps, and training grounds. We had sessions—first and most importantly to bring together and build relationships between the Egyptian women and ourselves. We created spaces where we laughed, danced, cooked, created, told our ancient stories, and learned the ins and outs of how we each related to the Great Force. It was an amazing time. Though

on one level I was "just a Hebrew slave," in this circle of loving and supportive sisters all hierarchies were leveled. This was a relic of the Old Paradigm, Pharaoh's daughter would often remind me. We had healing sessions where our most practiced witches would heal past traumas, making us more vital and clear for the Shift to come. We practiced opening up, letting go, and releasing expectations. Had any one of us tried to direct this next iteration of existence in a heavy-handed way we would have become the slaves and slave masters in our story of ideas and egos.

An excerpt of Pat's midrash on Exodus 2:1–2:10:

Pharaoh's daughter passed under the window of her father's meeting room. She heard his voice rise and his fist strike the table, "These Hebrews are swarming over the land. They must be stopped!" She felt a knot in her stomach. She hated it when her father wielded his power in cruel ways. She had Hebrew servants and had had a Hebrew nursemaid who cared lovingly for her when her own mother died in childbirth. Pharaoh had never recovered from the death of his queen. He blamed the women who had attended the birth, Shiphrah and Puah, still he was afraid of them, too. They were like witches and they knew things that even his most learned magicians did not know. Pharaoh's voice thundered, "When you attend the births of these Hebrews, kill the boys but let the girls live."

Pharaoh's daughter listened closely, crouched near the window. She heard Shiphrah murmur something and then the room grew silent. She hurried around to the other side to seem to bump into the two women as they exited the salon. "Oh, Hello!" she began, but the dark look in the women's eyes stopped her. These women had been like beloved aunts to the girl. When she achieved menarche, they instructed her in women's ways. They taught her methods to ease the cramping pains with herbs and tonics. They also told her how her mother's passage had been too narrow and tight and they encouraged her to walk and ride horses and be active to be more able to comfortably bear children when her time came. Yet, she too had narrow hips and they warned her about this. The daughter was old enough now that she understood the vastness of her father's power and his cruelty.

The women stopped before her. "Your father has decided to eliminate any newborn Hebrew boys," Puah said, her eyes flashed, "His own ministers have advised against this course." "He has asked, no, commanded us to murder them," Shiphrah added. The daughter replied, "You must not! He has never come to terms with having no son himself, he's jealous of the Hebrews and their families. He doesn't value a daughter as he would a son, but still, I think he can be distracted from this awful plan. He'll forget about it as other matters come before him and demand his attention."

Conclusion

Art is a vehicle that allows us to transcend linear time, to travel backward and forward into personal and transpersonal history, into possibilities that weren't realized and those that might be.[16]

Through this work we hoped to explore creative engagement as a means of what Art Green calls in his book *Radical Judaism* "going back to the mountain and hearing the word again," and of finding a "new sort of listening that is unique to this generation."[17] We sensed that the synergy of practicing *chevruta* learning via our two disciplines might yield a new method of midrashic inquiry. As inheritors of tradition we saw this project as a way to continue to breathe life into our texts and to allow our texts to breathe life back into us. As two people with different life experiences and knowledge bases, we hoped this project would enable us to deepen and transform our understanding of the Book of Exodus. As a mother and daughter we embraced the possibility of sharing our deepest interests together and learning from one another.

The work we did together, each bringing her unique experience and perspective to the project, is a manifestation of the collaborative post-hierarchical possibilities that exist and need to be nurtured in so many settings. Taking the *beit midrash* experience—close study of text, reading traditional and modern commentaries, discerning Hebrew word plays, etc.—and combining it with the Studio Process—activating the imagination, delving into the subconscious realm, following pleasure and play—has yielded insights into the text that neither could have accomplished alone. What has emerged is an holistic approach to accessing new information that makes space for multiple voices to be expressed and creates receptivity on multiple levels at once. At this time in history we are in need of new ways of relating to one another, to the Divine, and to the planet. If we approach our texts with intention they will generously provide what we ask for. When this is combined with the process of image making we can receive that which is beyond our cognitive grasp. The richness of our discoveries make us curious about what other stories and interpretations lie hidden in the hearts and minds of others. In this neo-rabbinic time, if we allow the entirety of our community and each of us in our uniqueness to flow into our stories, our stories will, in turn, flow again as the living waters they are meant to be.

The full Sh'mot project including images can be viewed at adinaallen.com and studiopardes.org.

Notes

1. Art Green, *Radical Judaism: Rethinking God and Tradition* (New Haven: Yale University Press, 2010), 83.
2. Margaret Naumburg, *Dynamically Oriented Art Therapy* (New York: Grune and Stratton, 1966).
3. Barbara Hannah, *Encounters with the Soul: Active Imagination as Developed by C. G. Jung* (Boston: Sigo Press, 1981).
4. Carl Jung, *The Red Book* (New York: W.W. Norton, 2009).
5. Joseph Campbell, *Masks of God* (New York: Penguin, 1964).
6. http://www.openstudioproject.org (retrieved on June 6, 2012).
7. http://www.studiopardes.org/pages/process.html (retrieved on April 15, 2012).
8. Pat B. Allen, *Art Is a Spiritual Path* (Boston: Shambhala, 2005), 11.
9. Geoffrey H. Hartman and Sanford Budick, *Midrash and Literature* (New Haven: Yale University Press, 1986), 15.
10. Allen, *Art Is a Spiritual Path,* 11.
11. Ibid., 67.
12. BT *Sotah* 11b.
13. Exod. 1:12.
14. Exod. 7:15.
15. Martin Buber, *I and Thou* (New York: Charles Scribner, 1970), 60.
16. Allen, *Art Is a Spiritual Path,* 1.
17. Green, *Radical Judaism,* 164.

Visual Midrash: The Role of Art and Artist in Our Seminaries

Jean Abarbanel and Anne Hromadka

For nearly twenty years the HUC-Skirball Museum was located within the HUC-JIR/LA Jack Skirball Campus. Through a program called MUSE, the museum encouraged faculty to integrate art into their classrooms using the permanent and rotating exhibitions. This joint program of the museum and the Rhea Hirsch School of Education ran from 1975 to 1983. In 1996, the HUC-Skirball Museum was moved from the HUC-JIR/LA campus to its current location on a fifteen-acre campus in the Santa Monica Mountains of Los Angeles.

Consequently, while the New York and Cincinnati campuses of HUC routinely hosted art programs and cultivated their on-site museums, HUC-JIR/LA now lacked the presence of a strong art program. Therefore, under the guidance of the dean and development offices, the College-Institute created the Enhancement Committee as an avenue to involve committed members of the Regional Board of Overseers and others dedicated to the life of the campus. Once formed, the main focus of the Enhancement Committee grew beyond campus aesthetics and simply installing rotating art exhibits to create meaningful experiences for the students using art as a mechanism for transmitting Jewish knowledge, values, and identities.

The first activity of the Enhancement Committee was to bring Tobi Kahn's exhibition *AVODA: Objects of the Spirit* from New York. On display from June 6 to August 30, 2003, this exhibition of ceremonial arts, fashioned by Tobi Kahn, was curated by Laura

JEAN ABARBANEL is cochair of the Western Region Board of Overseers' Campus Enhancement Committee at HUC-JIR's Jack H. Skirball Campus/Los Angeles.

ANNE HROMADKA is guest curator of the art collection and exhibitions at HUC-JIR's Jack H. Skirball Campus/Los Angeles.

Kruger, HUC-JIR/NY museum director, and was organized by the Avoda Institute, which is dedicated to providing a joyful understanding of Judaism through the arts. Activities were planned for Education and Jewish Communal Service students who were on campus for summer courses, in addition to a special session for early childhood educators cosponsored by the Los Angeles Bureau of Jewish Education. Moreover, Tobi Kahn addressed the entire campus community on an opening day ceremony in an inspiring presentation and then worked with select groups of students later that week.

The success of the Tobi Kahn exhibition affirmed the positive value of regularly integrating art into the life of the campus. Accordingly, the question became how to build on this new model of utilizing art as part of the learning experience.

In 2005, the next opportunity for serious artistic engagement occurred when a leading Jewish arts patron and independent curator, Nancy Berman, approached the College-Institute with a proposal for creating an Artist *Beit Midrash*. Eleven rabbinical students participating in Rabbi Lewis M. Barth's 2005 Midrash course were given the task of studying and collaborating with Victor Raphael, a Los Angeles–based mixed-media artist. The challenge for the class was to select key Jewish texts and ideas emanating from the course content to share with the artist. In turn, Raphael was to create a piece that accurately reflected this learning.

The essence of Rabbi Barth's class was the examination of the Hebrew text, *P'sikta D'Rav Kahana* 16. The students created an illuminating presentation on the relevant imagery and concepts that they had been studying. Through investigation, interaction, and reflection, art was used to amplify discussion, which lead to a transformation of the classroom itself.

Victor Raphael created three luminous mixed-media photographic art works for the classroom walls and embellished both sides of the entry door with designs of precious copper and metal leaf. This work, the result of his residency in the *Beit Midrash* program, is titled *Nachamu, Nachamu: The Heavens Spread Out Like a Prayer Shawl*. It remains in the classroom as a gift from the funder with signage outside documenting the project. The room is both a work of art and a classroom—both meditation space and learning place. It embodies the concept of study. By creating a beautiful and inspirational space for Jewish learning, it is clear from the responses of those who enter the space that this environment enlivens and deepens the everyday moments of teaching and understanding that takes place within. In addition to the enhancement of the physical classroom space, the project and its process demonstrated how artistic practice can be integrated into traditional Jewish learning and teaching.

As HUC students move into their chosen professions, they will take these innovative ideas and practices with them as illustrated by Rabbi Alissa Forrest (LA07). As a result of her participation in that course, Forrest created the first Jewish Art Camp at Temple Isaiah in Lafayette, California, in June 2008. She based the idea on the Midrash class explaining that the students "study a piece of Jewish text and then create a piece of art." The program, designed for children entering grades 1 through 5, started with students studying the story of creation. Forrest believes it is important to share this success with the Los Angeles campus because "those who supported these classes at HUC should know how they have translated into our rabbinates." Her experience in applying the lessons taught at HUC-JIR/LA to her work with children stresses the importance and roll of art in learning institutions. The HUC-JIR/LA Enhancement Committee goal is not only to provide adults with new ways to access our sacred texts, rituals, and contemporary experiences but to apply these lessons to learners of all ages. The value of reaching out to those who will be future educators, like Rabbi Forrest, is a gift that continues to give—*l'dor vador*.

It was clear both the Tobi Kahn and Victor Raphael projects on the Los Angeles campus had lasting impact. In both cases, the community was provided with direct learning opportunities engaging each artist in a variety of ways. Such projects served to highlight the ways in which art serves as an educational tool, expanding notions of contemporary Jewish study for HUC-JIR students. Accordingly, they served as a pilot for the Artist in Residence Program to Enhance Jewish Education.

In November 2006, HUC-JIR/LA applied for, and received, a grant from the Jewish Community Foundation of Los Angeles to create the Artist in Residence Program to Enhance Jewish Education. The primary goal of this residency program was to engage artists and their work as a means to enhance the learning experience and leadership training of students preparing for careers as rabbis, Jewish educators, and Jewish communal professionals. It was hoped that the program would present an expanded model of learning, introducing the concept of artistic expression as another language for understanding our tradition—an alternative midrash. HUC-JIR/LA Enhancement Committee believes that artists are educators with a unique vision and perspective for teaching and community building.

Over the course of two years (2007–2009), the Los Angeles campus hosted four artists, who interacted with students in the classroom setting and also cocreated works of art. Every artist led at least one lunchtime learning session during the course of their residency and had an opportunity to present their work to the community. During the residency program, each residency was tailored based on the unique talents and interests of the individual artist selected, as well as the interests of faculty who had elected to work with the artists, resulting in four distinct models:

- Peachy Levy, textile artist, participated as learner and instructor in two different courses. The courses included Rabbi Richard Levy's Festival *Machzor* class and Rabbi William Cutter's Modern Hebrew Literature course.
- Andrea Hodos, choreographer and dancer, participated as learner in one course taught by Rabbi Levy titled Homiletical Midrash, and was invited by multiple faculty members for a series of one-day guest lectures and workshops.
- Judith Margolis, visual artist, with an additional grant from a family foundation, was brought from Israel to participate in Dr. Tamara Eskenazi's Bible class on the *m'gillot* and lead several workshops. Her residency presented a model for working with an artist from abroad.
- Stacie Chaiken, actor and faculty member of the University of Southern California School of Theater Arts, was invited to teach her own elective course titled Storytelling I. This required approval from the Academic Governance Committee and the integration of her course description into the course catalog and registration protocols.

Each residency created different projects involving many students, faculty, and staff. Peachy Levy fashioned a seven-panel interactive sukkah, a lasting gift to the campus community. Each panel represents a doorway into Jewish tradition and is embellished with symbols taken directly from the Festival *Machzor* class content focusing on *ushpizin*.[1] Each year when the sukkah is installed, the HUC-JIR/LA community (the students, faculty, and staff) is invited to select a Velcro-backed fabric square and use fabric markers to write or draw images of the ancestors they would like to invite into the HUC-JIR/LA sukkah. They then attach their interpretations onto the fabric panels. These attachable Velcro-backed fabric squares were designed to engage students in annually inviting in new guests, teaching anew the custom of *ushpizin*. Peachy Levy explored her sukkah panel project in a final presentation to the students from Rabbi Levy's 2007 Festival *Machzor* class. This provided an opportunity for the students to share feedback on Levy's project as it related to the course material. The presentation led to students requesting a chance to participate in the dedication ceremony of the Levy sukkah for the school the following fall. The students expressed the desire to reflect on this experience in front of their peers. During the ceremony they spoke about being invited to participate in this work of art and how each panel shows various attributes of God so that when installed it symbolizes 'togetherness.' To create space for students and allow them to participate in the ritual of decorating and welcoming their ancestors strengthens notions of togetherness. The work serves to create both thought and dialogue.

Andrea Hodos's culminating presentation involved a group of students in creating a performance art piece presented at HUC-JIR/LA entitled *On Dry Ground: Faith, Fear and Transformation at the Edge of the Sea*. Judith Margolis created an original work of art that is installed on the campus. The subject matter for the painting grew out of images and ideas discussed during the Bible class on *m'gillot* and during the hands-on-workshops Margolis led with students. Stacie Chaiken's Storytelling I elective culminated in a weeklong series of prayer services, where students shared the stories developed during her class.

HUC-JIR/LA estimates that seventy students worked directly with the four artists during the Artist in Residence Program to Enhance Jewish Education. These students participated in one-day workshops taught by the participating artists or learned alongside them in the classroom. In all cases, smaller groups of students had unique opportunities to work closely with an artist developing new works of art. Rabbi Bill Cutter, professor of Modern Hebrew Literature, articulated the goals of the program when he said to HUC-JIR students participating in a presentation by Peachy Levy: "You are teachers and preachers. You can use this tool [art] Ms. Levy presented to you today in the future when you want a different way to explore texts with congregants, Jewish professionals, and lay leaders."

Andrea Hodos is known for creating "movable torah," combining innovative choreography, contemporary dance, and spoken word as ways to explore Jewish themes. Hodos invited students (many of whom had no formal dance training) to join her in creating a new performance piece, which was performed at the College-Institute in the spring of 2007. Three rabbinical students joined Hodos by developing content, contributing to the choreography, and participating in the performance. One former student who worked closely with Andrea Hodos was Rabbi Miriam Terlinchamp (LA10). Prior to rabbinical school, Terlinchamp attended an art school focused on visual arts. Dancing with Hodos was the first time she explored movement or kinesthetic learning techniques in connection with Judaism. This experience encouraged her to begin integrating arts into her seminary experience. Ultimately, she produced an exhibition that was installed at the Los Angeles campus as part of her thesis. Terlinchamp commented, "The arts program at HUC-JIR/LA allowed me to unite my passion for art and passion for Judaism. The programs opened the door for me to bring art into my thesis work, art into the prayer space, and art into my teaching. Currently, I am a solo rabbi at Temple Sholom in Cincinnati, Ohio. My art hangs on the walls of my office, and my congregation enjoys the benefit of a rabbi who learned that art has a place in creating sacred Jewish prayer and learning."

Actor and director Stacie Chaiken offered a semester-long course exploring the power of personal narrative to create exegesis. Over fifteen students, many of whom had no formal theater training, were enrolled in her class to develop this skill for their future role as rabbis. Rabbi Ari Margolis (LA10) was empowered by this experience to create a wonderful series of stories about a lamb to impart Jewish teachings to children. Rabbi Rochelle Tulik (LA09) created a powerful and moving prayer exploring personal destiny titled "Reflection on *Mi Chamocha*." Tulik's story was shared with Jewish Women's Theater group in Los Angeles and ultimately was included in their production *Stories From the Fringe: Women Rabbis, Revealed!* Both Hodos and Chaiken were powerful examples of how the arts can enrich the core values and teachings of a seminary.

Many recently ordained rabbis who participated in the artist in residence experience have integrated arts programming into Jewish synagogues and other nonprofit Jewish settings. Rabbi Lindy Davidson (LA10) previously utilized creative techniques in many aspects of her life. Her first experience at HUC-JIR/LA was to obtain dual degrees for Jewish Nonprofit Management from HUC and Public Art Studies from the USC Roski School of Fine Arts in 2005. As a Spinner Avoda Fellow in Jewish Arts, Davidson was encouraged to use her arts background and training to enhance her Jewish professional experience. With this strengthened background Davidson then entered into the rabbinic program. During her seminary experience, she had the opportunity to work with all four artists in residence. These experiences allowed her to pull from a variety of artistic disciplines in her current work for Wilshire Boulevard Temple in Los Angeles. For example, her creative endeavors include teaching a text study for a group of local visual artists using movement-based techniques.

Feedback garnered from student surveys showed that many involved were positively affected. Students saw the program as beneficial and an enhancement to their learning experience. Forty-five percent of those surveyed said this was their first opportunity to work closely with an established Jewish artist, and 78 percent said they would enroll in another class with an artist in residence. For example, Rabbi Julia Weisz (LA11) danced with Hodos in front of peers and colleagues without ever having taken a dance class. Over 74 percent felt that the artist's involvement had a positive effect on their classroom experience. Over 63 percent also felt that being part of this experience would affect their future approach to their rabbinate, including an interest to encourage a multidisciplinary approach to liturgical study. The students described multiple lessons learned from this experience: how to interact with Jewish arts and artists; how to view art as a teaching tool for their work in formal and informal learning, both with small and broader audiences in the communities they will serve; and to recognize that the integration of art can create a lasting impact. Their responses were gratifying and reflected back to us a perception that they not only understood the goals of the artist in residence program, but that it had accomplished those goals.

The artist in residence project resulted in a resource manual, *Engaging Artists in Residence in Jewish Educational Institutions:*

Reflections Usable in Many Jewish Settings, which includes examples of the request for proposals form, artist contract, and lessons learned. We strongly believe that the model is worth simulating. *The Reflections Guide*[2] is available for other institutions in the hope that it will highlight how the arts and artists can deepen an educational experience in our seminaries.

After the conclusion of the Artist in Residence Program to Enhance Jewish Education in 2009, HUC-JIR/LA has maintained a strong commitment to arts on the campus, including mounting nine exhibitions featuring work by more than eighty artists. The Los Angeles campus has also tried to continue student engagement by offering workshops and interactive exhibitions. HUC-JIR/LA and the Enhancement Committee began to work with the Jewish Artists Initiative (JAI), an artist-run organization committed to fostering visual art by Jewish artists and promoting dialogue about Jewish identity and related issues among members of the arts community.

This partnership with JAI has resulted in five exhibitions and several program opportunities. For example, HUC-JIR/LA served as a resource as JAI developed their Artist *Beit Midrash* project, modeled in part on the Victor Raphael HUC-JIR/LA class experience. The JAI model convened a group of artists for monthly meetings. HUC-JIR/LA helped link JAI with faculty, rabbis, and students who taught *Beit Midrash* sessions. Each session was led by a different rabbi or rabbinic student whose interpretation, style, and vision was unique. The sessions were stimulating, challenging, and inspired meaningful conversation. The JAI members were encouraged to use the study sessions to stimulate the creation of new works of art, while the HUC students used text study as a way to inspire creative dialogue.

In the fall of 2011, HUC-JIR/LA mounted an exhibition curated by Georgia Freedman-Harvey on behalf of JAI in collaboration with the college's Enhancement Committee. The exhibition, *Jewish Ritual: Rethinking, Renewed,* explored how contemporary artists think about and interpret rituals today. The curator included a project, entitled *Exposed Mezuzah,* by rabbinical student Ilana Schachter (LA12), originally commissioned by the URJ for their office in Los Angeles, which explores the use of technology and alternative texts in mezuzahs. This piece is part of a larger project exploring how the mezuzah can remain relevant, meaningful, and inspiring to the liberal Jewish community. It utilizes two methods to accomplish this goal. First, the mezuzah scroll uses an alternative text, one that does not speak of one's commitment to halachah but instead emphasizes holy Jewish values of which the URJ wants people to be reminded as they walk through its doors. Second, the mezuzah scroll, along with the translation of the biblical text, can be accessed using a QR (quick response) code—a style of graphical barcode used to encode information that a smartphone user can scan to access information on the Internet. By exposing the text, Ilana hopes that people will engage more intensely with it. Rather than simply acknowledging the presence of a mezuzah when walking through a doorway, scanning the QR code will expose the message of the mezuzah. During the exhibition, Ilana was also able to participate in a workshop where she invited participants to discuss the alternative text and interact with the QR code. Ilana explained how participating in this exhibition and workshop helped her gain new insights into her project. "*Jewish Ritual: Rethinking, Renewed* challenged the lines between art and Judaica. Participants were able to see and participate in rituals as an artistic practice. It allowed for the creation, reengagement, and renewal of their commitment to our faith. There was deep value in being able to see participants engage with this project within an artistic context."

The increased role of the arts at HUC-JIR/LA demonstrates that the arts serve a vital role in engaging a variety of learners and functions also as an entry point for a Jewish journey. Through enhanced study with artists, our learning faculty and students discovered a new language for Jewish expression and understanding. They learned that the arts, like the texts of our Jewish tradition, present another form of midrashic language, a way to express oneself beyond the written word, and that religion and the arts shape the soul. Art on our campus reinforces the variety of ways one can engage, educate, and reach out to others. Our graduates become cultural ambassadors as they continue along their journey bringing art into their future congregations and educational and organizational settings.

Notes

1. Welcoming the guests, generally ancestral Patriarchs, Matriarchs, and prophets of the Bible, but contemporized to include personal ancestors and desired guests.
2. The *Reflections Guide* is available at: http://bit.ly/HUC-JIRArtistGuide.

Jewish Art and Artists in the Seminary Setting

Jean Bloch Rosensaft and Laura Kruger

From its very inception as a modern rabbinical seminary in the late nineteenth century, HUC-JIR recognized that Jewish material culture was an essential resource for the liberal study of Judaism and the professional training of clergy and scholars. Learning at this American seminary was predicated on the principle of *Wissenschaft des Judentums*, the nineteenth-century German approach to scholarship that stressed a scientific orientation to the study of Judaism. This approach applied objective scholarly methods to Jewish history and thought and provided the intellectual impetus for collection efforts. Indeed, the urge to collect, preserve, and study Jewish religious or ethnographic heritage was the result of the emancipation and enlightenment of nineteenth-century European Jewry and was transplanted to these American shores.

The development of library, art, and artifact collections were part and parcel of the earliest decades of the College-Institute's existence and intended as research resources for faculty and students. The Library was established in 1875 with the acquisition of books and artifacts. The College-Institute's Union Museum in Cincinnati was established by the National Federation of Temple Sisterhoods in 1913 as one of the first formally established Jewish museums in the United States.

By the 1920s, through the acquisition of several major private collections and donations by individuals, the College-Institute's museum and library collections comprised objects dating from the Renaissance to the current day: Jewish ceremonial objects, Jewish graphic art, tapestries, ceramics, carvings, illuminated manuscripts

---

JEAN BLOCH ROSENSAFT is director of the HUC-JIR Museum in New York and assistant vice president for Communications and Public Affairs at HUC-JIR.

LAURA KRUGER is curator of the HUC-JIR Museum in New York.

and Esther scrolls, and the Eduard Birnbaum collection of musical manuscripts, the largest collection of Jewish music predating 1850 in the world.

Adolph S. Oko, the preeminent librarian who shaped the College-Institute collections, asserted that these collections provided the "external proof" for an evaluation of Jewish culture as the development of the Jewish people in dynamic interaction with the host cultures in which they resided, contributed, and simultaneously created their own culture. "The whole panorama of Jewish cultural history is spread out before the student—the objects used by the Jew in his religious worship, his achievements as artist and craftsman, as musician and architect, writer and philosopher."[1]

From the 1940s to 1960s, under the aegis of Dr. Franz Landsberger and Dr. Joseph Gutmann, the Union Museum's priorities were collecting, research, scholarship, and publication, leading to Landsberger's 1946 landmark volume, *A History of Jewish Art*, the first comprehensive survey of Jewish art ever written in English. Jacob Rader Marcus established the American Jewish Archives in 1947 to preserve Jewish learning in the aftermath of the Holocaust, with over fifteen million documents and artifacts relating to the history of Jews in the Western Hemisphere collected to date.

Complementing these resources was the development of the College-Institute's significant role in biblical archaeology, under the aegis of the noted archaeologist, Dr. Nelson Glueck, who served as the president of the College-Institute from 1947 to 1971. Dr. Glueck and the Nelson Glueck School of Biblical Archaeology at our Jerusalem campus directed extensive exacations and research at Tel Gezer (1964–1974), Tel Dan (1974–present), Aroer, Gilat, Shiqmim, Ira in the Negev, Horvat Rosh Zayit, the synagogue at Yesud Hama'alah in the Upper Galilee, Tel Tillah, and at Anathoth near Jerusalem.

The fruits of all of these efforts can be seen today in the vitality of the College-Institute's cultural institutions, exhibitions, artists-in-residence, and ongoing acquisitions: the Skirball Museum in Cincinnati (huc.edu/museums/cn), Skirball Center for Biblical Archaeology and Research and Museum in Jerusalem (huc.edu/museums/jr), the HUC-JIR Museum in New York (huc.edu/museums/ny), the Jack H. Skirball/Los Angeles campus (huc.edu/museums/la), the network of libraries at our four campuses (huc.edu/libraries), and the collections and galleries of the Marcus Center of the American Jewish Archives in Cincinnati (huc.edu/aja).

These resources are integrated into the fabric of curriculum and training at our institution in a multiplicity of ways. The core rabbinical curriculum challenges rabbinical students to formulate and respond to essential questions of meaning that lead to an articulation of a clear vision for Jewish life: "How does Judaism provide meaning to human existence?" and "Is there meaning to Jewish history?" The arts offer an enriching, conceptual component for their educational journey. The concept of *hidur mitzvah* (the beautification of the fulfillment of the commandments) comes alive as they directly encounter exhibitions of contemporary Jewish ritual art and the power of aesthetics in nurturing spirituality. They begin to understand a special dimension of their role as future leaders one day, when they will have the opportunity to encourage the participation of contemporary artists in their future congregations and communities in order to enrich worship, cultural programming, and Jewish identity and sustain Jewish culture.

When Dr. Lawrence Hoffman's students explored the groundbreaking and ongoing exhibition *Living in the Moment: Contemporary Artists Celebrate Jewish Time* at the HUC-JIR Museum in New York, they encountered innovative works of Jewish ceremonial art by artists from North America, Europe, and Israel. Dr. Hoffman's teachings on the power of aesthetics to foster spiritual experience, based on his pioneering work with Synagogue 2000 and Synagogue 3000, were amplified by the students' exposure to Judaica inspired by the new celebrations and commemorations that have emerged in Judaism since the latter half of the twentieth century, ranging from the feminist Miriam's cup and *simchat bat* and Rosh Chodesh ceremonial objects to ritual objects designed to commemorate the Shoah. Students learned that objects that facilitate the Jewish year and life cycle need not be reproductions in the style of nineteenth-century Europe to be "authentic" and that contemporary spiritual practice could be enriched by objects reflecting the aesthetic of their own day. Among Dr. Hoffman's students, Rabbi Marion Lev Cohen acquired a tallit, crafted of delicate lace and appliqué by artist Reeva Shaffer for this exhibition, to nurture her own spiritual practice.

Our museums provide a true laboratory for learning for all of our students, in which innovative strategies for informal education of diverse generations can be experienced and explored. Exhibitions, catalogs, educational materials, and curatorial staff are resources for their development of new curriculum, the honing of professional skills and pedagogical strategies, and the integration of arts education in engendering critical thinking skills, deepening understanding of Jewish identity and history, and familiarizing students of all faiths with Jewish heritage.

The students in Dr. Wendy Zierler's course on Modern Jewish Literature held a session on *I.B. Singer and His Artists* at the HUC-JIR Museum. The Nobel Prize–winning author's novels and short stories came alive through illustrations by such leading artists as Maurice Sendak, Larry Rivers, Raphael Soyer, and photographer Roman Vishniac. As the students gleaned new understandings and interpretations of the written word through vivid imagery, they were introduced to strategies that they could one day implement in their future professional settings. In fact, a number of HUC-JIR alumni have hosted this traveling exhibition at their congregations, where learners of all generations have entered Singer's imagination through text and the visual arts.

Recently, leading educators enrolled in HUC-JIR's Leadership Institute (in partnership with the Jewish Theological Seminary and funded by UJA/Federation of New York) participated in a workshop on teaching Hebrew through the visual arts. Acknowledging the challenges they encountered in promoting the study and utilization of modern Hebrew among their multigenerational learners, they embraced the possibilities offered by contemporary French graphic artist Joelle Dautricourt's *The Book of Happy Writing*. Fifty directors of congregational schools from throughout the greater New York region immersed themselves in the pedagogical possibilities presented by this exhibition of computer-generated prints, in which the artist explores the spiritual and mystical power of the twenty-two letters of the Hebrew alphabet. Their analysis of the overt and hidden meanings to be found within the artist's manipulation of Hebrew and Yiddish fonts led to *chevruta* study of prints from the portfolio, followed by presentations by each study group of the many ways in which they could use this exhibition to implement within their own schools and communities a broad range of creative, experiential learning experiences based on Hebrew letters.

Graduate students pursuing doctorates and master's degrees have unlimited access to our collections and unique, hands-on encounters with Jewish material culture that bring their scholarly research to life. Education students are encouraged to participate in our museum docent program, and some have prepared for professional careers as educators in Jewish museums. Jewish nonprofit management students fulfilling a dual Masters of Public Arts degree with the University of Southern California have helped shaped the arts offerings on campus and gone on to careers as independent curators and arts administrators. Cantorial students' recitals and senior theses are enriched by researching the unique and rare vocal scores in the Birnbaum Collection's treasures, connecting contemporary Jewish expressions in music and art, and engaging with visiting composers-in-residence. At a time when visual communication is preeminent in our society, these future rabbis, cantors, educators, nonprofit professionals, and scholars are prepared to take advantage of new ways in which to teach through the inclusion of the arts.

The students enjoy museum experiences that offer successful models for engaging the Jewish community and reaching out to unaffiliated Jews to encourage a connection to their Jewish faith and heritage. As they prepare for careers in synagogues, Jewish community centers, Federations, and communal agencies, our students are sensitized to the importance of the arts as an expression of contemporary Jewish creativity and a potent force in attracting younger generations.

During their studies at our campuses in Cincinnati, Jerusalem, Los Angeles, and New York, students encounter core and elective courses in which the visual arts play a meaningful role. For our first-year students in the Year-in-Israel Program, their discoveries at the Skirball Museum of Biblical Archaeology, at archaeological excavations, and at leading cultural institutions introduce them to the millennial scope of Jewish history and peoplehood. A yearlong history survey course taught by Dr. Carole Balin and Dr. Jonathan Krasner in New York culminates in a visit to the Metropolitan Museum, where students learn how a secular art and history museum in any city can serve as a potent context for teaching about Jewish identity and experience to others. Dr. Nili Fox's Bible students have a hands-on experience with antiquities at the Skirball Museum and Archaeology Center in Cincinnati or a visit to the Cincinnati Art Museum to view President Nelson Glueck's collection of Nabatean artifacts that places their studies in context, while Dr. Andrea Weiss's Bible students explored *Archetype/Anonymous: Biblical Women in Contemporary Art*, where artists applied feminist interpretations to challenge the stereotypes and androcentric nature of biblical record. Students in Dr. Eugene Borowitz's Reel Theology course, which integrated contemporary film into the study of Jewish religious thought, learned how to apply contemporary popular culture to the study of the ethical and moral issues of our time.

Team-taught electives in Jewish art, music, and literature offer an integrated understanding of Jewish cultural expression. Faculty teaching classes in Bible, midrash, Jewish literature, or history incorporate tours of related exhibitions. Contemporary artists exhibiting their work on campus are invited to meet with students and speak about their process in creating innovative works of ritual art or their approach to art as a form of visual midrash.

Beyond the designated museum spaces, art is deployed in lobbies, classrooms, meeting areas, and public venues throughout our campuses. Their omnipresence has wide-ranging impact. From the first moment one enters our buildings, the unexpected encounter with contemporary art serves to "brand" the Jewish identity of the campus environment and signals the creativity, innovation, and contemporary and progressive values that Reform Judaism upholds in addressing the needs of the changing Jewish community. The aesthetic beauty around you transports you from the mundane world outside of our seminary to an environment conducive to worship, study, and reflection. Art accompanies you to your studies in the classroom, to the synagogue for worship, or to your meeting in a conference room, and readies you for your purpose in being on campus. Our students assimilate this aesthetic context as part of their everyday experience, while their classes with museum professionals and faculty focus their attention on the spiritual, cultural, and educational opportunities offered by the arts that are modeled for them on campus and challenge them to one day enrich the aesthetic properties of their future professional venues.

The College-Institute's initial mission of collection, preservation, research, and publication, with an emphasis on serving faculty and students, has expanded over the past five decades to welcome the larger public. By offering educational and cultural enrichment to visitors of all backgrounds, our museums play an ever more important role in advancing knowledge, celebrating heritage, and promoting human understanding. As informal environments for teaching and learning, these collections and exhibitions provide a window into Jewish life, history, culture, civilization, and values and provide an infinite range of learning possibilities for students, scholars, and the public that encourage Jewish spiritual and cultural continuity as well as promote interfaith relations.

The greater Cincinnati region is welcomed by a core exhibition focusing on biblical antiquity, Torah and Jewish ritual, and the establishment of Reform Judaism in America. The artist-in-residence program in Los Angeles draws visitors downtown to the campus. In New York, groups tour significant exhibitions that have illuminated the Jewish values intrinsic to the aging process (*The Art of Aging*), broken the silence on family violence in the Jewish community (*Rage/Resolution*), explored contemporary artistic conceptions of borders and boundaries (*Envisioning Maps*), celebrated the creativity and Jewish subject matter of a pioneering feminist artist (*Judy Chicago: Jewish Identity*), or cast a Jewish lens on the use of textiles (*A Stitch in Jewish Time: Provocative Textiles*).

Currently, *The Sexuality Spectrum* at the HUC-JIR Museum in New York offers a groundbreaking exploration of sexual orientation through the creativity of over fifty contemporary artists. This exhibition explores a broad range of subjects, including the evolving social and religious attitudes toward sexuality; issues of alienation, marginalization, and inclusion; the impact on the family, child-rearing, and life stages; violence and persecution; AIDS/HIV; and the influence of the LGBTQI community on the Jewish and larger world. This collaborative project involves the guidance of HUC-JIR's Institute for Judaism and Sexual Orientation and the Blaustein Center for Pastoral Counseling. HUC-JIR's faculty and students have contributed essays reflective of their academic disciplines for the catalog, are integrating the exhibition into their teaching and research, and Dr. Nancy Wiener is incorporating the show into her professional development programs in the area of pastoral care. This exhibition exemplifies the spirit of the College-Institute's and the Reform Movement's shared commitment to free and open inquiry, inclusivity and outreach, and advocacy on behalf of human rights and the eradication of sexual discrimination.

Throughout their experiences with art and artists at the College-Institute, our students learn that we will be a continuing resource to them when they go out into their professional careers. We will provide ongoing guidance for their synagogue museums, advise them on Jewish artists and architects for their community's special commissions, and provide traveling exhibitions, generated by our HUC-JIR Museum (huc.edu/museums/ny/traveling_exhibitions.php), for their galleries, Jewish community centers, university art galleries, Hillel Jewish student centers, and local Jewish museums.

The art presented on our campuses is not intended for veneration —it is not art for art's sake alone. Nor are the artifacts of Judaism "mummified in cases, bereft of their original, authentic purpose," as eminent historian Dr. Arthur Hertzberg cautioned Jewish museum directors and curators at the Council of American Jewish Museums conference in New York in 1997. Our exhibitions and permanent collections are intended to promote Jewish practice and continuity, advance understanding of Jewish history and culture, demonstrate Judaism's relationship to the societies in which we dwell, and instill Jewish values of remembrance, tolerance, and social justice. By integrating art and artists in our seminary setting, we are providing an essential forum for contemporary artists expressing Jewish spirituality, experience, and identity, enabling students and visitors to apply the meaning of Jewish heritage to their lives, and fostering partnerships with others in extending multiethnic understanding.

In conclusion, visual midrash in the seminary setting enriches the education of future Jewish leaders, informs their integration of visual material culture together with text in the transmission of Jewish identity and memory, and sensitizes them to the values and opportunities for implementation of *hidur mitzvah* in their future professional settings. It inspires them to engage the participation, support, and creativity of contemporary artists in their communities and ultimately contributes to the vitalization of Jewish culture for future generations.

Note

1. Adolph S. Oko, "Jewish Book Collections in the United States," in *The American Jewish Year Book 5704*, ed. Harry Schneiderman (Philadelphia: The Jewish Publication Society of America, 1943), 84.

Faith in Irony: Judaica Today

Daniel Belasco

The field of contemporary Judaica is dynamic and ever-changing. In the twenty-first century, ritual objects have become opportunities for connection and discovery. Several talented artists are pushing the contemporary design interest in process to the extreme, testing the very notion of religious ritual as a renewable resource. While the older generation of modernists and postmodernists gravitate to the most familiar and central symbols and forms in Jewish ritual (yes, even Jewish feminism has its canon), younger artists prefer lesser-known types of Judaica, narratives, and symbols. They share a need to reinvent the traditions, but from a position of personal discovery and formal irony. In a notable evolution, their approaches to Jewish ritual objects are more closely related to jewelry than hollowware, drawing upon new ideas about the social construction of the body and the relationship between objects and identity.

Contemporary Judaica is defined more by process than aesthetic or media. This article surveys five key methods used by artists and designers in the creation of contemporary Judaica. These methods are: chance operations, mash-up, hybridization, repurposing, and inversion. They represent an international approach to ritual today that is evident in Europe, Israel, and the Americas. The subtle transformations that occur within these processes of reinventing Judaica harbor creativity and connect ancient ritual to contemporary life in a way that is often fresh and unexpected.

DANIEL BELASCO's books include the exhibition catalog *Reinventing Ritual: Contemporary Art and Design for Jewish Life* (2009) and *500 Judaica: Innovative Contemporary Ritual Art* (2010). He teaches Contemporary Art at the Jewish Theological Seminary and holds a Ph.D. and MA in the History of Art from the Institute of Fine Arts, New York University. This article is adapted from previous articles that appeared in *Metalsmith* v. 31 n. 2 (Summer 2011) and *Bezalel Proceedings of History & Theory* 16 (April 2010).

Chance Operations

A number of artists making avant-garde Judaica rely on chance and randomness. Uncertainty is a way for artists to achieve critical distance to turn a ritual object into conceptual art. Good examples of the use of chance are the seder plates by Israeli designers Johnathan Hopp and Sarah Auslander. The plates are made from random dinner plates found in the flea market in Jaffa, where Hopp currently maintains a studio. The assorted plates possess varied abstract, vegetal, and other patterns. Hopp and Auslander baked a decal image of a traditional seder plate directly onto each plate. The artists never knew what the result would look like when they withdrew the piece from the kiln.

Several transformations occur in these plates. First, the decal overlaps the original pattern on the plate. Sometimes the decorations blend unpredictably well, and other times the contrast is jarring. The colors and glaze of the plates also may change in the refiring. Overall, the high degree of chance and uncertainty that the process brings is satisfying for a sensibility that prefers open systems. It's as if John Cage were to make a ritual object. I also like the punk quality of the decal, which rudely asserts itself against the domestic order of the original plate. Surprisingly, the refiring serves a traditional ritual function as well. Baking at such high temperatures "koshers" the plate for Passover, burning off impurities and any trace of bread or other *chameitz*.

Mash-up

The look of objects produced through the process of chance can be compared to the mash-up, a term popularized in recent years to refer to the overlaying and unexpected harmonizing of different voice and sound tracks in music (Danger Mouse's mash-up of Jay-Z and the Beatles might be the most famous example). Collage and montage have been a part of modernism from the beginning. But what makes the technique of mash-up novel is that it requires the artist to get into the structure of systems in order to see where part of one can be logically grafted to part of another. Mash-up requires both a high degree of craftsmanship and sophistication. There is a fundamental irony to the process—the surprise of radical juxtaposition—but the visual satisfaction comes not from dissonance but from synchronization.

In postmodernism, juxtaposition was used to upset the viewer. In post-postmodernist mash-ups, juxtaposition sooths and assures the viewer that meaning can be created out of the vast complexity of the universe.

The term is not often applied to the visual arts, especially Judaica. Yet the mash-up has become an important graphical strategy employed by a variety of artists interested in fusing Jewish ritual and everyday life to create new hybrid forms. The method is simple: Take a Jewish symbol or image and infuse with secular content. The maneuver sheds light on the assumptions that underpin two or more systems of thought. A good example of this is British artist Suzanne Treister's *Alchemy* series. Taking alchemical symbols, including the kabbalistic tree of life, Treister maps across them the headlines and thumbnail images from the newspaper she was reading that day, blurring distinctions between high and low, mundane and catastrophic, such as in her piece *The Independent, 28 June, 2007*. The mash-up can be enacted the other way too. Artists map Jewish ideas and images to a secular organizational structure. Israeli graphic designer Dov Abramson's print *Shoah: A Table of Elements* carefully calibrates the relative significance and groupings of Holocaust memory by precisely locating its elements within the periodic table (page 123).

Hybridization

The American silversmith Anika Smulovitz works in the hybrid aesthetic of today, whereby artists approach creative problems through functional analysis that results in a crossbred work. She perceives the Torah pointer—the stylus-like implement held by the reader to follow the text without touching the sacred parchment—as full of possibility. At once, the beautifully crafted yads are sleek, minimalist, tapered silver tubes of a lovely size and weight that perfectly serve the function of a traditional Torah pointer in respecting the holiness of the scroll by avoiding directly contact with bare hands. Yet, in addition, each of the pointers possesses a scientific instrument. One yad has a small magnifying glass at the tip that points to the text. The other yad has a compass embedded in the other end. A third has a wheel representing the nomadic history of the Jews (page 122). These empirical tools represent the critical historian wishing to deconstruct or otherwise navigate deeper into the text.

Smulovitz researched critical debates in Judaism, which she wanted to represent in the typological language of ritual objects. Smulovitz was interested in the historical arguments over who wrote the Torah. Scholars have gathered textual evidence of multiple authors of the holy book. Such a stance directly challenges the point of view that the Torah, every word, was handed directly down from God to Moses to the Jewish people. Smulovitz, in her *yads*, has reinvented a ritual object that accommodates both sides of the debate. These works possess a strong conceptual and critical content laced with irony, yet at the same time are beautifully crafted functional objects that play by the traditional rules. These pieces are polylingual, speaking in multiple artistic voices. There is a yearning among American Jewish artists who have visceral memories and experiences of Jewish ritual, but no deep understanding of them, to create experiential ritual objects.

Repurposing

To repurpose one type of Jewish ritual object for another Jewish use is an ongoing practice through the centuries. People turned wedding dresses into Torah curtains and Torah shields into Chanukah lamp backs. Today we are witnessing an efflorescence of this tendency to remix sacred materials. In the last few years artists have reused candlesticks, which normally come in pairs, as the units of seven- and nine-branch menorahs.

A variation on the theme occurs in the *Mixalabra,* a cast silver Chanukah menorah recently produced by Umbra in their U+ line of higher-end design. It was on view front and center in Umbra's booth at the International Contemporary Furniture Fair in New York City in 2009. Modified casts of nine mismatched candlesticks are arranged in a circle on a tray. A tall stick at the center serves as the *shamash.* The entire work is in brightly polished silver, and comes off a little blingy for my taste. The Canadian designer, Matt Carr, said the owners of Umbra felt there was a lack of well-designed Judaica on the market and charged their designers to come up with something, and so Carr gathered a collection of random candlesticks from a thrift store near the Umbra HQ in Toronto for inspiration. With its source materials cast and reworked, the piece does not initially read menorah, but certainly is a bold take on the traditional form, especially for a mainstream company that I associate more with soap dispensers than Jewish ceremonial objects (though hand washing certainly is a key ritual in its own right). Overall, something was lost in translation. Maybe it's the homogenization of the diverse candlesticks into a single material.

In a similar vein, the Israeli designers Reddish Studio reclaimed orphaned candlesticks in various homes and flea markets and assembled them into a single seven-branch menorah. The sticks seem to float in the air, suspended from their tops by a metal frame. The candlesticks are presented as found objects, so their diverse ages and styles talk to each other. Because the ancient seven-branch menorah is largely symbolic and not used in any popular domestic ceremony like its offspring the Chanukah lamp, Reddish Studio's piece reads as more sculpture than functional object, although the holes of the sticks remain open and could hold candles. This menorah is an elegant statement of the nature of a Jewish community as a collection of different people brought together and given form through the continual repurposing of ritual.

Inversion

Central in the contemporary process of creating Judaica is the rethinking of the relationship between the decorative and the functional. The core idea in postmodernism was to invest the decorative and its objects, once dismissed as useless and meaningless, with value and purpose. What's interesting about the current trend is that a number of contemporary Israeli designers take the decorative a step further and invert the roles of the functional and nonfunctional, the object and the ornament. Recent works have been inspired by the tablecloths and lace doilies that were part of the interior decoration of Israeli households once aspiring to import Old World sensibility into postwar concrete apartments. In Israel today, perhaps aware of the achievement of commercial abundance, industrial designers are reimagining the material culture of past as ritual objects for the present, so that a soft, delicate material can become a rigid and structurally sound form capable of performing the rituals.

Sahar Batsry's *Volcano* (2007) turns the idea of a tablecloth into a soft seder plate. A white molded silicone disk serves as a "plate" supporting six etched glass dishes. The elastic properties hold in place the embedded dishes, which when used contain the symbolic foods discussed in the Haggadah. Small perforations around the plate's perimeter recall the source inspiration in lace. The piece is flexible, so it requires a flat surface to be fully functional as a plate. Thus the piece metaphorically transforms the entire table into a plate by blurring the distinctions between object and furniture. *Volcano* rethinks the tripartite relationship among furniture, cover, and object: no longer a three-element combination, but all fused into one elegant object.

Talilia Abraham, also a designer in Israel, created a finely worked pierced metal that mimics lace. This type of unexpected hybrid of the hard and the soft can be found in a lot of jewelry and tabletop objects these days. But Abraham's workshop hand etches the pieces to get an added delicacy, while most other examples in international design rely on laser cutting. Abraham, as part of her large line of baskets and containers, created a basket to hold matzah during the Passover seder. The piece, called *Dantela* after the type of heirloom lace that inspired it, directly endows the decorative look of lace with a new purpose. Thus the "lower" valued decorative item is "elevated" to status of ritual object to frame unleavened bread, eaten during Passover to recall liberation from slavery in Egypt. The feminist politics resolve clearly in this piece. Abraham reinvests an anonymous craft practiced by women for centuries. While these handicrafts are now largely industrialized, Abraham revives their patterns as tribute to the women of the past and as a strong statement of her presence and autonomy. *Dantela* is a feminist ritual object par excellence, literally bringing the history of women's creativity to the Passover table.

Conclusion

The radicalism of contemporary processes of Judaica emerges from an estrangement from the origins of ritual, which the artist seeks to overcome through formalized methods and techniques that embrace the vagaries and transformations of daily life. Artists take an existing ritual object and want to update it, transform it, and make it contemporary. The art historical parallel is perhaps neo-Dada. Rituals and ritual objects and materials themselves are treated as manipulatable found objects. In the words of Jasper Johns, "You do something, then do something again." Formal invention results from the dedication to experimental process.

The cutting-edge work, especially seen in younger artists born in the 1970s and 1980s, combines the best of postmodernism (diversity and history) and modernism (clarity and significant form). They are sophisticated works that simultaneously enhance and question ritual. Judaica has almost always expressed its hybrid style as sourced in local culture and Jewish traditions. The urge today is to blend and morph specifically Jewish symbols and rituals with pop culture, science, food, fashion, architecture, and commercial imagery and materials. Contemporary artists have seized upon the inherent diversity and pluralism of Jewish culture, using formal wit to negotiate differences. Perhaps the best means of expressing a post-ethnic Jewish identity in ritual objects is to pinpoint intercultural and open-ended qualities with new forms and materials.

*Deuteronomy/*D'varim: *Moving Forward Creatively*

On the Path to Jewish Universalism: Art and Literature in Modern Hebrew Culture

William Cutter

Don't try by measures or weights
To capture this grandiose state:
With his razor the barber, all lather and foam,
Can never be captured in essay or poem.

Natan Alterman, a rendering by William Cutter
Shirim al Re-utha Ruach (Nonsense Poems)

I. Introduction: Visual, Tactile, Verbal—A Look at a Zionist Aesthetic

Each year I hold one session of a poetry seminar in the home of the Levy family, prominent philanthropists and collectors of Jewish ritual objects. Of course we enjoy the morning near the beach, a light meal, and the words of these generous collectors as to why and how they gather physical objects and material cultural artifacts into their gorgeous glass cases. Then, in the presence of countless *Havdalah* sets, seder plates, and *Kiddush* cups—finials and mantles, silver treasures that tell the story of a hundred lost communities—we read Yehuda Amichai's deceptive little segment from "*Patuach Sagur Patuach*" (the translation of Chana Bloch and Chana Kronfeld):

RABBI WILLIAM CUTTER, Ph.D. (C65) has just completed forty-seven years of teaching at HUC-JIR, where much of his scholarship has concentrated on aesthetics and education. He was also founding director of the Rhea Hirsch School of Education, the Kalsman Institute on Judaism and Health, and cofounder, with Nancy Berman, of the HUC Museum Education Project (MUSE).

The original Hebrew versions of the poems by Lea Goldberg, Tuvia Ruebner, Uzi Shavit, and Asher Reich are taken from Professor Holtzman's book *Melechet Machshevet*.

A collection of ritual objects in the museum: spice boxes
With little flags on top like festive troops
And many fragrant generations of sacrifice,
And the memory of many Sabbath exits that did not exit in death.
["the night of death" to capture the play on words—*motzaei Shabbat/motzaei mavet*]
And happy menorahs and weepy menorahs and oil lamps
With the beaks of chicks pouting like children singing,
Their mouths wide open in desire and love.
And long metal hands to point out everything
That is no more.The human hands that held them—
Long since underground, severed from the bodies.
Seder plates that rotate at the speed of time,
so it seems they are standing still, and Kiddush cups
in a row on the shelf like soccer trophies
Or victory cups from the track and field of generations.[1]

And so my students learn that what is important in Jewish culture is not limited to the words of the Rabbis or the commentators or the respondents or even the sociologists of the twenty-first century. Jews found value in their objects, if they could afford them, and Jewish writers have found ways to prove with a thousand words what objects and pictures mean to them. Objects and pictures are another form of commentary, and a stimulus to further commentary.[2]

But the present essay is about the conjunction of the verbal and the visual within one work, and the meaning that the conjunction has for Jewish aesthetics, and particularly for the success of the Zionist and/or Hebrew imagination. Sociologist Graciella Trachtenberg has written extensively about art and nationalism, tracing the significance of Jewish engagement in graphic or plastic arts and connecting developments in those fields to what many of us call "The Zionist Project"—a project that has included world-changing developments in language, definitions of sovereignty, and relations between the tiny country in the Middle East and its Western models.

II. The Centrality of the Written Word—
Are There Prohibitions Against Depiction?

As we know, religious themes served as the primary inspiration for much of the early visual art in medieval Europe. The

Christian motives of that art cooperated with the Jewish resistance to visual representation, because of which Jews had not been very much in the arts game. But times have changed, and they had even changed to an extent before modernity challenged the rules about such things, even before Spinoza opened the door to a Jewish secularity. Early motives of art as elevation and spiritual uplift have intensified in our more secular times when new ideas and new forms created new arts and new attitudes. In any event, "elevation" has come to mean something different from pure religious inspiration, and in secular Judaism's modernity, critics and the public continue to debate whether "art" should include some kind of social obligation along with its purely aesthetic—or formalistic—elements. One might think of the classical template for the value of art as being aesthetics combined with utility (*dulce et utile*).[3]

But in spite of our exposure to new art forms, Jewish writing has remained the form with which most of us (rabbis especially) have become familiar. We are people of books, to be sure—and The Book behind all those books prompted centuries of caution about the dangers of visual representation. New understandings by creative scholars like Kalman Bland and Richard Cohen[4](and others) as well as Trachtenberg have forced us to reexamine the old prohibitions, or even the influence of those prohibitions, on Jewish societies. The coming together of the written word and the fashioned image is a merger of modern motives that is addressed in one of aesthetic criticism's more awkward words: "Ekphrasis," defined elegantly by W. J. T. Mitchell as "a verbal representation of a visual representation."[5]Avner Holtzman's book *Melechet Machshevet* (*Fine Arts*) is the most comprehensive examination of this aesthetic phenomenon for Jews, and my work here would have been impossible without his important book, and without my lengthy conversations with him. Prof. Holtzman has catalogued over seventy poems in which graphics are the theme—ranging from Dan Pagis's meditations on the Louvre as location, to poets reflecting on famous works of art like the *Mona Lisa* or Rembrandt's biblical representations.[6]

Poets new and old have been drawn into the iconography of the great art of the world, and from a variety of launching pads: residence in Europe, attendance at art academies, rebellious attachments to Christian imagery, and more.

III. Icons and the Verbal Icon

The prominent literary critic William Wimsatt provided the phrase that helped form the bridge for my essay:"The Verbal Icon," in his book of that name, written in 1956.[7] Jews the world over have contributed mountains of verbal iconography, and—since entering the academies—a great deal of language about visual iconography as well. And Israelis—the current bearers of the Hebrew cultural tradition—exhibit a particularly intriguing version of this blending. Since Israeli intellectuals come out of a writing tradition in the first place, and since they are empowered by a world of travel and a certain amount of cabin fever, it is no surprise that modern Israeli poets have thought and written much about the visual arts in their lives. And we sometimes forget that older generations of Hebrew writers began their careers in various European centers where art museums were a prominent part of cultural life, and several of these writers also tried their hands as painters.[8]Avner Holtzman, has argued:"Hebrew literature has been an exceptionally powerful intermediary in the adoption of a visual art culture into the general Hebrew culture."[9]And it began early, as we shall see.

Jewish "national sovereignty" has managed to take a place in the increasingly global world of arts and letters, of business and finance, of transportation and power politics. The Israeli cultural world is rich in theatre and museums, and one can spend weeks in Israel going from formal theatre to improvisational settings, from important museums to Gordon Street's galleries, and wonder at the simultaneous Jewish character of Israeli cultural life and its liberation from that Jewish character. Can whatever Jewish qualities we find in the art be due to the centrality of language in the life of Israelis? Can commentators like David Hazony[10] and Leon Wieseltier be right that it is the Hebrew language that is the great anchor to the Jewish past, and the cement for the various branches of the Jewish polity?[11] If so, then writing about the art experience might be considered a natural outcome of this shift that is so unique to Jewish modernity. Collecting art is already a major Jewish pastime among the wealthy, and while much of the big league collecting by Jews is of general world-class art, some have specialized in Israeli painters and sculptors, and it hasn't seemed to hurt the prestige of Jewish collectors if—as part of their passion—they include pictures by Pascin and Modigliani or Soutine, and important Israeli artists like Gabi Klezmer, Reuven Rubin, Moshe Gershuni, Ana Ticho, and Pinchas Cohen-Gan. But Jewish reference is no longer the main thing for serious connoisseurs, and more purely formal matters have finally become part of our treatment of Jewish culture.

My Spirit Is Too Weak—Keats and Mortality

For John Keats and others of that romantic age, the reference to a previous work of literature or sculpture was part of a commitment to what we might call "The Classic"—whose existence remains for those romantics an appreciation of a glory age and a touchstone that has its own virtue. Hence Keats writes of "Sitting Down to Read King Lear Once Again"; he composes an ode to Homer, "Ode on a Grecian Urn," and other constantly suggestive references to old and ripening images of the culture. Keats could more or less count on the fact that his readers knew the classic objects of his gaze and rumination that resulted in vigorous intertextuality.

That classic reference to a cultural familiarity is to some extent like the frequency with which modern Israeli poetry utilizes the *Tanach* for a variety of its ruminations on politics, national identity, and personal struggle.[12] The *Tanach* operates in much modern Israeli literature and in a variety of modalities that manipulate our concepts of *mashal* and *nimshal*. The love of *mashal-nimshal* dialectic along biblical lines had an early progenitor in Tschernichovski's affection for King Saul, in whose rebellion the poet saw a vigor that was missing from the Jewish people in his surround. The play has continued up to the present day, and with different motives, in the poetry of almost every modern Hebrew poet.

IV. Hebrew Poetry's Archetypal Homage to the Classic Statue

The most famous Hebrew poem by Tschernichovski was stimulated by the contemplation of a statue: "In the Presence of Apollo" (1892) (*LeNochach HaPesel Apollo*—some would suggest an "oppositional stance" is embedded in the preposition). Tschernichovski wrote a few poems of reflection on non-Jewish classics and found newness in an attachment to someone else's old past—an image that stands iconically for an idea that is the actual subject of the poem. In the instance of Apollo, his poetry was less about the object itself and more about the object as a counter-symbol of modern Jewish longing. "We once had a God like you, but since that time,the Jewish people has become old and weak, and must break the shackles of its illness" (my paraphrase).Professor Holtzman, by the way, alludes to the title of Tschernichovski's poem in the subtitle of his book, *Hebrew Literature in the Presence of the Plastic Arts*, a clever use of the phrase with just a hint of acknowledgment that the whole arts enterprise has a touch of the rebellious and even idolatrous—at least for some communities.

Excerpts from "In the Presence of Apollo":

I have come to you, forgotten God of an ancient world,
A God of primal moons and other days,
Who ruled the potent streams of exuberant creatures,
The waves of their power and the surfeit of youth!
A god of mighty generations when giants were in the land,
Who conquered with his might the very boundaries of those who dwelt on high
. . .
Here I am the first of those who have returned to you
A moment in which I feared the dying of generations,
The season in which I would break the chains of my soul
My living soul, that clings to the earth.
The people has become old—and its God has aged with it!
. . .
And so I come to you.
I have come unto you, and I bow before your statue,
Your statue—the very symbol of the light in life;
I bow and kneel to all that is good and lofty,
To that which is lifted up in the fullness of the universe
To that which is marvelous in all of Creation,
To that which is elevated in the secret places of Creation,
I bow to life, to power and to beauty,
And I bow to all the pleasured weave, that the corpses of man
Have despoiled with their rotting seed,
Those rebels of life from the hand of the almighty and the rock
The God of the Gods of wondrous deserts,
The God of the Gods who conquered Canaan in a storm
But whom they have bound in straps of *t'fillin*.

William Cutter, unofficial translation

Staying with the ironic suggestion that there is idolatry in the activity of gazing on a Greek statue at all, one must note that the "bowing" of the young Jewish man takes place in the presence of a God, and in the presence of the representation of the God: two for the price of one. Not only do we violate the commandment against representation, but we seek out some other nation's representation and then we bow to it! Plato's cave never had such interesting dwellers!

So one could say that here Apollo serves only as a foil for the fantasy idea that the God of the Hebrews was once a vigorous God; after all in the *Tanach* God has the properties of vigorous youth and anger and conqueror, and as the people aged, God aged into a God of laws and a kind of impotent organizer of halachic behavior who has "lost his voice" (as in *"ein shom'in levatkol"*)—which for many Enlightenment intellectuals prompted another kind of impotence. For Tschernichovski the Hebrew God is a reflection of the Hebrew people, and—as was the case with so many of the early Zionists—God became irrelevant when He became the God of the Jews instead of a god of the Hebrews.

Tschernichovski's God-Apollo ought to stand for the contrast to what we've got—perhaps even as an offshoot of Nietzsche's trope that God is dead. The simplicity of that notion was a powerful message to the young intellectuals of the late nineteenth century and early twentieth century. It is not too much of a stretch to move from a reclaimed powerful god-image to a reclaimed image of Zionism's "renewed man."

As revolutionary as was Tschernichovski's poem, the Jews of the Enlightenment were no strangers to art museums or to the statues that were established in the capital cities of Europe. Late *maskilim* like Reuven Asher Breinin, Mordechai Ehrenpreis, and Micah Yosef Berdyczewski were known to visit museums and comment on the art—surely in their eagerness to be a part of world culture. While most of the attention of the intelligentsia was devoted to writing and to creating new texts of Jewish thought or belles lettres, the plastic arts played a significant role in the lives of those Jews who traveled. And so intellectuals like Berdyczewski and Yitzhak Isaac Lubetski or Lubetski's cousin Reuven Asher Breinin wrote of the art they visited in museums—and were especially vigorous in their discussion of the Impressionists. Some of the early writers tried their hand at the plastic arts as well. The visual arts were beginning to redefine the modern Jew, along with the more extensive literary efforts that are better known to us. For the longest time critics debated the value of the visual arts and sought within those arts statements of moral or social weight, questioning from time to time an art they obviously loved: the Impressionism of the late nineteenth and early twentieth century that seemed to some of them to be too devoted to the principles of beauty without the weighty subjects that would justify their importance in the world. (See below Holtzman's discussion of Asher Reich's poem on Cezanne.)

The struggle between a purer aesthetics and an aesthetics with social message or moral meanings seems, with time's perspective, to be an indicator that the Jewish intelligentsia was not immediately comfortable with the new place of "art for art's sake," and one can see traces of the concern with this issue in numerous essays and intellectual debates at the end of the nineteenth century. Decadence, for example, often hovered as a threat to the moral posture that some critics felt ought to be part and parcel of the new art. Liberation, yes; but not an absolute liberation from the moral imperative.[13] But time marches on, and in the last two or three generations, Israeli criticism has produced an extraordinary and sophisticated critical intelligence. Young Israeli scholars have traveled widely, served as faculty in American universities, taught as visiting professors at Oxford and Cambridge, served as research assistants to the likes of George Steiner, purchased condominiums in New York City—have, in fact, joined the cultural elite of the Western world at every level. In a sneaky backdrop scene in the Israeli popular film *Footnote*, an Israeli consultant is overheard on his cell phone telling a friend about his coming trip to New York: *"Ba'Pierre, kamuvan, aheret Zilah lo hay-etah no-saat iti."* (Of course we're staying at the Pierre; otherwise Zilah wouldn't be willing to join me. This was a nasty insider joke from the director, Joseph Cedar.)

V. The Surprise of Christian Iconography, and Natan Zach's Complicity

As I suggested earlier in this essay, one cannot talk about the history of art in the West without connecting the themes of that art to the religion that dominated European life and thought. If you studied art in an American university, you learned all the rules of composition, of color and even of theme, through the eyes of Christian painters and their efforts to represent the early scenes of

Christianity. It is sometimes surprising to us moderns to find that many modern Jewish poets have somehow found subjects in the great art of Christian representation. I cite at first two interesting examples, the first is by Lea Goldberg, one of the leaders of both poetry and criticsm between 1936 and 1971 when she died, and known to most Americans through important translations found in song and the *Reform Jewish Siddur*, especially *"Lamdeni Elohai"* ("Teach me, O God"). [I introduce Malka Shaked, a less well-known poet, to be sure, but a woman with a profound relationship to the Jerusalem environment, which is saturated with Christian history and reference.[14]]

Lea Goldberg's *Halom Na-arah* (A Girl's Dream)
(referencing Saint Mary Magdalene, by Carlo Crivelli, the Kaiser Friedrich Museum in Berlin)

I dreamed that I—am you,
And that Crivelli's Magdalene serves me a boiling beverage, pure
In a diamond goblet with golden surface
And her curl—a delicate curled snake
As she passes by, touching my cheek,
And my body is drunk with the fragrance of Tuberosa [Lilies].
I dreamed that I—am you.
And the face of a pale woman
Is erased forever from my memory
And I thirst for Magdalene.

And I could not escape the terror of the dream
And there was no escape from Mary Magdalene.
William Cutter, unofficial translation

Numerous poems by contemporary Israelis reflect their visits to museums, their understanding of the place of early Christian symbolism within the intellectual life of the West. Natan Zach, among contemporaries, has been fascinated with the themes of Christian imagery and ideas of word become flesh.[15] No surprise this, in one sense, because the "normalization" that Zionism sought included almost every phase of life. In the Goldberg poem, the application of the religious themes of the painting to the personal status of the individual poet is an equally telling aspect of the poet's response to the visual experience and certainly can be generalized to a sense of Hebrew cosmopolitanism.

One would be hard pressed to argue that there is a specific virtue in the use of Christian images as part of the trend towards personalization and formalist preoccupation. I would rather suggest that the poet becomes part of the tradition of reflection on the art experience, and among some poets a sense of liberation from Jewish strictures. (See below my discussion of Kartun-Blum's discussion of Yonah Wolloch.) In the following poem, Malka Shaked exhibits a kind of stealthy sophistication in which the Christian art imagery emerges—not from her visit to European museums, but from living and loving in the very environment that gave birth to Christianity and to Christian art.[14] The Christianity in the Jerusalem environment often eludes us as we pursue our daily rounds as part-visitor, part-resident of the "Holy City":

When like a sleepwalker I see you
Through my half closed lids
Walking around at night—a prisoner
Barefoot, figuring the narrow space
Between the walls
And measuring your breathing
So as not to stir the bedlam
In your body.
And not to arouse my pity
Or my love crazed by pain—
I think about the Crucifixion.
Not what happened in Jerusalem
In the Valley of the Cross which enchanted us
When we picked the timid primroses
Of love in the wanton Spring;
But I think about the deeper vale
Of the Crucifixion that was experienced
By those who loved Him most
And who once again set it before their eyes
In a thousand icons and pictures
Plucked arrows bloody
Like open wounds.
And I ask myself "how
Would they love Him
If he was to return and be crucified
Return and be crucified in front of them
Not for them—and in vain?"

William Cutter, authorized translation,
reprinted from the *CCAR Journal*

The poet weaves a clever series of bands: her natural attachment to Jerusalem with traces of Christianity in the very place where she and her lover enjoyed their youthful springtime; and the Jerusalem that enchants Christians for having been the center of Christianity's origins. But then she injects one of art history's most important theoretical questions: the difference between the historical Jesus and what might have happened on the actual cross to the Jesus imagined through centuries of art and representation. She thinks about the Crucifixion when she watches her lover suffer the torments of the night, when his breath comes with difficulty and he must pace the floor alone. She thinks not of the historical crucifixion, but of the crucifixion as experienced by all those people who witnessed the event through the medium of the great art of the ages. But the simile doesn't stop there; it causes her to ask which Jesus she is remembering: the one who actually died in front of the people or the one for whom the people have assumed that he died "for" them. This is an aggressive hermeneutic tactic and a powerful goad to our becoming conscious of the role that art has played in the development of people's memories and sense of spiritual reality. Do we learn more or less from the experience of a real event? And how does our representation of an event figure in our adoption of that event as operative in our lives? For Malka Shaked the Christian classic is the most suitable image for thinking about dying in vain, for questions of representation, and for the gap between historicity and historical imagination.

VI. Further Rebellion from the Woman who Put on *T'fillin*

Some of Yonah Wolloch's poetry (her name is spelled several ways) has granted her a particular notoriety that links her sexuality and her poetic innovations to a classic sensibility. Ruth Kartun-Blum has given Wolloch a special place in a discussion of intertextuality that began as Eforymson lectures at HUC-JIR in Cincinnati. Her book *Profane Scriptures* includes a remarkable treatment of Wolloch's poem "The Troubles of Donna Teresa" but includes additional material that remains a relevant discussion of postmodern writing and intertextuality nearly two decades after the lectures were delivered—by which date some of the discussion was already well-seasoned. Wolloch's textual strategies are described with insight and postmodern savvy by the Israeli critic. Here is the poem:

Donna Teresa's gorgeous troubles/
Did not captivate my heart today/
I seem to have grown very weary
I despised myself all these years
While ceaselessly
Your nostrils quiver Donna Teresa
Have you not had enough of your sensations
Her house she set in crystal
And softened it with velvet
Wallowing in beauty
And still her nostrils quiver
Legionaries above her in swift flight
The insteps of their boots beating
And Donna Teresa collects falcons . . .

Although I will not include the entire poem, I will cite Blum's exposition that includes Wolloch's feminism, her interest in personal mystical experience, and her assimilation of the great Bernini statue of St. Teresa as the source of her poetic stimulus. How like Wolloch to find in the great Catholic Saint a model for the independent and rebellious woman and to draw on a religious sculpture to launch a consideration of personal and feminine ecstasy and independence: nostrils quivering, wallowing in beauty, and collecting falcons!

VII. A Contemporary Narrative Instance—
A. B. Yehoshua's Game of History and Personal Spirit

Among dozens of examples of the attraction to Christian iconography, a remarkable instance of the Jewish-Israeli connection to Christian iconography occurs in the recent novel of A. B. Yehoshua: *Hesed Sefaradi* (*Spanish Grace*, to be translated by Stuart Schoffman). In this novel a theme of representation carries forward to the age of cinema; and the idea of *t'shuvah* combines the double entendre of "returning" through memory and of returning from the "sin" that such memory evokes. Yair Moses, prominent Israeli filmmaker, is invited to a retrospective of his films in the famous Spanish pilgrimage town of Santiago de Compastella. Arriving late at night to the history-laden medieval town, he and his former starring actress, Ruth, sleep in the same hotel room in a parador (inn) across the square from the amazing pilgrimage cathedral associated with St. James. By the dim night light Moses catches a glimpse of an impressive reproduction (that hangs just over their bed) of an aged man—a prisoner apparently—bending forward to take milk from the gorgeous breast of a young woman. Too tired to ponder this vision, Moses goes to sleep, until morning when he is able to examine the picture more closely and to think about its implied narrative. The painting, depicting an act of "Roman Grace" (or charity) remains throughout the novel both as a metaphor and a part of the plot. And the content of the picture is revisited with reinterpretations—both imaginative and historical. I will not give away the story, but will quote just the first substantive scene in which the picture *Carita Romana* appears:

> Moses seeks the name of the artist and finds only two words in elaborate script: Carita Romana, in other words, Hesed Romi, and in a flash of distant lightning it is just possible that this strange and audacious picture, hanging by chance, as it were, in a hotel room in Spanish Galicia, was known to Trigano [his scriptwriter]. Is it even possible that in this early morning light, with random simplicity, he has uncovered in Santiago de Compostella, the hidden source that sparked the imagination of his scriptwriter, the stubbornly persistent uncompromising talent, that caused the men to cut off relations. Is it possible that this mythological picture was the inspiration for Trigano's extravagant scene which was designed to shock at the end of [what turned out to be] their final picture together. [And which turns out to be a bit of a shock at the end of the novel!]

The portrait becomes the object of an ongoing meditation throughout the narrative—and a visual trope as well as an intrinsic part of the plot. Yair Moses has been is invited to Santiago de Compostella as honored guest for a retrospective of his early films. Adhering modestly to the biography of Yehoshua himself (down to the hearing aids that pre-occupy the director and an early concentration on the surreal—although Yehoshua is certainly not a has-been) the retrospective features films from the early part of a great career. Like its author, the story's protagonist is conscious of his art. Moses betrays a tendency to revisit the earliest artistic trends of his life. Moses' midnight entrance into the parador guest room is both comic and ominous, and that entrance hints of relationships with countless religious and secular figures who contemplate the significance of confession, repentance, and unconditional love. Important steps in the narrative include hiring the town expert to explain the provenance of the original painting and the director's effort to imitate the action as metaphor as he is about to wind up his professional life. Yehoshua's novel is perhaps the most audacious use of pictorial art yet created in Israeli fiction and is the gathering place for the novel's several characterizations and plot complications, as well as its themes of memory, repentance, confession, and responsibility. The central work of art around which the novel is based offers both tragic and comic perspectives on the life of a great Israeli artist in an art, movie making, which is itself a critical element in the modernity that has drastically altered the landscape for discussion about art, representation, and the function of art and entertainment in a modern world. Moses seeks, for other purposes that I won't reveal here, the perfect breast that can capture the "message" in the original reproduction (an intended oxymoron in case you have any doubts). The novel is as close as we can come to Keats's reflections on the Elgin Marbles.

These three bold representations of a Christian theme and their function within equally bold Jewish contexts might be enough to demonstrate the power of art to move us away from our way of having looked at Judaism and the Jewish world. Israeli culture is our greatest ally in the emergence of Jewish national consciousness, but it has also helped us hold on to tired clichés, norms, and canons that have driven our Jewish cultural and academic assumptions. Although a serious look at any phase of Israeli culture will reveal a greater cosmopolitanism than some Zionist sensibilities tolerate, among the greatest challenges to clichés includes Shaked's memory of a monastery as a place of lovemaking, Wolloch's use of St. Teresa to express feminist power, Yehoshua's appropriation of a Christian image for reflection on the Israeli film industry, and several poems by Natan Zach that have added the New Testament to the reservoir of associations and stimuli. The visual arts have, in many ways, been responsible for changing the very landscapes of Modern Hebrew Literature.

VIII. From Christian Imagery to Secular Art

Yet, even in the art-for-art's-sake environment that is now permissible in Israel, the question has been kept alive by such critics as Avner Holtzman, who has seen even in the less ethically loaded poetry of such as Asher Reich, the importance of social message. Let us look at a decidedly secular icon and Impressionist monument painting and its accompanying Israeli poem to expand the horizon of this discussion.

Most of us know Cezanne's painting in one form or another of *The Card Players*. It is one of the average museum goer's favorite paintings: two simple French men at cards, with a bottle of wine between them and a deck of cards, their pipes, and funny provincial hats. There are several versions of the painting, which—or so it seems—was as much an opportunity for Cezanne to rehearse technique and formal issues of painting as for any particular point of view beyond appreciation for the simple person or the genre portrait. A segment of *The Card Players* has recently been celebrated at auction in New York.

> What has destiny hidden there in that sleeve
> On the narrow table where all of the past
> Is hidden in one packet like the future?
> Which one shall be brought low today, and perhaps tomorrow will be lifted up?
>
> William Cutter, informal translation

Professor Holtzman sees in the picture an echo of the *Un'taneh Tokef* and argues that such echoes continue the Jewish ethical concerns about art's responsibility. I leave that reading to my reader, although there surely is here a sense of "the parable of life" in the painting.

Several aspects of this larger question of Hebrew culture and art remain undisclosed here: the concentration of ekphrasis among certain poets, the European origins of certain poets, portraits of famous literary figures, and art in which poetry appears (thus reversing the ekphrasis). There is more to be said, and there will be even more as time goes on, as the Israeli cultural environment shifts forward.

Five Ways to Look at a Scream

For some reason, several poems of the 1980s were composed as responses to the famous *Scream* of the Norwegian painter, Edvard Munch. One of the versions of this picture has also just sold at auction in New York, for a staggering sum. Although skeptical of the picture's intrinsic value, Holland Cotter attempts to explain the picture's allegorical relevance for our age;[16] and I assume that Israeli critics have tried no less to see in "the scream" some of the angst associated with the life of Europeans in the Middle East. (Think of Amos Oz's *Sippur Shel Ahava Vehoshech* [*A Story of Love and Darkness*].) The first Israeli writer to reflect on Munch was, no surprise to me, Micah Yosef Berdyczewski. Berdyczewski was especially eager to use his new found city Berlin (1893) as a cultural well from which to draw his insights about culture and the place of the Jewish people within the broader world of culture. Munch was in Berlin at the time, and represented, or so it seems, the "expressionistic way" of reflecting experience. It was a tone that fascinated Berdyczewski and that stimulated much of the aesthetics of the later nationalist poet, Uri Tsvi Greenberg. Both intellectuals found in Munch the visual voice of an age. Later, however, as late as 1982, *The Scream* became the visual stimulus for several interesting poems by Sh. Shalom, Tuvia Ruebner, Moshe Dor, and Uzi Shavit. I have chosen to show two paths to Munch from Ruebner—a much underappreciated poet in America—and critic, poet and editor Uzi Shavit, one of the leaders of the literary universe within Israel today.

Ruebner:
What have they done to you? What have they done? What—
Stillness on stillness—
No to silence
Nor still
Mouth.

Shavit:
In the beginning was
The image: the burning red, the heaping up
Of evening sky, like blood
Oozing from a wound
Open, wave upon wave,
Uninterrupted; The rounded black blueness
Around and around, hugging gently
The golden fjord, the darkened yawn, the functionality
Of the ice, stretched out in all of its straight cold;
The endless cry in space; ever so slowly
The blood has left his face, the color
Gone, like the fog
Of morning, like the Cheshire
Cat, that leaves behind
Just his smile.
Alone and lost
In the wide expanse, on black and white shutting
His ears, with widened eyes that see nothing at all, the Scream
Remains.

William Cutter, unauthorized translations

Shavit's poem appears to reference the fact that Munch created two versions of the picture, and Shavit uses that fact as a narrative on the story behind the scream, or on the story that flows from its contemporary meaning. He thus joins the endless tradition of commentary on another artifact, another situation, another "is" in human experience: our legacy, which is enriched by the dialogue between what looks like pictures of physical objects and what looks like words about pictures of physical objects. This is the cosmopolitan trope that resides just under the surface in all Israeli culture, threatening continuity on the one hand and enhancing the probability that Hebrew culture will play a definitive role in extending Jewish life around the world. We surely are living and reading and looking for a new Judaism that awaits yet further undreamed of *parshanut*. And Hebrew culture is one of the guarantors.

IX. Conclusion: Accommodation, Nationhood, and Commodity

As Graciella Trachtenberg has demonstrated, the development of art cultures is both a product of and a stimulus for an emerging economic prosperity, cosmopolitanism, and leisure. The inevitable commodification of art (which cannot happen with literature, except in the case of manuscripts) should not detract from the fact that the aesthetic possibilities of all arts are enhanced through the cross-referencing and the consciousness of tropes that come when a writer creates on a sheet of paper a metaphoric entity that encounters another person's way of looking at reality in another way. This development in the "Jewish arts," the escape from pragmatic function, and the introduction of foreign terrain is one of the evidences of the success of the Jewish national experiment, the Zionist Project.

Notes

1. Yehuda Amichai, *Open Closed Open* (*Patuach Sagur Patuach*), trans. Chana Bloch and Chana Kronfeld (Jerusalem: Schocken Books, 1999), no. 15, p. 11.
2. I indulge a personal comment that over twenty-five years ago I argued (in a review of Barry Holtz's excellent *Back to the Sources*) that our source study should always consider visual along with verbal representation.
3. For a discussion of that principle, which underlies a lot of modern criticism about Israeli arts, see several essays in Hazard Adams, ed., *Critical Theory Since Plato*(New York: Harcourt Brace Jovanovich, 1971).

4. Kalman Bland, *The Artless Jew, Medieval and Modern Affirmations and Denials of the Visual* (Princeton, NJ: Princeton University Press, 2000); Richard Cohen, *Jewish Icons: Art and Society in Modern Europe* (Berkeley and Los Angeles: University of California Press, 1998). One can even find in Carmi's Penguin anthology some classical genres that are surprisingly "pictorial." T. Carmi, *The Penguin Anthology of Hebrew Verse* (New York: Penguin Books, 1981).
5. Cited in Ruth Kartun-Blum, *Profane Scriptures* (Cincinnati: Hebrew Union College Presss, 1999).
6. Avner Holtzman, *Melechet Machshevet: Tehiyat haUmah, HaSifrut ha Ivrit LeNochach HaOmanutha Plastit* (*Art: The Resurrection of the Nation; Hebrew Literature in the Presence of the Plastic Arts*) (Tel Aviv: Zemorah Bitan and Haifa University, 1999); Avner Holtzman, "Changes in the Position of Plastic Art in Hebrew Literary Thought," *Tarbitz* 63 (1994): 555–95.
7. William Wimsatt, *The Verbal Icon* (Lexington: University of Kentucky Press,1954), along with numerous articles and essays co-published with Cleanthe Brooks and Monroe Beardsley.
8. Holtzman, *Melechet Machshevet*; Holtzman, "Changes in the Position of Plastic Art in Hebrew Literary Thought."
9. See ibid., 15–30,for especially illuminating comments in these regards.
10. David Hazony, "Speak Hebrew," an op ed essay in*The Forward*, April 9, 2012.
11. Leon Wieseltier in several of his popular essays and public statements.
12. In this regard, see (and purchase) Malka Shaked's *Lanetzach Anagnech* (Tel Aviv: Yediot Aharonot Press, 2001), a collection of over six hundred poems grounded in biblical reference and anthologized according to book of the Bible. Shaked's collection includes long theoretical discussions of the different uses to which the classic source can be put, and an extended consideration of the tension between *mashal* and *nimshal*, "sacralization" and "secularization."
13. Hamutal Bar Yosef, *Decadent Trends in Hebrew Literature: Bialik, Berdycheski and Brenner* (Beersheba: Ben Gurion University, 1997).
14. See my translations of Malka Shaked's work: William Cutter, "Poetic Situations in Honor of Ezra Spicehandler: New Poems by Malka Shaked," *CCAR Journal* (Summer 2003): 59–75.
15. On this subject, see Ruth Kartun-Blum, *Thoughts on the Psycho-Theology of Natan Zach's Poetry* (Tel Aviv: Hakibbutz Hame'uchad, 2009).
16. Holland Cotter, "If I Had the Cash, I Wouldn't Buy That," *New York Times*, May 4, 2012.

Mishkan and Sukkah: Toward Jewish Sacred Space

Amy Reichert

> We are all infatuated with the splendor of space, with the grandeur of things of space . . . Indeed, we know what to do with space but do not know what to do about time, except to make it subservient to space. Most of us seem to labor for the sake of things of space. As a result we suffer from a deeply rooted dread of time and stand aghast when compelled to look into its face.
>
> Judaism is a religion of time aiming at the sanctification of time . . . Jewish ritual may be characterized as the art of significant forms in time, as architecture of time.
>
> A. B. Heschel, prologue to *The Sabbath*

Is Heschel correct? Are we enslaved to the "things of space" and liberated from them only through Jewish ritual time? Heschel places the expressive power and spiritual center of Judaism squarely in time, dismissing space as the realm of base materialism.

As we wade through the repetitious listings of materials and methods that describe the construction of the *Mishkan* in *Parashiyot T'rumah* through *P'kudei,* we may indeed be left with the feeling that the poetry and power of Judaism is in time rather than space. How can what looks like a hardware shopping list contain the spiritual essence of Judaism? In this article I will suggest that in fact these difficult passages describe a uniquely Jewish model of sacred space that can resonate with us today.

> You shall make the planks for the Tabernacle of acacia wood, upright. The length of each plank shall be ten cubits, and the width

AMY REICHERT is an architect and designer of Judaica, whose work can be seen in major museum collections. She received her BA and MArch from Yale University, and teaches at the School of the Art Institute, Chicago. Website: judaica.amyreichertdesign.com. This article is dedicated to the memory of her mother, Edith Klein Reichert.

> of each plank a cubit and a half. Each plank shall have two tenons, parallel to each other. Do the same with all the planks of the Tabernacle . . . Forty silver sockets under the twenty planks, two sockets under the one plank and two sockets under each following plank. (Exod. 26:15)

In synagogue one often hears an especially enthusiastic "*chazak*" at the end of the reading of the book of Exodus. Perhaps it expresses a kind of relief at completing five portions that are largely catalogs of elements of the *Mishkan* and its accouterments. For most congregants, these *parashiyot* are about as exciting as the instructions and parts list of an IKEA dresser—without a clear diagram of what the final assembly should look like.

Loops, sockets, tenons, etc.—this is a very strange and dull way to describe a building. What if, as your architect, I described my vision for your new home at our initial meeting: "Your house—it'll be great—there will be 23 doors, each door will have 3 solid brass hinges with ball-tipped pins, and 2 ½ feet from those hinges will be a knob, and the knob will latch into a nickel plated strike . . . You're gonna love it!"

Hardware schedules are among the most tedious documents in architectural practice. Why is the first and arguably the central building project in our tradition described in such alienating terms? What does it mean to focus on connectors and planks?

I believe the Torah is telling us, in the prominence and repetition of these fittings, that the prefabricated, temporary nature of the *Mishkan* is central to its function as a dwelling place for God. The description of the *Mishkan* as a kit of parts reminds us that it is to be taken down and re-erected. The building does not stand as a monument against time, but lives in time, to be dismantled and reconstructed, constantly to be reborn. To use Heschel's terms: if Shabbat is the "architecture of time" the *Mishkan* is architecture *in* time.

The *Mishkan*'s temporal quality becomes clearer if we look at other buildings described in the Torah. Consider, for instance, the tower of Babel. As Nechama Leibowitz says, "the purpose of [this] awe-inspiring monument erected by the technical skill of men was to enable people to forget their insignificance and transient nature."[1] The tower was man's attempt, through burnt brick, to make a name for himself, to reach the heavens in a monumental structure that attempts to defeat time. The punishment for the arrogance motivating this building project was dispersion, confusion, violence, and chaos—annihilation of what was a unified community:

> Let us, then, go down and confound their speech there, so that they shall not understand one another's speech. Thus the Lord scattered them from there over the face of the whole earth; and they stopped building the city. (Gen. 11:7)

In Babel and later in the Egyptian pyramids, the act of building is fueled by the condition of slavery. In Babel, the people became enslaved to an egocentric ideal. Their misdirected building projects, imagined for the sake of man's glory ("to make a name for ourselves"), aimed to reach heaven by physical means instead of spiritual ones. They sought to bring man up to God instead of entreating God to descend to man. Similarly, in Egypt, building projects served as a justification for literal enslavement, and in turn reflected the enslavement of the Egyptian people to a cult of immortality.

In the inert masonry of Babel and the pyramids, the parts fuse to become a monolithic whole. Many ancient monumental structures had no mortar and no reinforcement, the sheer mass of stone piled upon stone kept things in place. Pieter Bruegel's great painting of Babel listing under its own weight vividly depicts the folly behind this gravity-bound mountain building .

Contrast this with the delicacy of the *Mishkan*, whose ropes and tent pins tether it to the land. It is gravity-less, resting lightly on the earth. Even when assembled, the *Mishkan*'s means of construction are made explicit, transparent to us. We understand by looking at how it is erected, used, dismantled, and carried. It exists as a place, then ceases to exist. It makes its fragility, its transience, visible.

But even without seeing the *Mishkan*, we can learn some of its deepest spiritual teachings from the way it is described in the Torah. Consider just two: its form and the process by which it is constructed.

The Form of the *Mishkan*

Despite the huge number of verses describing the *Mishkan*, we get no feel for the building's overall impact. We must do without adjectives—was it sublime? Awe-inspiring? At least beautiful? The character of the structure only becomes clear when we are confronted with its antithesis. We are drowsily reading along the passages on the *Mishkan*, when the high drama of the Golden Calf disrupts the narrative. The people demand a concrete creation that will stand before them, unlike Moses who has disappeared for an extended period. They are ecstatic over the statue's seductive form, its limited, constant nature. The Golden Calf is solid, it contains no interior space in which to dwell. It is representational (of an especially problematic image, possibly the highest god of Egypt, Ra)[2] while the *Mishkan* is abstract. The calf incites idolatry, while it is near impossible to fetishize a tent pin, to invest a socket with magical qualities.

The solidity of the molten calf contrasts sharply with the *Mishkan*. The *Mishkan* is a set of nesting containers. From the smallest utensils to the overall tent of meeting, all parts are vessels: menorah, lavers, incense holders, ark, tents. These containers have empty centers, waiting to be filled by oil, water, fire, stone, and cloud.

James Kugel describes the spiritual import of the container form:

> The purpose is to open up a space, a possibility, in the heart . . . After the people of Israel had been led out of Egypt and slavery, God ordered them to build for him a certain structure, called in Hebrew *mishkan* . . . Why should they build it—could not the Creator of the universe have chosen some magnificent feature of the natural world that He had fashioned in which to, as it were, dwell, rather than relying on merely human artisans? But the point was, as I said, for them to open up a space in order to allow Him to fill it. And this is the most basic principle of our way, to open up such a space in our lives and in our hearts. Then such a space will have the capacity to radiate outward.[3]

The hollowness of the *Mishkan* allows it to become a dwelling place for God and symbolizes a kind of openness of spirit we need to cultivate in ourselves.

The Making of the *Mishkan*

The *Mishkan*'s array of fabricated elements were the end result of the donations brought by the Israelites, then shaped by their enthusiastic labor. By focusing on the number and variety of these elements, the Torah tells us something significant about the community itself:

> Its members are different from one another . . . they are orchestrated together for a collective undertaking—one that is involved

> in making a distinctive contribution . . . The beauty of a *kehillah* . . . is that when it is driven by constructive purpose, it gathers together the distinct and separate contributions of many individuals, so that each can say, "I helped to make this." That is why, assembling the people on this occasion, Moses emphasizes that each has something different to give: "Take from what you have, an offering to God. Everyone who is willing to bring to God an offering of gold, silver and bronze . . . All you who are skilled among you are to come and make everything the Lord has commanded . . ." (Exodus 35:4–10)
>
> The greatness of the Tabernacle was that it was a collective achievement—one in which not everyone did the same thing. Each gave a different thing. Each contribution was valued—and therefore each participant felt valued.[4]

I suggested earlier that the kit-of-parts typology of the *Mishkan* makes us aware of its relationship to time. Here, the loop-and-tenon structure is a mirror of the community that built it—the individual components are still recognizable even once the building is complete. To direct the *k'hilah*, Bezalel and Oholiab are deputized as project foreman and assistant for their qualities as "men of wisdom" both in artisanship and community organizing:

> And Moses said to the Israelites: See, the Lord has singled out by name Bezalel . . . He has endowed him with a divine spirit of skill, ability, and knowledge in every kind of craft and has inspired him to make designs for work in gold, silver, and copper, to cut stones for setting and to carve wood—to work in every kind of designer's craft—and to give directions. He and Oholiab . . . have been endowed with the skill to do any work. (Exod. 35:30–35)

This is the first time in the Torah that individuals are singled out for skillfulness and craftsmanship, and the Israelites rise to meet the standards set by the two chiefs. Creating the *Mishkan* parts demanded careful, precise work in order to make all the interlocking elements fit together. How different is this picture of humility and focus from the frenzy that accompanied the creation of the Golden Calf: "The danger of a *kehillah* is that it can become a mass, a rabble, a crowd. That is the meaning of the phrase in which Moses, descending the mountain, sees the people dancing around [the Golden Calf]":[5]

> Moses saw that the people were running wild, and that Aaron had let them get out of control and so become a laughing-stock to their enemies. (Exod. 32:25)

The perfect cooperation that the people exhibit in crafting the *Mishkan* becomes the paradigm of work in the Torah. When all the parts of the *Mishkan* are made, Moses himself erects the tents. Only he can put the structure together, because only he has been shown what it should look like. Everyone else, even Bezalel and Oholiab, have been laboring in faith, without an image of the final product. At the very end of *P'kudei*, the *Mishkan* is complete. If all has been made with the right skill and intention, if Moses has anointed, blessed, and assembled it properly, God descends in a cloud. The cloud not only fills its house, but envelops it. What a curious structure! Not only does it dissolve when taken apart in order to journey on, but it disappears from view when consummated. It is a structure that the community can identify with, yet it ultimately remains obscure.

The *Mishkan* is a temporary container, dependent on intense communion with others. Although it is a structure from our ancient past, its example of living lightly on the earth, divinely inspired craftsmanship, and collective creativity still resonates today.

Making Sacred Space Today: The Sukkah

How can we make sacred space today? We can learn something about this from the *Mishkan*, as well as from the other temporary structure commanded in the Torah: one that, unlike the *Mishkan*, we are supposed to keep in our midst in every generation.

While the *Mishkan* was the desert dwelling place for God, the sukkah was the desert dwelling place for man, together they formed an itinerant community. We are commanded to re-create a sukkah each autumn, in order to recall that stage in our sacred history. This commandment presents each of us with an opportunity to explore ideas of sacred space in our own backyards. How can the relationship between *Mishkan* and sukkah inform our constructions? As an architect and Judaica designer, I've found it helpful to think about the sukkah as a space for three sacred encounters: Encounter with Text, Encounter with Nature, and Encounter with Others. And each of these encounters can be enriched by viewing it in relation to the *Mishkan*.

Ecounter with Text

While the *Mishkan* was the direct, earthly incarnation of a "fiery model" shown to Moses on Mount Sinai, the designs of sukkot come to us mediated by texts. Our challenge is to move out of Talmudic debate and into design. After all, we are charged to build and dwell on this holiday, not just to study. Our mission, therefore, is to translate textual insight into construction.

> From Leviticus 42:3:
>
> You shall dwell in sukkot seven days; all that are home-born in Israel shall dwell in booths, that your generations may know that I made the children of Israel to dwell in booths, when I brought them out of the land of Egypt. I am the Lord your God.
>
> From Talmud, BT *Sukkah* 11b:
>
> "I provided Sukkot for the Bnei Yisrael." Rabbi Eliezer explained, the Sukkot of the verse were the Clouds of God's Glory. Rabbi Akiva translated the verse literally. The Bnei Yisrael made themselves tents in the desert, and it is to these tents that the verse refers.

What is the debate between Eliezer and Akiva? For R. Eliezer, the mitzvah is an attempt to reenact the supernatural sukkot, the clouds of glory hovering over the Israelites as they traversed the desert. According to him, we must leave our houses and move into temporary shelters whose entire essence represents dwelling in the shadow of God. We must open ourselves up to the ephemeral, mystical protection of dwelling in God's presence.

Conversely, for R. Akiva, a hut is just a hut. The mitzvah requires humble, ramshackle booths, to enable a reenactment of the historical period upon which the holiday is based. According to R. Akiva, our experience should parallel the physical conditions that the Israelites endured.

We can move out of the text, and into construction if we think in terms of what I think of as "visual midrash," an artistic practice that can parallel our tradition of textual interpretation. I have created two art pieces that embody this debate between R. Eliezer and R. Akiva, viewable at judaica.amyriechertdesign.com. Sukkah I illustrates the basic concept of hut and cloud coexisting. The hut is a simple, post-and-beam structure, rectangular in plan, with rough linen walls and exposed connectors.

If the walls of the sukkah belong to the humble hut of R. Akiva, the roof echoes the celestial covering of R. Eliezer. The sukkah roof echoes a cloud by being elevated above the walls, floating free of the rectangle below. The roof floats at the maximum distance above the walls allowed by the Rabbis, three *tefach* (handbreadths).

Beyond the powerful metaphors of cloud and hut, Talmudic discussions reveal a deep understanding of the central role that design and aesthetics play in spiritual life. The many rules that the Rabbis lay out regarding sukkah roof, walls, and plan point to a sensitivity to the human experience of architecture. Much of the discussion reveals an awareness of how dimension can shape the perception of space. When is a roof so far above a wall that it ceases to be a shelter? When is a wall so far from the ground that it doesn't give a sense of enclosure?

> A great building, in my opinion, must begin with the unmeasurable, must go through measurable means when it is being designed and in the end must be unmeasurable . . . You must follow the laws but in the end when the building becomes part of living it evokes unmeasurable qualities.[6]

The dimensions of the *Mishkan*, the house for God, are unmodifiable. They are strictly set by the choreography of the ceremonies to take place there. The dimensions of the sukkah, man's house, are minimal and maximal limits, allowing us to play within them—to live within the complex interaction between the measurable and the unmeasurable.

Encounter with Nature

The ephemeral quality of the *Mishkan* tells us that this is a building that treads lightly on the earth. The sukkah has a strong connection to nature even beyond the temporary quality it shares with the *Mishkan*. The spirit of Sukkot demands that we construct the thinnest possible membrane between ourselves and the elements—it insists that, while the roof provide more shade than sun, it must allow us to feel the falling rain on our skin. We must constantly be aware of the very tenuous protection that physical shelter *alone* provides. In Sukkah II as in Sukkah I, the hut is enclosed by simple linen walls. By using fabric instead of fixed, solid panels, I hoped to emphasize the fragile boundary between domestic interior and wild nature outside.

In this sukkah, I wanted to explore the values expressed in some further rules for creating kosher roofing: First, it must be made of material that was once growing but is no longer attached to the earth. This is a very beautiful idea about how handicraft and the artistry of nature can come together to express the concept that we are God's partners in creation.

Second, the beams that support the roof here are made of "urban forest" reclaimed lumber. Their use was initially inspired by the use of natural tree trunks as expressive elements in the Japanese tea house, but they also reflect a basic Jewish value of *bal tashchit* (not wasting). Discussions of this principle usually concern the cutting down of trees. Urban forest wood is harvested from trees in suburbs and cities that have been cut down for other reasons—construction, road work, etc. As well as the spiritual value of using trees that have already been felled for another purpose, we have the advantage of a lower carbon footprint (minimal transport) and a connection to the local environment.

Encounter with Others

We have seen that the building of the *Mishkan* created Jewish community. While the commandment to build a sukkah rests on the individual or family, there is a strong impulse to connect with others during this holiday. I'd like to propose that we see our final encounter, with others, through the lenses of social justice and universality.

Sukkot is essentially a holiday of exile. The existential condition of homelessness, at the very core of the festival, is the focus of our experiment in moving out of our comfortable homes and into flimsy huts. The sukkah should serve as a reminder that we have the luxury of leaving our minimal dwelling after only seven days. One has only to look at the *favelas* of Rio de Janeiro or the shanty towns of Bombay to realize much of the world lives in such huts fifty-two weeks a year.

Hospitality is a related value of the festival. While sukkot are built by individuals, they are by nature ownerless. We are compelled to offer food, drink, and companionship to anyone who walks into our sukkah, and acting in such a manner will cause God to dwell among us. Here too, the sukkah as built reality is a visual representation of another of Judaism's core concepts. The flimsy nature of our temporary homes and the empathy it invokes towards the homeless reminds us of James Kugel's idea that the *Mishkan* is the physical manifestation of an "opening of the heart," to let God in, or, in this case, to let a stranger in.

Sukkot is often referred to as the most universal of Jewish holidays. All sukkot gesture toward a sort of messianic sukkah where all nations will live in peace. As in the *Mishkan*, the cloud coming to rest is the sign of the realization of sacred space: "If in the wilderness the clouds of glory separated between Israel and the nations of the world, in the future these clouds will expand and encompass all men, so that they will constitute a single family finding cover in the shadow of Heaven."[7]

Conclusion

The ideals of the *Mishkan* live on in the sukkah. These two structures reveal to us the deepest value of art: that we can use the medium of the material world to create spiritual meaning through beauty, critical engagement with community, and a visual dialogue with our legacy.

Notes

1. Nechama Leibowitz on Babel (Gen. 11:1). Nehama Leibowitz, Studies in Bereshit (Genesis) in the Context of Ancient and Modern Jewish Bible Commentary (Jerusalem: World Zionist Organization, 1974).
2. For a fascinating exploration of the Golden Calf as Egyptian god, see Allan Langner, "The Golden Calf and RA," *Jewish Bible Quarterly* 31, no. 1 (2003): 43–47.
3. James Kugel, *On Being a Jew* (Baltimore: Johns Hopkins University Press, 1998), 36.
4. Jonathan Sacks, *Covenant and Conversation* (New Milford, CT: Maggid Books, 2010), 285–86.
5. Ibid., 285.
6. Louis I. Kahn, *Conversations with Students* (Houston: Rice University School of Architecture and Princeton Architectural Press, 1998), 69.
7. Yehuda Shaviv, "A *Sukka* of Peace," The Israel Koschitzky Virtual Beit Midrash, http://www.vbm-torah.org/sukkot/suk67ys.htm.

Daring to Alter a Perfect Twentieth-Century Sanctuary to Meet the Needs of the Twenty-First Century

Roy A. Walter and Garey F. Marks

In many ways, we rabbis need aesthetics in our work. Some of us may have a more refined sense of, or are better educated about, aesthetics than others. But all of us use the arts to some degree in our work. At a minimum, we congregation rabbis use theater arts and music in the dramaturgy of worship and literary arts in our creative services and *divrei Torah*.

Aesthetics are also part of, and important to, the architecture of the spaces in which we worship, learn, and gather. Occasionally we get to change those spaces when we refurbish or remodel them; in rare instances we even have the opportunity to start from scratch, as in the construction of a new building. But whether we're using or reworking existing space, aesthetics should be a central part of the process for both the rabbi and the laity.

I am proud to say that aesthetics has been an integral component in most aspects of the synagogue I served for forty-one years. From the main building, which was completed in 1949, to the addition of a chapel on site and another chapel at our cemetery, to the rebuilding of our religious school, to the addition of a parking facility and the remodeling of our sanctuary last year, the rabbis have been intimately involved in planning every project. We have worked closely with the lay leadership, taking great care not only to preserve the integrity of our architecture, but also to see that the space is functional, flexible,

GAREY F. MARKS, AIA, is a partner in Marks and Salley, Inc., Houston, Texas and senior vice-president of Congregation Emanu El, Houston, Texas.

ROY A. WALTER (C70) served as assistant, associate, and senior rabbi of Congregation Emanu El for forty-one years and currently serves as rabbi emeritus.

accessible for all, beautiful, and, in the case of our worship spaces, inspiring. Indeed, I would say that pride in our building is part of our history: the grandchildren of our founders remain lovingly involved in overseeing and maintaining the building's artistic integrity—and one of them coauthored this article.

In addition, over our sixty-eight years of existence we have proudly acquired an amazing collection of art that is on display throughout the building: paintings, lithos, photographs, sculptures, and ritual objects. The art, while decorative, also serves us inspirationally and educationally. At least once a year, our Art Committee creates a special thematic exhibit of our art that is used programmatically by our auxiliaries, and our religious school and Continuing Education Committee often build courses around the exhibits. Our art gallery, though small, also serves as an outreach to the broader community.

Of course, the importance of the beauty of worship space is not a new concept in Judaism. It goes back to the Tabernacle and the Jerusalem Temple. Our ancestors knew that "there is space and there is *space*." Or as they might have said, "There are tents and there is the *Tabernacle*. There are buildings and there is the *Temple*." The materials they used, we know, were the finest; the architect and designer were chosen by God. Indeed, as the Torah itself tells us, their design and work were nothing less than inspired by God.

The key to good architecture is the nexus of form and function in each space. If space is beautiful but unusable or inaccessible, or if it is functional but uninspiring, it falls short of a synagogue's needs. It should be the ongoing task of synagogue leadership, lay and rabbinic, jointly to develop and maintain the close relationship between the spaces and their uses, between their integrity and their artistry.

To that end, I recently had the joy of initiating the redesign of the pulpit of our sanctuary and working with the committee in charge to effect the change. The pulpit is a gem, and the suggestion that we might somehow alter it and maintain its impeccable design did not come easily to me without a degree of anxiety. The pulpit was originally built as a preaching pulpit, but with the passage of time we found the need, as most congregations have, to "bring the pulpit down to the congregation," to make the worship experience more intimate. Until the point of redesign, we were actually working against the design of the room in our efforts to do so. How to retain the grandeur of a space with soaring ceilings and a large seating capacity, and yet make it more intimate, was a challenge. Following are the thoughts of an architect, the grandson of a founding member who chaired the committee and responded enthusiastically to my proposal that we attempt the redo. Through his words, you will discover for yourself that his love of, and respect for, our worship space shines through.

Garey:

I remember at an early age, sitting in our sanctuary, staring at the ceiling and marveling at how the oak-clad beams seemed to soar up and out through the large expanse of clerestory glass. I did not realize it then, but what must have been an innate interest in design was being influenced by my temple's interiors. Fast-forward through architecture school, a return home, a position on the synagogue's Building and Grounds Committee, and subsequent "advancement" to lay leadership; I was presented with, and enthusiastically accepted, the senior rabbi's request to partner with him (and with the board-chosen religious architecture design firm) in helping to plan the renovation to the now sixty-three-year-old sanctuary. Albeit a project with a very personal and historic connection, the previously mentioned basic principles of any successful design (form-follows-function, program-begets-solution) were requisite. But what presented a unique and more exciting challenge was the obligation to create an updated, multifunctional space (meeting the transition from preaching pulpit to interactive service), while respecting a place of worship that has inspired and uplifted five generations.

Of course the main purpose of a sanctuary is to create a space to pray and to feel a closeness to God, the design and construction of which is no easy task. Equally challenging is recognizing that what formulates a synagogue's structure, what physically enables it to meet its congregational needs at its inception, will very likely need reprogramming in the future. In our case, the architectural firm charged with designing a building to accommodate nine hundred families in 1949 most likely did not imagine its meeting the needs of two thousand families sixty-plus years later.

Remarkably, the architects succeeded in their endeavor, and for almost sixty-two years, our sanctuary, with its flexibility to expand from 850 seats to 2,500 seats by opening a folding wall between the sanctuary and social hall, has indisputably provided such a space. And by comparison to the neoclassical style of many synagogues built in the early 1900s, Emanu El's designers—protégés of iconic architect Frank Lloyd Wright—incorporated many Wrightian details and materials. Rather than stones such as granite and marble, Emanu El's architects opted for a sunset-toned brick on the building's exterior, transitioned the masonry to the interiors, and successfully blended it with the warmth of medium-red oak. And as is typical of many Wrightian interiors, the entry portals to Emanu El's sanctuary were lowered to a more residential, welcoming scale before rising abruptly to forty-plus feet. This contrast in scale and proportion gives one a sense of welcome and awe.

But notwithstanding the architectural firm's insight, and regardless of those nine hundred families and their rabbi's incredible vision, none could imagine how the practice of Reform Judaism would evolve from its liberal approach of attempting to assimilate into American society to a more traditional and interactive service.

In 1949, Emanu El opened its sanctuary doors to its congregants, who were presented with a service, led by its rabbi, who preached from a centrally located, somewhat lofty podium, positioned on an elevated bimah rather detached from the congregation (or so I felt), and with no inclination to connect physically with them. There was also no cantor.

Fast-forward to current times. For years now Emanu El's clergy has consisted of three rabbis and a cantor. Our rituals now include a more traditional, relaxed, less choreographed service. Our senior rabbi had long envisioned bringing the service physically closer to the congregants, to allow him and the rest of the clergy to interact with the congregation on a more intimate level. In order to bring that change about, the architects, the rabbinical staff, and the lay-led building committee presented the board and ultimately the congregation with a design that restructured the bimah. The original, smaller podium was replaced with one that could accommodate as many as six or eight, and its architecture was detailed to be less imposing and more reflective of a traditional, simple table, designed for reading Torah.

But the most dramatic change came with the reconfiguration of the bimah to include an intermediate, lower level, which not only facilitated a closer, physical connection to the congregation, but also enhanced the intimacy of the service. Now, over sixty years since its founding, Temple Emanu El's sanctuary has not only accommodated its growing population, but has successfully transformed itself to meet the current structure of modern Reform Judaism. In so doing, Emanu El has stayed true to the vision of its founding families and their rabbi: to gather its congregants in a space that is inviting and inspirational.

As you can tell from Garey's comments, we worked closely together. I had the idea of what we needed functionally, and he had the skills to transform my thoughts into a reality. Working with Garey helped me better understand the challenges of accomplishing our goals, and I learned how to be more attuned to the details than previously. I learned that the shape of the lower bimah was especially challenging because of the shape of our sanctuary. We had to sacrifice a few rows of seats and followed the lines of the upper bimah down to the lower level by creating a wide, open, angled staircase that brings your eye upward toward the ark, even as the focus is on the service conducted from below. The design of the new lower podium mirrors the grill work on the ark doors in an attempt to create symmetry and harmony between the new and old spaces. The proportions of the lower bimah were critical, and we actually created temporary structures of several sizes to determine the correct dimensions. Realizing the growing use of technology in the sanctuary, we also added all kinds of outlets that will allow us to use the room creatively as we move into the future.

All of Garey's and my efforts, I believe, succeeded because we were true partners in redesigning a space we both love. The aesthetics of our sanctuary continue to inspire all who enter. We both believe the founders, who poured their heart and soul into creating so magnificent a worship space, would be proud of what we have done.

Transforming a Congregation through the Arts

Cheri Ellowitz

Since September 2006 the power of the arts has transformed The Temple-Tifereth Israel (TTTI) in Beachwood, Ohio. Our planned, focused, and vision-driven approach impacts learners of all ages, offers opportunities to people from the broader community, and has most clearly enhanced our religious school program. A building that previously had even the youngest children sitting in chairs with worksheets now has classrooms bustling with movement and activities of all sorts, hallways filled with color and excitement, and participants of all ages experimenting with varieties of approaches to Jewish learning. This did not happen by replacing staff and faculty, but by transforming them.

In 2004, under the leadership of Senior Rabbi Richard Block, TTTI received a generous, multiyear grant from the Jewish Education Center of Cleveland (JECC) to partner with them and the Laura and Alvin Siegal College of Judaic Studies in an endeavor entitled Building Leadership Capacity for Educational Excellence and Congregational Transformation (now known as the Learning and Leadership Initiative). Phase 1 encompassed a six-month period of planning the Task Force. Professional representatives of each of the sponsoring organizations, the lay chair of the initiative, and an advisor experienced in synagogue transformation projects established the three basic outcomes for the initiative: (1) educational innovation

CHERI ELLOWITZ (MAJE/MAJCS HUC-LA/USC 1982) is the director of Education at The Temple-Tifereth Israel in Beachwood, Ohio. She has served in similar positions in Reform and Conservative supplementary and day schools for thirty years in Cincinnati, Houston, and Los Angeles. She is also the author of Jewish educational materials published by URJ Press and others, such as *Pass the Torah, Please, Is This Apple Kosher?* and the *Mitkadem* Hebrew Program. Nothing pleases her more than spending time with her children.

An earlier version of this article appeared in the online edition of *Jewish Educational Leadership* (Lookstein Center for Jewish Education) 9, no. 3 (Summer 2011)

and excellence, (2) leadership development, and (3) congregational transformation. When Phase 2 (the Task Force) was completed, a Temple Learning Council had been established to implement The Temple's new Vision for Learning and to oversee the educational programs of TTTI. One of two areas of immediate concern that they chose to address was arts education (the second was adolescent education). The arts were viewed as an area that could touch all ages and areas of temple life. We wanted an early initiative to have potential for multigenerational programming that could reach out to many people's interests and enliven the synagogue.

The Temple Learning Council established an Arts Education Working Group comprised of both lay and professional members with varied experiences in Judaism, education, and the arts. We gathered names of potential members from interested Task Force participants, congregants who were knowledgeable about the arts or education, and community members expert in either the field of education or the arts. At least one temple faculty member is included on the Working Group, which is cochaired by a lay volunteer and a member of our education staff. Their charge was to imagine what Jewish arts education at The Temple could and should look like and to develop a proposal for implementation.

The Working Group spent their initial months learning and reading about Jewish education and arts education. They experienced different methodologies themselves, and they had many discussions of great impact and passion about religion and art. Meetings always began with a text study. Because of the topic of this group, the learning was facilitated through the arts. One example is a lesson that had us view several paintings on the same biblical text, read the text, and discuss the artists' interpretations and ours. On another occasion we used movement to explore a teaching. We read articles, from Jewish and secular sources, regarding the arts and education between meetings, and had directed discussions to lead us toward our goals of determining how "learning through the arts" should be expressed at TTTI. Facilitators of the meetings included the education staff that were part of the Working Group, the lay chair, and occasionally one of the members of the group.

The first significant outcome of their work came in the form of Enduring Understandings regarding Jewish arts education, Enduring Understandings are educational language for "big ideas" or core values on which a teacher and curriculum designer bases the particulars of a program. They are the guiding values that stay with the learner throughout life, long after the details of the lessons are gone. These statements express the group's beliefs about how integral to learning and Judaism the arts are:

- Jewish arts education inspires the integration of Judaism into daily life.
- Jewish arts education is a means to transform Jewish ideas, images, and feelings into an art form.
- Jewish arts education redefines a participant's awareness of the aesthetic qualities in art and embraces the concept of *hidur mitzvah* (making a mitzvah beautiful).
- Jewish arts education is a means to explore spirituality and connection to God.
- Jewish arts education engages multiple learners through diverse modalities.
- Jewish arts education is joyful and gratifying.
- Jewish arts education engages multigenerational learners throughout a lifetime.

This work paved the way for the Working Group to conceive of their ultimate vision for the future of arts education at The Temple. The first stage of implementation was a Jewish Arts Festival for The Temple community that would be participatory, with individuals and families joining workshops learning about Judaism through different artistic media (plastic arts, music, drama, dance, movies, etc.). They chose the Festival as the pilot program because it would be a multigenerational, stand alone event that would allow us to experiment with a variety of modalities. The vision for the event included the following:

> This is not a showcase of individual talent, but rather a collective experience that emphasizes process over product, participation over indifference, effort over talent.
>
> Congregants who attend the Arts Festival will not recognize their environment. Walls will be rejuvenated by vibrant paintings. Silent hallways will burst with music. Children will run to their classrooms, parents in tow, desperate to show their work. For one week, The Temple will be transformed and transfixed by the power of Judaism through the arts: the power to uplift, the

power to educate, and the power to inspire a new commitment to our Jewish community at The Temple-Tifereth Israel.

As soon as the Working Group's proposal was accepted by the Learning Council, a committee was established to execute plans for the Arts Festival, which would become known as FestAviv, The Temple's Spring Festival. Currently anticipating the fifth FestAviv, the program has surpassed the vision of its creators. More than a thousand participants of all ages attend workshops and presentations where Judaism is experienced and explored through the arts, from singing to orchestra presentations, to sidewalk chalk art, to paper cutting, to cooking, to movie viewing and discussion, to dance interpretation, to clay, to silk painting, and on and on. Each workshop is led by an artist who blends teaching of Jewish text and learning into the expression of their art. The Director of Education at The Temple works with each artist to assist in the creation of the lesson and sometimes to select a partner to teach the Jewish content (often a religious school teacher). This program is only possible because of the collaboration of devoted lay volunteers and of all of The Temple departments (clergy, administration, education, maintenance). One of the goals and outcomes of the Learning and Leadership Initiative has been to better familiarize departments about each other's work and programs. Working together on these temple-wide events has contributed to the transformation for which we hoped. Each year FestAviv centers on a different theme, allowing for focused learning and new workshops. Our themes have been: *L'Dor V'Dor*, Israel's 60th Birthday, Eco-FestAviv: Sharing and Caring for the Earth, and The Art of *Tikkun Olam*. (To see a video of FestAviv 2007 and photos of FestAviv 2008, go to http://festaviv.blogspot.com/.)

The long-term, and crucial, vision of the Working Group included transforming the formal educational program through professional development for the teachers in our supplementary and preschools. Teachers in our religious schools are extremely devoted to the temple. The majority of them at that time had been teaching in the school for fifteen to fifty years. This was the necessary opportunity to include the entire faculty in training for a new approach that would challenge them and have them work together as a faculty. The educational program for them would begin within six months of the acceptance of the proposal by the Temple Learning Council and continue over a two-year period. The Working Group proposal states:

> The second prong of our long-term Arts Initiative will be to establish arts education professional development that provides and promotes ongoing instruction to our professional staff in the area of arts integration education. Gradual curricular change will occur at the Religious School in a manner that is educationally sound; arts will be integrated in the educational program to underscore the lessons, not replace them. Holistic educational reform, such as is contemplated here, cannot happen only through artist residencies. It can only happen when teachers are trained to use the arts as effective and unique teaching tools. This professional development program should be led by experts in arts and Jewish education and teachers must be paid for their time.

As envisioned, the immediate execution of professional development in arts education for all teachers (religious school and preschool) at The Temple would be key to implementing this vision. The first year, teachers were charged with developing a class project that could be displayed at FestAviv. The project was to be process-, not product-, oriented (as the Working Group proposal stated), and it was to be derived from their class curriculum, not the FestAviv theme, so as to allow teachers to view arts education as a new approach, not an add on. For most teachers this presented a challenge as they were just beginning to develop an understanding about "learning through the arts."

Examples of how this might manifest are:

- In the difference between offering students a pattern or two with which to create a very lovely *Kiddush* cup to take home and hope it might be used versus spending time creatively examining the themes in the *Kiddush*, imagining different ways creation and freedom can be expressed through movement, drawing, and words and then having the students create their own *Kiddush* cup designs with various materials and sending it home with copies of the traditional blessings and one written by the student on the themes.
- In the difference between learning about one's family history by interviewing a family member versus choosing one of the ancestors learned about and then further investigating Jewish history of that time period. The project follows with the student dressing up as that ancestor, writing a letter to a family member in another part of the world at that time or a personal diary entry, and having a sepia photo taken of them in the

costume. A "museum" display can be put together of the photos and the writings.

We developed a two-year professional development program for the teachers that ultimately changed the way our classrooms look and function today. By bringing in Debbie Krivoy of Avoda Arts for the first workshop, we set the philosophical groundwork. In her five hour session Debbie clearly defined the difference between "teaching and doing art" and "teaching Judaism through the arts." While there can be a place for both in Jewish education, to enhance learning at The Temple our initiative sought to expand our teachers' abilities to explore Judaism creatively, in this case by using artistic methodologies. Once the faculty understood this most important concept, we were able to follow with practical, skill-based workshops, such as storytelling, puppetry, using objects (ritual objects, photos, etc.) to teach history, cooking, drama, and art midrash.

We also presented sessions that stressed pedagogy. In one such session the teachers experienced three models of teaching: advanced organizer, synectics, and Storahtelling. With each model the same Torah text was presented followed by some sort of artistic expression of the text, using the particular model of teaching. It has been essential to our vision for professional development to impart the ideals of flexibility, creativity, and experimentation.

Today our weekly classes substantiate real outcomes from the Arts Education Initiative. Each year, FestAviv or not, we have a display of class "art" that is evidence of learning of at least one aspect of their curriculum. We developed a form for teachers to complete at the beginning of the school year asking:

- What part of your curriculum will your arts program address?
- What is the "Big Idea" (Enduring Understanding) that is inspiring your project? What's the main concept or idea that you want your students to learn from the curriculum?
- What will your students be able to do or express through or after the learning? *Students will be able to:*
- List three different ways that this learning can be expressed in an artistic form (painting, sculpting, dance, drama, puppets, gardening, etc.):

As we work individually with teachers, they improve each year in their understanding of the concepts of "big ideas" and ability to design artistic exploration that is an integral part of the curriculum, not an art project that can be completed in two weeks. Through our yearly documentation, we have evidence of teacher learning and definitive progress toward our vision of learning through the arts.

Naturally our teachers' new skills and attitudes affect all of their teaching, not just the "project" that we ask them to do, so a new vitality is apparent in our classrooms. Worksheets have virtually disappeared. Working together on an undertaking such as FestAviv also brought the faculty together more closely as a group. Grade level teachers work collectively on group projects; the entire school has a deadline for an "all community event" in which they play a central role.

Today the contributions of the Arts Education Initiative are evident throughout The Temple in subtle and obvious ways. We added a part time Temple Arts Director. His responsibilities are synagogue-wide and through his work we developed a variety of educational and informal opportunities, such as:

• *Temple Arts Program Committee*—a lay committee charged with implementing the original Arts Education Proposal accepted by the Temple Learning Council. They monitor the status of existing programs and continue to develop new ones. One of their immediate tasks was to create a mission statement that would guide their work: *The mission of the Jewish Learning through the Arts Committee is to enrich Jewish learning and community through opportunities for creative expression.*

- *FestAviv*—now a biennial program, each event includes twenty-two to thirty-nine workshops with approximately twenty to thirty artists/teachers and more than a thousand participants over two days.
- *Klezmer U*—a teen klezmer band for students in grades 7 to 12. Learning about klezmer music and its origins is part of the program. They perform several times a year at The Temple and at other venues, such as the Jewish Home for the Aged.
- *TGIS* (*Thank God It's Shabbat*)—a new, informal Shabbat service, featuring contemporary music and open discussion on the *parashah*.
- *Smart Sundays*—Classes for teens and adults that are arts-based taking place during Sunday school.

Collaboration among departments within The Temple has been a benefit of this initiative. Clergy have taken great interest in expanding their teaching range to include arts-based programs, participating as Smart Sundays and FestAviv teachers. We are privileged to have The Temple Museum of Religious Art, a department of The Temple with three spaces for displaying the synagogue's Judaica collection, including a gallery at the Maltz Museum of Jewish Heritage located adjacent to The Temple. Previous to the Arts Initiative, The Temple's Museum Director had minimal contact with students and families through a couple of family programs a year. Today, the museum, its galleries, collection, and director are highly integrated into many aspects of our arts education and schools' programs—from preschool through high school, from classroom activities to family education programs. Much of our learning would feel incomplete without access to the rich ritual and artistic resources that we have in The Temple's historic collection and vibrant opportunities that new exhibits bring.

Today there are newer members, parents, and faculty who tell us that they think of us as the "Arts Synagogue" because that is the way that they have always known The Temple-Tifereth Israel. For those of us who have been at the synagogue for more than five years, this is an amazing statement because Jewish Learning through the Arts was launched in spring of 2007 with the first FestAviv. We have received continual support from the Jewish Community Federation of Cleveland through the ongoing advocacy of the JECC and funding from their Fund for the Jewish Future and other funders.

Using the lens of the arts, whether to expand one's ritual experience, to invite a student to experience another time period, to invest one's emotions in a piece of text—this is the aspiration of teaching through the arts. The concept of teaching Judaism *through* the arts rather than doing art projects is paramount to the vision of transforming learning and allowing students of all ages to experience Judaism for themselves. With or without a museum we all have beautiful ritual objects, photographs, and pictures at our disposal, and we oftentimes don't need to bring people from out of town to find experts in fields of professional development. What we do need is a vision of what we want to accomplish and a plan of how to get there. We also need to recognize that the vision takes nurturing over time. With patience and a plan, it's amazing how soon people think it was always how you meant it to be!

Faith in Art: Visual Culture and the Future of Judaism

Lance J. Sussman

In December 1969 I went to Israel for the first time. Everything about that trip was transformative. Traveling with my summer friends from Camp Harlam (UAHC), flying on a "Jewish airplane," and seeing the coastline of the Jewish state for the first time all were powerful experiences for me. But perhaps the most surprising experience during those magical two weeks was my encounter with public art in Israel. By age fifteen, I had already visited numerous leading art museums with my family. My childhood synagogue, Oheb Shalom in Baltimore, Maryland, itself was an important architectural statement created by Walter Gropius, a leader in the Bauhaus movement. But nothing fully prepared me for coming face to face with powerful, dramatic, public art portraying Jewish and Israeli themes with boldness and a uniquely modern beauty.

After arriving at the old Ben Gurion airport with its open metal hangers, cracked sunflower seed–covered sidewalks, and pungent cigarette smoke, we were whisked off toward Haifa. Because it was already night and I was exhausted, I did not really "see" Israel until morning. Stepping out of the old guest house, I was immediately confronted with David Polus's little-known sculpture *Israel Saba*, a two-figure metal statute, which could have worked perfectly as the cover for Amos Elon's iconoclastic 1971 book, *The Israelis: Founders and Sons.* For me, Polus's work provided the perfect Zionist framework for my first journey to Israel: a biblical grandfather walking with his arm around a farmer-soldier kibbutznik. Much more than my first encounter with the Western Wall, Polus's sculpture, the Billy Rose Art Garden in Jerusalem, and the

LANCE J. SUSSMAN, Ph.D. (C80) is senior rabbi of Reform Congregation Keneseth Israel in Elkins Park, Pennsylvania, and national chair of the CCAR Press. He teaches classes in Jewish History at Princeton and Temple University. His article "Transcending an Artless Tradition" appeared in *Reform Judaism* (Winter 2010).

white modernism of Tel Aviv connected me visually with Israel and instilled a sense of excitement in me about the possibilities of a modern Jewish culture. Although art and architecture remained a private interest for many years, my decision to study to be rabbi eventually took priority and other interests prevailed.

In recent years, however, I found myself increasingly returning to images as a source of religious inspiration and Judaic knowledge. Quite unexpectedly, my vision was threatened by premature cataracts and a retina that detached twice. Surgery, eye patches, and double and triple vision all made sight much more important to me. I started to look at the world differently. I discovered a universe of discourse among the visually impaired. The Macular Degeneration group, which met at the far end of our synagogue, were no longer exotic guests, but "my people." My sight improved and ultimately was fully restored; however, my thinking about the importance of the visual in life and in the dynamic of the synagogue will never recover.

Having been trained as a historian at HUC-JIR/Cincinnati (Ph.D.,1987), I made a decision to start studying Jewish art historically and to produce a yearlong series of PowerPoint lectures on the history of Jewish art for my congregation's Adult Education program. The lectures, which covered Jewish art from its emergence in Ancient Israel to the present. were so well received, I began to prepare additional illustrated talks on a variety of individual artists, among them Chagall, Ben Shahn, Roman Vishniak, and the designer of our synagogue's primary stained glass windows, Jacob Landau. I also prepared thematic PowerPoint presentations including one on "Women and Art in the Jewish Tradition" and a multipart series on "Art and the Holocaust: Before, During and After." Our regional rabbinic organization, DVARR (Delaware Valley Association of Reform Rabbis) was kind enough to invite me to present several of my talks at one of their annual retreats several years ago. Not only did we look at pictures together, but we also read biblical and Rabbinic texts on idolatry, *hidur mitzvah*, and the relationship between them. Jewish Art History and Holocaust and Art became electives in our confirmation academy, and eventually outside groups and schools began making similar requests.

In my career, studying Jewish art had rapidly moved from personal interest to a central activity in my pulpit and academic work. The next step was to bring art (or, better, an awareness of art) into our worship space. Using a laser pointer, I started highlighting the art of our sanctuary during services to help "open the eyes" of my congregation to the possibility of using visuality in prayer. I focused a High Holy Day sermon (with mixed success) on art in the Jewish tradition and challenged my congregation to think about why modern Jews are both dedicated patrons of the arts as well as artists, yet major art museums remain nearly without any Judaic images for a host of reasons including a widespread assumption that Judaism is an imageless tradition; Chagall, of course, being the most important and often only exception. By contrast, where do you regularly find art relating to the Jewish experience in a major metropolitan museum? The gift shop!

Jewish art, I concluded, cannot just be about nostalgia, tourist junk, and frivolous tchotchkes! What about prayer? Can't synagogue prayer include images? Is there a way to employ the strategies of illuminated medieval Haggadot in the *t'filot* of our congregation by providing compelling images as a regular part of the worship experiences? Visual *t'filot* during Shabbat services, a PowerPoint congregational Passover seder, and "in service" visual presentations by our *b'nei mitzvah* students were all soon finding their way into our prayer experience. I also began illustrating special sermons (delivered after *Kaddish*) with PowerPoint presentations. Dozens of powerful images ranging from biblical archaeology to stirring natural scenes to faux colored dreamscapes by Chagall accompanied all the major rubrics of prayer at Keneseth Israel. Attendance jumped upward. Now, we are installing large retractable screens in our synagogue and built-in high power projectors. "Rabbi," I have been told repeatedly, "I never looked up at services before and I like seeing pictures of the Wall when we pray for the peace of Jerusalem and starry night scenes when we read *Maariv Aravim.*"

I have come to the conclusion that visual culture and visual *t'filot* can and should play a major role in the Reform Judaism of the future. We live in a visual age. From major league stadiums to LED billboards on superhighways, images, and increasingly electronic images, are defining our culture. Reform Judaism began by bringing the pipe organ into regular synagogue worship. It reinvented itself by learning how to make the six-string guitar the Davidic harp of our age. Our future, I believe, is inextricably tied up with the use of images and, most importantly, computer-generated images, because of the endless capacity that technology has to recover the art of the past and generate new art for the present and the future. Just as the medieval church was able to teach its nonreading adherents through the medium of stained glass, we can teach our post-reading members through contemporary visual culture and technology.

In order to most fully use the visual arts to perpetuate and deepen Judaism in our time, we need to move beyond Judaism's traditional ambivalence toward art. Art itself is not idolatrous. The second commandment, as is evidenced by the explosion of art in the Orthodox community today, can be understood very narrowly in terms of restrictions. Sensuousness and nudity present a second set of challenges as do the use of non-Jewish religious images in a synagogue setting. Can Buddhist images be used the way Buddhist sounds are in the synagogue? Can Chagall's use of a Jewish Jesus ever be displayed or discussed within our congregations?

My research into the history of Jewish art has convinced me that except for digital technology, none of this is really new. During the Italian Renaissance, the Jews of Rome flocked to see Michelangelo's *Moses* in a church on Shabbat afternoon. By contrast, the Jews of Florence did not seek inspiration from the same sculptor's heroic depiction of King David as a young man. We, too, will have to make choices but first we need to cultivate and refine an interest in Jewish art in service to the living experience of Judaism in our own time.

I believe synagogues need visual art committees, that the national movement needs to take art seriously as a primary path in the definition of a new and revolutionary Reform spirituality, and that HUC-JIR needs to teach Jewish art and explore how art has and can impact Jewish life as is being done at the ATID Yeshiva in Jerusalem and at least in the Graduate Program of the Jewish Theological Seminary in New York. The agenda is almost endless and to begin we need to learn how to ask questions about how art can be used to preserve and nurture Jewish life for the present and the distant future.

What are some of those questions? Here is a brief sampling: What should we exhibit in our synagogues, display on our walls, and hang in our sanctuaries? What kind of labels and explanations should we prepare? How many images of dancing Chasidim do we need in Reform synagogues? Should we feature emerging artists who use Jewish ideas and inspiration in their work? Do we engage the local art community and commission new ceremonial art, installations, sculpture, and paintings? Should children's art be displayed in our sanctuaries? How can we teach Torah through art? Do we request docented tours of our great museums to learn to see them through Jewish eyes? How effectively can Jewish art move beyond nostalgia into a means of engagement? Can we redirect Jewish patronage of the arts in general toward the creation of a deeper art-based culture in the Jewish community? How do we learn to have more faith in art and allow art to help us deepen our faith and our connections to Judaism and the Jewish people?

Visual art, like a pipe organ or a guitar, may not have the capacity to define what we believe. However, it does have the power to help us better understand and relate to what it is we hope to accomplish as a community. The long debates about the existence of Jewish art and the question of art or fine art are over. It is time our movement heeded Martin Buber's challenge to the Zionist Movement at the beginning of the twentieth century and elevated the place of visual art in our work.

From the Bezalel of Exodus to the establishment of the Bezalel School in Jerusalem, Judaism has generated a visual culture. The time has come for us to reenvision our foundational texts as well as textualize the images that define our lives as Jews. We need to move beyond tourist art and gift shop art. We need to extend art education from our preschools and summer camp arts and crafts shacks to our adult education programs and worship committees. We need to see our prayers and illustrate our sermons. We need to create meaningful images for our members who live their lives in an age of images. We need to reinvent our synagogues by applying museum understanding of visual culture and new museological methods to them without turning our synagogues into museums that simply put "the past under glass." Similarly, we need to harness the teaching and cultural power of our museums, Jewish and communal, in service to the needs of our faith. Ultimately, we need to find ways to understand ourselves as being created in the image of the imageless Creator. Like Moses, let us find skilled artists who are filled with the spirit of God and let us again rediscover how to root reform worship in the beauty of holiness.

Poetry

I Was at Sinai

Rick Lupert

I was at Sinai

I remember what I was wearing
what the ground felt like
who was standing next to me

the looks on everyone's face
when Moses came down with the stones
telling us, *this is gonna be good*
pay attention people
you'll be telling your children about this

I was at Sinai
my wisdom was young and old then
now I'm just old and my wisdom
has left the building or
maybe it's still at the mountain

I was at Sinai well before they put in the gift shop
Back when the only gift was a Golden Calf and in the end
no one wanted it
Not our best moment, but it was *our* moment
we've had so many moments
like remember the time when . . .

RICK LUPERT is a Los Angeles poet who edited the anthology *A Poet's Haggadah* (www.poetseder.com). He has authored numerous collections of poetry (all available through his Web site www.poetrysuperhighway.com) and is a regular participant in the Hava Nashira Jewish music educators retreat at Olin-Sang-Ruby Union Institute.

When I was at Sinai
we didn't look at our watches
Forget about the fact that there weren't watches
we didn't even want them

Don't you get it, we're still there now
we are all a part of the circle
we are the beginning and the end
we receive it every day
This is your permanent online status

Sinai was the first place we held hands
but not the last, in fact I never let go
we are still holding hands
I choose to be a part of the circle
as if I have a choice

I could ignore the circle
travel a thousand miles from the circle
but turn around and see I haven't gone anywhere
It's a big circle orbiting *you* Sinai
where the property values are holding steady

Oh Sinai, to say I was with you is to pretend I left
is to conceive I was ever anywhere else

Oh Sinai, I tweet your commandments to the masses
I spin around in your circle
I see the world through your eyes

your holy eyes

Exercises in Uncertainty that Resolve in Embrace

James Stone Goodman

Try sitting by yourself waiting—
you are alone looking out a window, now throw up your arms
let yourself be taken up by the hands of a God,
look out over the mist of your city
let your vision drift up to the sky set with clouds.
Let your God expand just then.

Hold on, let your large God
lift you. Ascend, look down, send a message
from your perch in the sky, draw it like a billboard
with a ribbon of light set against the threatening clouds,
blow the clouds away if you can, if you can't
let your God try.

RABBI JAMES STONE GOODMAN (C81) serves Congregation Neve Shalom and Central Reform Congregation in St. Louis, Missouri. He is also a musician who has produced six CDs, combining music, story, and poetry.

The Story of a Ring

Navah-Tehila

Enschede, Holland
Once there lived a beautiful woman
in a city in the east of the Netherlands
Rivka—was perhaps her name—
received a gift of love
from David—was perhaps his name:
a golden ring with three embedded stones
two sapphires and a brilliant.
Then came the war
and brought along an evil man
a Nazi collaborator who became the Mayor.
Rivka, David, and their children had to go
where to we do not know
They had to leave their lovely house
with all that was therein.
The golden ring
the beautiful ring with two sapphires and a brilliant
given in love by a man to his wife
by a David to a Rivka
disappeared.

Utrecht
Many many years have gone by.
Two weeks before she passed away
an old sick mother
surrounded by her family, says:
this ring, which I have worn,
does not belong to me
it came to me from my brother's wife
daughter of a Mayor, a Nazi collaborator.
This golden ring, says the dying mother,
came from the Jews

NAVAH-TEHILA is a composer of Jewish liturgical music, an artist, and teacher. She was the first (singing) woman rabbi to serve the Liberal Jewish Community in Utrecht. The poem was composed in Utrecht in November 2011.With thanks to family T.

a golden ring with two wornout stones
—one sapphire forever lost.

The mother is dead, the aunt is old
the children long to return the ring
but how and to whom?

Contact with a rabbi:
could we give it to the Jewish museum?
But as no owner's name is known
—a Rivka, Miryam, or Tzipora?—
this is not the place.
The golden ring with two wornout stones
Finds its way to the synagoge in Utrecht,
No, not in body but in soul.
Gold and stones are sold and melted
A *yad* is made with which to read Torah
with love.
The ring in spirit is Jewish again
is home again
in Utrecht
in our beautiful shul.

Book Reviews

Blood, Resurrection, and New Paradigms in Dialogue
A Review Essay

Daniel F. Polish

Reviewing

Resurrection: the Power of God for Christians and Jews by Kevin J. Madigan and Jon D. Levenson (New Haven and London: Yale University Press, 2008), 304 pp.

Blood and Belief: The Circulation of a Symbol Between Jews and Christians by David Biale (Berkeley, Los Angeles, and London: University of California Press, 2007), 316 pp.

A certain number of years ago, a lifetime actually, the Hebrew Union College was invited to sell its campus in Cincinnati and form some sort of relationship with the Divinity School at the University of Chicago. For a number of considerations, economic and practical, that proposal was declined. But beneath the rejection was an implicit assumption that there would be no educational advantage in placing these two sets of students in proximity. Much has changed in that intervening lifetime. A number of recent books reflect the extent to which a portentous but little-discussed paradigm shift has taken place in the studies of Jewish and Christian traditions—indeed in the study of Jewish and Christian religiousness.[1]

Of course already at that time there were significant numbers of scholars and thinkers who studied the two traditions in tandem.[2] But even with those notable outliers, scholars in the fields of Jewish studies and Christian studies tended to conceptualize their fields of specialization in isolation from each other. The academic paradigm was that of silos: two separate realms fundamentally independent of one another. That paradigm still persists in the minds of many. There are many other paradigms for this relationship, some overlapping, some mutually exclusive. One understanding held by many (the proverbial "if you woke someone up in the middle of the night" response) is that the two traditions are essentially the same except that Jews (the reason varying depending on your theology) do not believe in Jesus. More sophisticated is the model that recognizes that historically Christianity emerged out of the Judaism of a particular time, and then went "in a radically different direction." Some suggest that Christianity represented a "reaction against" the Judaism of its time and thus went off in a diametrically opposite direction. Others would argue that not all the directions that the new tradition went in were so opposite, or even radically new. Still others include in their understanding the recognition that the two traditions, no less than groups of Jews and Christians, continued to interact over the millennia exchanging concepts and practices between themselves in addition to the well-documented modes of opposition between them.

Many of these paradigms suggest that there is much to be gained by studying the two traditions in conjunction with one another. Certainly it has long been a commonplace for Christians to assert that there was value in learning about the Jewish tradition as a way to understand the context out of which the Jesus community emerged. Or as a way of understanding the root onto which the branch of their tradition was grafted. It has long been recognized that Jews gain a richer understanding of the Second Temple/first century period by including Christian texts in the mix of more-or-less primary sources. Such conjoint study may offer members of both traditions a greater depth of insight into those issues over which the divorce of the two traditions was contested.

In a number of significant recent books, a newer paradigm is either proposed or assumed that represents a tectonic shift in understanding of the history of the relationship of these two traditions. This new paradigm will require scholars to study each of them in dramatically new ways in which engaging with the reality of their interaction is unavoidable. Indeed, this new paradigm may have profound implications for the way exponents of the two traditions make sense of themselves and one another and change the ways in which their adherents interact in the future. This new paradigm is implicit in James Kugel's magisterial, *Traditions of the Bible* (Harvard University Press, 1998), which treats Rabbinic Torah commentary and Christian exegesis of the Old Testament as parallel midrashic structures for apprehending the text. The new paradigm is given most explicit expression in Biale:

> Judaism and Christianity rest on the same sacred scripture. But Judaism is no more a biblical religion than is Christianity; it is, instead, the rabbinic interpretation (or interpretations) of biblical religion. Both Judaism and Christianity should therefore be seen as Second Testaments, two religious formations that emerged in late antiquity out of the same literary, cultural, and religious milieu. (p. 3)

And later, the two traditions developed, not in isolation, but in relation, and reaction, to one another. What underlies both of the books under consideration and all the other works that embrace the new paradigm is the conviction that there is no way to make sense of postbiblical Judaism or Christianity except in relation to one another. We can no longer employ the metaphor of mother/daughter to express their connection to one another; rather that of siblings, with all the complex dynamics associated with that relationship.

The Madigan/Levenson book has its own interesting history. It grew out of an earlier book by Levenson, *Resurrection and the Restoration of Israel: The Ultimate Victory of the God of Life* (Yale University Press, 2006). In that book Levenson deals with the idea that at the end of time, God will "resurrect the dead and restore them to full bodily existence" (p. ix), an idea widely held to be consequential in Christian tradition but absent in normative Judaism. Levenson argues that this idea is, on the contrary, central to the thinking of the Rabbis. More innovatively he persuasively demonstrates that the elements that would ultimately be employed in constructing this idea system can, in fact, be found in the *Tanach* itself, especially prominently in the later books.

Madigan and Levenson, colleagues at Harvard Divinity School, pick up that theme and extend its implications. The book does retrace some of the arguments of Levenson's earlier work. Its special contribution is what it adds to the discussion of that first work. Taking as a given the idea that constituent elements of the theme of resurrection are to be found in Hebrew scriptures, the authors go on to argue that this biblical material provided the raw material for further development in the two faith traditions. They explore the parallel development of two very different elaborations of the theme in those two traditions. It is not that Judaism and Christianity understand the concept in the same way. As the authors assert:

> The theologies and practices of Judaism and Christianity are not only different but even, in some ways, mutually exclusive, and in

> drawing the parallels that we have, it has not been our intention to imply otherwise. Jewish-Christian dialogue is authentic only to the extent that it includes comparison as well as contrast, an examination and frank discussion of both the commonalities and the points of difference. (p. 256)

Their fundamental point is that the very different ways resurrection is understood have their roots in the same source material. This is an unfamiliar assertion, and a significant one. The common sources and the very different ways they are reconfigured make fascinating and challenging reading. The net effect of this presentation is not merely to present anew the "Jewish roots of Christianity," but to invite us into a reciprocal exploration. The book presents us with a Judaism and a Christianity that are not antithetical to one another; but are, instead, two distinct extrapolations from the *Tanach*. Such an awareness invites a further reconsideration about the way we perceive the very traditions themselves.

The book serves a purpose beyond the academic. The centrality of the theme of resurrection in Christian tradition directs our attention back to its parallel evolution in Judaism, impelling us to a revised, and fuller, understanding of Judaism itself. Like the earlier *The Death of Death* by Neil Gillman (Jewish Lights, 1977) this book and Levenson's first book on the subject serve as a call to the modern reader to reappropriate this ancient theme for their own religious life—a resurrection of resurrection as it were.[3]

In *Blood and Belief*, David Biale presents nothing less than a study of the wide variety of ways blood has figured in the Jewish and Christian traditions. The very framing of the question is inventive and audacious. Biale takes us through a magisterial tour of each of the traditions, as well as the frequent ways they have interacted over blood as both a concrete reality and symbol. Thus he discusses themes we could anticipate: the use of blood in Hebrew scriptural sacrifice, and as an element in the Christian Eucharist, as well as the medieval and post-medieval blood libels. And he presents full and rich discussion of issues we might not have anticipated: the role of that same Eucharist in those blood libels—as well as the accusations against Jews of desecrating the Host; the role of martyrdom in the two traditions; blood as a marker of group identity; blood as a gender marker, and its different valuation between Jews and Christians.

The book makes for fascinating and challenging reading. It is more wide-ranging than can be suggested in a listing of its themes. What other book have you read that includes a presentation of Freud's understanding of the "essence" of Judaism (p. 184) and blood imagery in the poetry of Uri Tzvi Greenberg (pp. 194-198)? Which is not to say it does not have its faults. Biale, an intentional provocateur, may indeed raise the blood pressure of some readers. He is too frequently given to overgeneralization—at some points outright tendentiousness. Yet even here, if certain themes and interpretations that Biale presents were not normative in one or both of the traditions, certainly there were streams within them that articulated similar perspectives.

Perhaps the book's greatest significance lies beyond its specific discussion of the role of blood and blood imagery in the Jewish and Christian traditions. We come to grasp more fully the role of blood in each tradition by exploring what it means in both. In this, Biale models the promise of the new paradigm. For true as it is in studying the role of blood in tandem, such an approach is no less useful for so many elements in these two traditions.

Blood and Belief is consistently stimulating and especially suggestive in indicating possibilities of interaction between the two traditions (hence the subtitle) and mutual influence. It is here that Biale is especially useful, reminding us that neither tradition employed blood imagery in isolation, but in constant reference to the other. Whatever blood may have meant for Jews or Christians at any point, such an understanding undoubtedly made reference to the understanding of that substance in the other tradition. Biale's sensitivity to this complexity and to its significance is exemplified in such challenging observations as his discussion of the reciprocity of understanding surrounding the issue of the medieval blood libel:

> It is not sufficient to look only at how Christians imagined the Jewish consumption of Christian blood; we must also consider how Jews may have projected their own fears and desires upon the host culture. The Jewish response to the blood libel will tell us a great deal about how a minority protects its identity by sanctifying its own blood rituals. (p. 3)

The reminder of that mutual cross-referencing and cross-pollinating is of great importance, even beyond the specific subject at hand, in shaping a more fully developed understanding in general of the relationship of these two communities—both for good and for ill—over the last two millennia.

The Jewish and Christian communities of faith have been thrust by history into a more constructive and mutually respectful relationship. We are still feeling our way into this new way of relating to one another. At this point it expresses itself most easily in shared response to problems in the wider world. Undoubtedly a significant part of this process must ultimately involve a reshaped understanding of the nature of our relationships in the past—and the ways we have influenced one another in our respective processes of development. Books such as these are an indication of the direction of that necessary future conversation, and significant resources for it.

Notes

1. The inconceivability of any interconnection is reflected, more popularly, in the trope of an old series of jokes whose setup begins, "a rabbi, a priest, and a minister . . . ," which rest on the once-implausible occurrence of any such conjunction. Perhaps because it is no longer so implausible, we do not hear as many such jokes today.
2. To cite just a few of many: Martin Buber, *Two Types of Faith*; Leo Baeck, *Judaism and Christianity*; Samuel Sandmel, *We Jews and You Christians*; Will Herberg, *Protestant, Catholic and Jew*.
3. Significantly, we are seeing a reappropriation of the theme *t'chiyat hameitim* in Reform liturgy.

DANIEL POLISH is rabbi of Congregation Shir Chadash of the Hudson Valley, in Lagrange New York. His most recent book is *Talking about God: Exploring the Meaning of Religious Life with Kierkegaard, Buber, Tillich and Heschel* (SkyLight Paths, 2007).

I Have a Story to Tell You
Edited by Seemah C. Berson
(Waterloo, Ontario: Wilfrid Laurier University Press, 2010), 311 pp.

The title of this volume aptly describes the contents: a collection of oral histories of Jewish immigrants to Canada in the early twentieth century. While the editor initially intended to focus on why so many of these Jewish immigrants went into the needle trades, her interviews led her to expand this to portray a broader panorama of Jewish life at the turn of the twentieth century. Interviewees describe where they came from, how they journeyed to the New

World, what they did when they arrived, and their work in the garment industry.

The first dozen stories in the book focus on describing life as it was in the Old Country. This helps the reader understand the background these immigrants came from and (to use the editor's phrase) the "cultural baggage" they brought with them. These immigrants came from Eastern Europe—Russia, Bessarabia, Poland, Lithuania, Latvia, the Ukraine. A few came from cities, but the majority came from shtetlach, small villages where their families worked as tradespeople, owned small farms, or had stores. Many lived on the edge of poverty, and raising funds to send a son or daughter to the New World required considerable effort. Some came from communities that had suffered pogroms. The early twentieth century was a time of considerable political and social unrest in Eastern Europe. As one interviewee described it, "We didn't know who was shooting at night and in the morning we'd have a different government." The Revolution of 1905 had swept across the Russian empire, and strikes and political demonstrations were common occurrences. Frequently these actions ended in violence, and all too often that violence was directed against the Jews.

The immigrants interviewed in this book came to America for the same reasons most immigrants leave their native land: to seek better opportunities and to escape persecution and discrimination. Why Canada? In the minds of these immigrants they were going to America. There was no distinction between the United States and Canada—to them it was all "America." The reason they chose Canada was usually because they "knew someone"—a distant relative, a family friend—who could put them up and help them get started. And so they settled in Montreal, Toronto, Winnipeg, or Vancouver.

The thread (no pun intended) that links these stories is that all the interviewees worked in the needle trades. They went into this business because, in the words of one interviewee, "We didn't have anything else to do." Added another: "You didn't have to be a full-fledged tailor. If you could make something—sew buttons, make buttonholes or something—you're already in the trade." Often they began as sweepers, then moved up to become "operators" (those who ran the sewing machines), pressers, and finally cutters, the elite of the needle trades. Conditions for these workers were not unlike those in the sweatshops of New York's Lower East Side during the same era—doing piecework, working long hours, earning low wages. It is fascinating to hear in their own words how these immigrants coped and how they managed to learn new skills and to advance themselves.

Eventually many of them did, in fact, become owners of their own companies. One person describes it this way: "They did not want to work all their lives for somebody else . . . they wanted to be on their own. And in the needle trades it is the easiest way. If you know the trade, as soon as you get yourself two machines, you can yourself become a small contractor. You take out work from bigger manufacturers and in this way you gradually work yourself up to three, four machines . . . In the needle trades it is very easy to become a boss." In fact, one interviewee remarks that the basic reason so many Jews were in the needle trades is because the manufacturers were mostly Jews.

The other thread that links these stories is that most of the people interviewed had been activists in the trade union movement, leading the fight for better working conditions in the needle industry. Part of the "baggage" they brought with them to Canada was a revolutionary consciousness and a zeal to fight oppression. Some had already been involved with the establishment of trade unions in the Old Country; many were committed socialists and a number became members of the Communist Party of Canada. They brought with them the tradition and spirit of revolutionary class-consciousness. They were determined to fight for decent wages, shorter work hours, job security, and minimum health and sanitary guarantees.

The men and women interviewed had been dedicated to the union movement, and they retain this loyalty. They eagerly display their union cards and extol their union pensions. They would not have considered working in a non-union shop, even if it meant their families suffered. Several of the interviewees had served as officers in the union. The Eastern European Jewish immigrants tended to support the more progressive wing of the union and were more aggressive in preventing collaboration with manufacturers and in demanding shorter hours and better pay. They were leaders in the formation of the Amalgamated Clothing Workers of America, the socialist directed wing of the labor movement. Their stories provide a fascinating insight to the struggles going on in the labor movement during the 1920s–1930s.

One of the chief weaknesses of this work is the lack of an index. For example, several interviewees talk about the Shiffer & Hillman Strike, a major garment workers strike that took place in Toronto in 1930; it would be interesting to be able to compare their impressions of this event. An index would also enable the reader to compare stories by place. For example, how the workers in Montreal interacted with the French Canadian community.

It is both a strength and a weakness of the work that the editor appears to have done minimal editing of these oral histories. This allows the reader to hear the voices of these now elderly women and men as they recall their early lives. On the other hand, this sometimes leads to some rambling and repetition in their narratives.

This volume is an excellent supplement to the objective histories and factual reports of the period. It reveals the personalities behind the early needle trade union struggles and brings to life the journey from the Old Country to Canada at the turn of the twentieth century.

SUSAN JACOBSON, MSLS, was born and raised in Montreal, Quebec. She was an academic librarian for over thirty years, most recently at the University of Illinois at Chicago. Both her grandfather and her father were in the needle trades (or *shmata* business as it was more commonly known).

Call for Papers: *Maayanot*

The CCAR Journal: The Reform Jewish Quarterly is committed to serving its readers' professional, intellectual, and spiritual needs. In pursuit of that objective, the *Journal* has created a new section known as *Maayanot* (Primary Sources). The new rubric made its debut in the Spring 2012 issue.

We continue to welcome proposals for *Maayanot* —translations of significant Jewish texts, accompanied by an appropriate introduction and annotations and/or commentary. *Maayanot* aims to present fresh approaches to materials from any period of Jewish life that, including but not confined to the biblical or Rabbinic periods. When appropriate, it may be possible to include the original document in the published presentation.

Please submit proposals, inquiries, and questions to *Maayanot* editor, Daniel Polish, dpolish@optonline.net.

Along with submissions for *Maayanot,* the *Journal* will continue to welcome the submission of scholarly articles in fields of Jewish Studies, along with other articles that fit within our Statement of Purpose.

The *CCAR Journal: The Reform Jewish Quarterly*
Published quarterly by the Central Conference of American Rabbis.

Volume LX, No. 1. Issue Number: Two hundred thirty-five.
Winter 2013.

STATEMENT OF PURPOSE

The *CCAR Journal: The Reform Jewish Quarterly* seeks to explore ideas and issues of Judaism and Jewish life, primarily—but not exclusively—from a Reform Jewish perspective. To fulfill this objective, the Journal is designed to:

1. provide a forum to reflect the thinking of informed and concerned individuals—especially Reform rabbis—on issues of consequence to the Jewish people and the Reform Movement;
2. increase awareness of developments taking place in fields of Jewish scholarship and the practical rabbinate, and to make additional contributions to these areas of study;
3. encourage creative and innovative approaches to Jewish thought and practice, based upon a thorough understanding of the traditional sources.

The views expressed in the Journal do not necessarily reflect the position of the Editorial Board or the Central Conference of American Rabbis.

The *CCAR Journal: The Reform Jewish Quarterly* (ISSN 1058-8760) is published quarterly by the Central Conference of American Rabbis, 355 Lexington Avenue, 18th Floor, New York, NY, 10017. Application to mail at periodical postage rates is pending at New York, NY and at additional mailing offices.

Subscriptions should be sent to CCAR Executive Offices, 355 Lexington Avenue, 18th Floor, New York, NY, 10017. Subscription rate as set by the Conference is $100 for a one-year subscription, $150 for a two-year subscription. Overseas subscribers should add $36 per year for postage. POSTMASTER: Please send address changes to CCAR Journal: The Reform Jewish Quarterly, c/o Central Conference of American Rabbis, 355 Lexington Avenue, 18th Floor, New York, NY, 10017.

Typesetting and publishing services provided by Publishing Synthesis, Ltd., 39 Crosby Street, New York, NY, 10013.

The *CCAR Journal: The Reform Jewish Quarterly* is indexed in the *Index to Jewish Periodicals*. Articles appearing in it are listed in the *Index of Articles on Jewish Studies* (of *Kirjath Sepher*).

ISSN 1058-8760

ISBN: 978-0-88123-197-7

GUIDELINES FOR SUBMITTING MATERIAL

1. The *CCAR Journal* welcomes submissions that fulfill its Statement of Purpose whatever the author's background or identification. Inquiries regarding publishing in the CCAR Journal and submissions for possible publication (including poetry) should be sent to the editor, Rabbi Susan Laemmle, in electronic form via Laemmle@usc.edu. Should problems arise, call 323-939-4084.

2. Other than commissioned articles, submissions to the *CCAR Journal* are sent out to a member of the editorial board for anonymous peer review. Thus submitted articles and poems should be sent to the editor with the author's name omitted. Please use MS Word format for the attachment. The message itself should contain the author's name, phone number, and e-mail address, as well as the submission's title and a 1–2 sentence bio.

3. Books for review and inquiries regarding submitting a review should be sent directly to the book review editor, Rabbi Laurence Edwards, at LLE49@comcast.net.

4. Inquiries concerning, or submissions for, *Maayanot* (Primary Sources) should be directed to the *Maayanot* editor, Rabbi Daniel Polish, at dpolish@optonline.net.

5. Based on Reform Judaism's commitment to egalitarianism, we request that articles be written in gender-inclusive language.

6. The *Journal* publishes reference notes at the end of articles, but submissions are easier to review when notes come at the bottom of each page. If possible, keep this in mind when submitting an article. Notes should conform to the following style:

a. Norman Lamm, *The Shema: Spirituality and Law in Judaism* (Philadelphia: Jewish Publication Society, 1998), 101–6. **[book]**

b. Lawrence A. Hoffman, "The Liturgical Message," in *Gates of Understanding*, ed. Lawrence A.Hoffman (New York: CCAR Press, 1977), 147–48, 162–63. **[chapter in a book]**

c. Richard Levy, "The God Puzzle," *Reform Judaism* 28 (Spring 2000): 18–22. **[article in a periodical]**

d. Lamm, *Shema*, 102. **[short form for subsequent reference]**

e. Levy, "God Puzzle," 20. **[short form for subsequent reference]**

f. Ibid., 21. **[short form for subsequent reference]**

7. If Hebrew script is used, please include an English translation. If transliteration is used, follow the guidelines abbreviated below and included more fully in the **Master Style Sheet**, available on the CCAR website at www.ccarnet.org:

"ch" for *chet* and *chaf* "ei" for *tzeirei*

"f" for *fei* "a" for *patach* and *kamatz*

"k" for *kaf* and *kuf* "o" for *cholam* and *kamatz katan*

"tz" for *tzadi* "u" for *shuruk* and *kibbutz*

"i" for *chirik* "ai" for *patach* with *yod*

"e" for *segol*

Final "h" for final *hei*; none for final *ayin* (with exceptions based on common usage): *atah, Sh'ma*, but *Moshe*.

Apostrophe for *sh'va nah*: *b'nei, b'rit, Sh'ma*; no apostrophe for *sh'va nach*.

Hyphen for two vowels together where necessary for correct pronunciation: *ne-eman, samei-ach*, but *maariv*, Shavuot.

No hyphen for prefixes unless necessary for correct pronunciation: *babayit, HaShem, Yom HaAtzma-ut*.

Do not double consonants (with exceptions based on dictionary spelling or common usage): *t'filah, chayim*, but *tikkun*, Sukkot.

www.ingramcontent.com/pod-product-compliance
Lightning Source LLC
LaVergne TN
LVHW050620100826
845148LV00011B/1667

9780881231977